D1590597

Douglas Bruster's provocative study of English Renaissance drama explores its links with Elizabethan and Jacobean economy and society, looking at the professional status of playwrights such as Shakespeare, and the establishment of commercial theaters. Stressing that playhouses were, first and foremost, places of business, he argues that a significant proportion of the drama's practical energy went toward understanding the material conditions that maintained its existence. He sees this impetus as part of a "materialist vision" which has its origins in the climate of uncertainty engendered by a rapidly expanding London and its burgeoning market. Exploring, for example, the economic importance of the cuckold theme, the role taken by stage objects as commodities, and the commercial significance of the Troy story as staged in Shakespeare's *Troilus and Cressida*, Bruster returns the theater and the plays performed there to their basis in the material world. In doing so, he offers new ways of reading the drama of Renaissance England.

CAMBRIDGE STUDIES IN RENAISSANCE
LITERATURE AND CULTURE 1

Drama and the market in the age of Shakespeare

Cambridge Studies in Renaissance Literature and Culture

General Editor
STEPHEN ORGEL
Jackson Eli Reynolds Professor of Humanities, Stanford University

Advisory Board
Anne Barton, *University of Cambridge*
Jonathan Dollimore, *University of Sussex*
Marjorie Garber, *Harvard University*
Jonathan Goldberg, *The Johns Hopkins University*
Nancy Vickers, *University of Southern California*

The last twenty years have seen a broad and vital reinterpretation of the nature of literary texts, a move away from formalism to a sense of literature as an aspect of social, economic, political and cultural history. While the earliest New Historicist work was criticized for a narrow and anecdotal view of history, it also served as an important stimulus for post-structuralist, feminist, Marxist and psychoanalytic work, which in turn has increasingly informed and redirected it. Recent writing on the nature of representation, the historical construction of gender and of the concept of identity itself, on theatre as a political and economic phenomenon and on the ideologies of art generally, reveal the breadth of the field. *Cambridge Studies in Renaissance Literature and Culture* is designed to offer historically oriented studies of Renaissance literature and theatre which makes use of the insights afforded by theoretical perspectives. The view of history envisioned is above all a view of our own history, a reading of the Renaissance for and from our own time.

Opening titles

Drama and the market in the age of Shakespeare
DOUGLAS BRUSTER, University of Chicago

The Renaissance dialogue: literary dialogue in its social and political contexts, Castiglione to Galileo
VIRGINIA COX, University College London

Drama and the market in the age of Shakespeare

Douglas Bruster

Assistant Professor of English, University of Chicago

Published by the Press Syndicate of the University of Cambridge
The Pitt Building, Trumpington Street, Cambridge CB2 1RP
40 West 20th Street, New York, NY 10011–4211, USA
10 Stamford Road, Oakleigh, Victoria 3166, Australia

© Cambridge University Press 1992

First published 1992

Printed in Great Britain at the University Press, Cambridge

A catalogue record for this book is available from the British Library

Library of Congress cataloguing in publication data
Bruster, Douglas.
Drama and the market in the age of Shakespeare / Douglas Bruster.
    p.   cm. – (Cambridge studies in Renaissance literature and culture : 1)
Includes bibliographical references and index.
ISBN 0 521 41664 7
1. English drama – Early modern and Elizabethan. 1500–1600 – History and criticism.
2. Dramatists, English – Early modern, 1500–1700 – Economic conditions.
3. Shakespeare, William, 1564–1616 – Contemporary England.
4. Shakespeare, William, 1564–1616 – Knowledge – Economics.
5. English drama – 17th century – History and criticism.
6. Theater – Economic aspects – England.
7. Drama – Econopmic aspects – England.
8. Literature and society – England.
9. Economics in literature. I. Title   II. Series
PR658.E35B78   1992
822'.3'09–dc20   91–45712   CIP

ISBN 0 521 41664 7   hardback

for Elizabeth D. Scala and Virginia Katherine McMath

Contents

Preface

This book explores how English drama responded to the market, even as it sprang from it, during the Renaissance. Faced with a relatively unfamiliar but expanding network of commercial exchange, playwrights fastened onto a variety of strategies to understand the dynamics of the market. They did so, of course, from within it, in conjunction with playhouses that were quickly becoming fixtures in the landscape of early modern London. Thus the first part of my argument in this study focuses on the institutional situation of London's playhouses – that is, on how and why theaters came to be theaters when they did – as particular historical pressures called for new means of understanding the material foundations of urban life. Then, in chapters devoted to the economic basis of the cuckold myth, the objective inscription of identity in Elizabethan and Jacobean farce, and the staging of London's market through the Troy tale in *Troilus and Cressida*, I explore how dramatists came to mythologize the elaborate realities of London's material base.

One strategy involved exploiting the traditional links between sexual and economic transaction, using erotic possession and possessiveness as symbolic doubles for the economic. Although the links between the sexual and the monetary have long been a customary site of cultural exploration, the literature of the Elizabethan and Jacobean eras displayed a special, if anxious, fascination with the topic. As the social relationship between people and things became increasingly more complex, Elizabethan and Jacobean comedy – its farce in particular – subsumed subjectivity within the objective. Props in Renaissance farce became markers of value and status, encoding identity into worth counters which, passed from hand to hand, often acted as reservoirs of erotic potential. Consciously or unconsciously, playwrights connected identity with ownership, rendering the relationship between property and person as one of almost complete interdependence.

Seeing formal exchange rooted ever more firmly within the boundaries of the city itself, writers of the period also sought to interpret the dynamics of London's market through folk metaphors, agrestic figures which would allow them to gloss the urban market and the concepts of labor and property in anatopical, or "other-placed," terms. Rural tropes like cony-catching and cuckoldry, for instance, provided ready, if temporary, help in the construction of a vocabulary for a changing social and financial economy. The myth of the patient, knowing cuckold, or "wittol" became the dominant literary paradigm for interpreting the concept of profit in the literature of the 1590s and early 1600s. The often misogynistic scenario of marital infidelity offered an attractive double for commercial speculation: like the wittol, who usually winked complacently at his wife's adultery in return for pecuniary or social gain, the literary merchant was frequently characterized as necessarily patient, one who willingly entrusted goods of value to others to enhance his financial status. Like the trope of cony-catching, the cuckold myth traced its roots to the rural and bestial – to animals like the cuckoo, the stag, and the bull – and formed what might be called a portal trope between country and city. Because they were rural at base, and because the countryside was seen as a center of natural struggle, both figures offered themselves as metaphors with which Elizabethan and Jacobean playwrights could explain the savagery of urban competition.

For all its apparent novelty the market also called up, in the literary imagination of Renaissance England, echoes of property exchange and the acquisitive impulse as shown in stories set in London's international rivals, past and present. Such cities as Vienna, Verona, Malta, and Cyprus took an important role, of course, in staging the urban market in (and of) Renaissance London. London also looked to ancient cities for its urban mythology. As the prophet Oseas, chorus of Thomas Lodge and Robert Greene's *A Looking Glass for London and England* (1588), warns the theater audience about the events recently revealed in "Nineveh": "London, take heed, these sins abound in thee" (1.3.144).[1] Already possessing celebrated mythological/historical links to London, the city of Troy provided an especially attractive model which dramatists could use to describe and anticipate the social implications of a commercial culture. The story of national conflict deriving from an act of theft, of course, appealed to the historical and moral imaginations of Renaissance playwrights in a time of increasing international tensions over military and mercantile supremacy. Thus, a play like Shakespeare's *Troilus and Cressida*, with its wealth of commercial imagery and topical allusions, drew on the established complexity of London's literary ancestor in the construction of a narrative full of contemporary – and commercial – import.

These three general strategies with which dramatists attempted to come to grips with social change – linking the sexual and the economic, the urban and the rural, and the ancient with the modern – allowed them to explore and define the character of the socioeconomic changes affecting London. Describing the often mystifying nature of the city's relationship with the market, playwrights sought to reconcile the worlds of the near and the far,[2] the subject with the object, and the past with the present. Their attempts to do so brought them face to face with the complexities of the material world.

Acknowledgments

A number of people have generously helped me with this project. I want to thank in particular Daniel Aaron, William Bond, G. Blakemore Evans, Marjorie Garber, Roland Greene, Walter Kaiser, Jeffrey Knapp, Robert Knoll, Barbara Lewalski, John G. Norman, Elizabeth Scala, David Steiner, John Tobin, Robert Watson, and Robert Weimann.

A note on texts

Where possible, I have in this study modernized the spelling and punctuation of quotations from Renaissance texts. Upon their first citation in a chapter, plays (and selected primary texts) referred to are followed by a date indicating their estimated year or years of composition; the dates for plays are supplied by Alfred Harbage, Samuel Schoenbaum, and Sylvia Stoler Wagonheim in *Annals of the English Drama, 975–1700*, third edition (London: Routledge, 1989). I use the Wagonheim updating of the *Annals* aware of the negative review by Anne Lancashire (*Shakespeare Quarterly* 42 (1991): 225–30), which points out a number of mistakes and omissions in the new edition. Most of Lancashire's objections concern issues that do not, in most cases, affect the validity of the dates provided in Wagonheim's text. Needless to say, all dates should be understood as approximate. Unless otherwise noted, references to Shakespeare are taken from *The Riverside Shakespeare*, ed. G. Blakemore Evans (Boston: Houghton Mifflin, 1974). References to Jonson's plays are from the modernized spelling edition of *The Complete Plays of Ben Jonson*, ed. G. A. Wilkes, 4 vols. (Oxford: Clarendon Press, 1981–82), based on the edition of C. H. Herford, Percy Simpson, and Evelyn Simpson. Quotations from Heywood's plays are drawn from *The Dramatic Works of Thomas Heywood*, 6 vols. (London: 1874; rpt. New York: Russell & Russell, 1964). Quotations from Webster are from *The Complete Works of John Webster*, ed. F. L. Lucas, 4 vols. (Boston: Houghton Mifflin, 1928). References to E. K. Chambers' invaluable study, *The Elizabethan Stage*, 4 vols. (Oxford: Clarendon Press, 1923), are given simply as "Chambers" (along with volume and page number) in the notes.

Did not Will Summers break his wind for thee?
And Shakespeare therefore write his comedy?
All things acknowledge thy vast power divine
(Great God of Money) whose most powerful shine
Gives motion, life.
> Chremylus to Plutus, in Thomas Randolph's *Hey for Honesty* (1627)

This study evolves out of an apparent cultural paradox: during the late
Elizabethan and early Jacobean era – a time that many commentators
agree constituted a signal transitional period in English history – London
responded to the rapidly intensifying pressures of social change by
institutionalizing its theater. Throughout the early and middle sixteenth
century, players had traditionally adapted themselves and their theatrical
productions to the spaces at hand – to inn-yards, city streets, and the
interiors of various and varied buildings. With the opening of the Red
Lion in 1567, the Theater in 1576, and the Curtain in 1577, however, there
came a general, significant movement from itinerant playing to acting in
fixed playing spaces. For the first time, acting companies began to enjoy
the use of semipermanent, purpose-built structures for the marketing of
dramatic entertainment, staging productions in playhouses that would
become regular fixtures in the urban geography of Renaissance London.[1]
That these acting companies ceased having to adapt themselves to changing performing conditions (or rather, ceased having to do this on such a
regular basis) just when the social landscape itself became especially
changeful – this constitutes what seems to be a paradox underlying the
physical institutionalization of English drama during the Renaissance. As
sociology has taught us, however, such a paradox may be merely apparent: with what Max Weber called 'rational industrial organization' going
hand in hand with the historical unfolding of the market system in the
West, a certain level of centralization has almost inevitably accompanied
social change. Products of this process, the Renaissance playhouses can
be seen less as anomalies, perhaps, than as the logical outcome of a
historical pattern of social development.

1

The erection of London's amphitheaters came as a gesture, by those involved in the business of playing, toward a kind of professional stability, a gesture which attracted considerable notice in London at the time. Those whose objections to playing had long taken on primarily moral overtones now responded to the theaters in terms of direct institutional rivalry, seeing in the establishment of the public playhouses false temples that could detract from churchgoing and drain money from church coffers. Throughout the late 1570s, attacks on playing and playgoing invariably stressed the patent evils of a fixed theater. Resentful of the players' new status and prosperity, William Harrison lamented shortly after 1576 that "It is an evident token of a wicked time when players wax so rich that they can build such houses."[2] In a 1577 polemic against "dicing, dancing, plays, and interludes," John Northbrooke, a Gloucester minister, inveighed against houses specially "builded for such exercises," those places "which are made up and builded for such plays and interludes as the *Theatre* and *Curtain*."[3] And in a sermon preached at St. Paul's in November of 1577, one T. W. (Thomas White?) exhorted his audience to

Look but upon the common plays in London, and see the multitude that flocketh to them and followeth them: behold the sumptuous Theatre houses, a continual monument of London's prodigality and folly ... and if it be not suppressed in time, it will make such a Tragedy, that London may well mourn while it is London, for it is no playing time.[4]

Like Harrison's offhand jeremiad, T. W.'s sermon grudgingly recognizes a historical truth: something different about the "time" had indeed allowed, even sponsored, the construction of semipermanent playhouses. What before had been a relatively haphazard, mobile enterprise now began to claim a permanent status. The strong undercurrent of jealousy evident in the mention of the "multitude" that flocks to the "sumptuous" playhouses and the manner in which theatrical terminology ("it will make such a Tragedy") slides into and (however intended) ironizes T. W.'s moral are of course significant, but one might also note the logical contradiction between labeling the theaters a "continual monument of London's prodigality and folly" and the ensuing, antitheatrical diagnosis. That is, while the description of the playhouses as apparently permanent fixtures in the local landscape would prove to be more accurate than he might have imagined, on the latter point – his declaration that "it is no playing time" – T. W. could not have been more wrong.

Between the erection of the first purpose-built playhouses and the closing of the theaters in 1642, in the estimate of Andrew Gurr, "well over fifty million visits were made to playhouses."[5] This unprecedented rate of playgoing in London was matched by a heightened concern, by investors, shareholders, and those who operated the playhouses, for the increase and assurance of profits. Indeed, "playing time" became a serious, highly competitive commercial enterprise. The construction, in the Fields and Liberties of London, of amphitheaters designed especially for theatrical productions enabled theater-owners and managers not only to improve the practical conditions of performance, but also to control admission to the playhouses and obtain from each member of the audience the required admission fee – always a potential problem in outdoor and temporary venues. In this way the specialization of function of the Renaissance playhouse evolved alongside commercial concerns even as it responded to a material transformation in the size of the city's potential playgoing audience. The topographical "fixing" of the theater which seems, in retrospect, to belie the fluidity so characteristic of London and England during the Renaissance can be seen then as a corollary, rather than contradiction, of the pressures of historical change. Its institutionalization came as a response to this change; a practical acknowledgment of the early modern push toward centralization, it testified in suggestive ways to the far-reaching effects of social transformation.

Correspondingly, London's playhouses can best be understood in terms of commerce, as centers for the production and consumption of an aesthetic product. During the Renaissance, the cornucopian plays which even today appear to offer almost everything to almost everyone delivered many myths in different voices to audiences which seem to have been themselves extremely heterogeneous.[6] What Norman Rabkin calls the "common understanding" – the tendency or ability of Shakespeare's plays to offer (even affirm) simultaneously, without contradiction, contradictory themes, messages, and ideological stances – was, I would argue, ultimately a product of early modern market forces which shaped dramatic commodities to answer the various manifestations of social desire, desire addressed by the titles, no less than the content, of plays like *As You Like It* (1599) and *What You Will* (1601).[7] More interesting to me than whether a particular thematic reading of the plays "holds true," then, is how, and why, it came to be the case that so many readings "hold true" – that is, how, and why, the drama became and remains the equivalent of what Brecht, speaking of radio, would later call an "acoustic department store."[8]

Thus it is the theater's role as part of the market – itself inextricably linked to the forces of social change – with which I am most concerned in the following study. Like the theater, the market took its first permanent roots during this period: the two "institutions," in fact, share a similar physical chronology. Thomas Gresham began construction of the Royal Exchange in Lombard Street in London in 1566–67, just as the Red Lion playhouse opened for business and only a decade before the opening of the Theater and Curtain. Four-stories tall, the Royal Exchange came to be known popularly as "Gresham's Exchange," and was dedicated in large part to matters of national and international finance, changing foreign money and distributing new coinage. In addition, the piazzas surrounding it contained around a hundred individual shops – shops "richly furnished," as John Stowe remarked, "with all sorts of the finest wares in the city."[9] A visitor from Germany in 1592 called the Exchange "a palace, where all kinds of beautiful goods are usually to be found."[10]

Not quite a year after the erection of the Globe on the Bankside in 1599, in the same year that the second Blackfriars and the Fortune would open their doors to playgoing audiences, Elizabeth signed the documents legitimizing the operations of the East India Company. And in the spring of 1609, four years after the opening of the Red Bull and one year after the commencement of theatrical activity at the Whitefriars, Robert Cecil opened the New Exchange (sometimes called "Britain's Bourse") on the Strand frontage of Durham House in London. Like the Royal Exchange, the New Exchange was – in the words of Lawrence Stone – "a sort of stock exchange and estate agency . . . a kind of bazaar for the upper-class clientele which normally passed along the Strand between the Law Courts and the royal palace at Westminster, and the Inns of Court and the City to the east."[11] And, even as the Blackfriars playhouse capitalized on the atavistic "liberty" that the former monastery had brought the parish, the New Exchange testified to the post-Reformation character of its time of construction in the very materials that made up its foundations: the first building stone for its construction came from (then standing) monastic buildings at Saint Augustine's in Canterbury.[12]

I offer these historical instances out of a belief that, together, they come not as random or coincidental events, but rather as part of a larger historical trajectory: the dawn, in London, of institutionalized capitalism. Writing dramatic commodities for consumption in public and private theaters – and even for sale at book stalls – professional playwrights during this period frequently alluded to the energies of the developing market. Around 1605, during the flurry of economic activity characterizing the two decades bordering the monarchial transition, Thomas Heywood literalized the connections between market and theater in the Second Part of *If You Know Not Me, You Know Nobody* by presenting a scenario purporting to show how Thomas Gresham had conceived, supervised – even laid the first masonry for – the Royal Exchange. At the fictional cornerstone ceremony Alexander Nowell – reknowned scholar and "Dean of Paul's" – borrows the architect's plans for the Exchange from Gresham and, looking them over, mentions its unusual design. He notes especially a "fair / Space" which "Seems open," and asks Gresham: "your conceit for that?"[13] Gresham responds:

> This space, that hides not heaven from us,
> Shall be so still; my reason is,
> There's summer's heat as well as winter's cold;
> And I allow, and here's my reason for't,
> 'Tis better to be bleaked by winter's breath,
> Than to be stifled up with summer's heat.

Open to the elements, the Exchange is depicted as a kind of *argentaria mundi*, a "bank of the world" where the counsellors of seasonal change feelingly argue for the naturalness of commercial exchange – all performed under the open gaze of heaven. Heywood's description of the design's open "space" also makes the Exchange sound much like the physically exposed *theatrum mundi* of the Elizabethan amphitheaters – in one of which this description would have first been heard. The play was most likely the property of Queen Anne's Men when initially acted in 1605, and thus probably put on at the Curtain. Constructed less than a decade after the Exchange, the Curtain, like its companion amphitheaters, resembled Gresham's building in its "fair space," open to both the cold of winter and "summer's heat."

Further similarities between the Exchange and London's amphitheaters are suggested when Heywood's merchant continues his architectural blazon by describing another part of the Exchange, the "Pawn" or covered walkway featuring a row of shops in the upper gallery:

> Here, like a parish for good citizens
> And their fair wives to dwell in, I'll have shops,
> Where every day they shall become themselves
> In neat attire; that when our courtiers
> Shall come in trains to trace old Gresham's Burse,
> They shall have such a girdle of chaste eyes,
> And such a globe of beauty round about,
> Ladies shall blush to turn their vizards off,
> And courtiers swear they lied when they did scoff.

Gresham fashions his description for Nowell, connecting his Exchange with a moral and hygienic Protestantism. In its emphasis on the visual, however, his portrait of the shop gallery also brings to mind London's theaters. Like Elizabethan actors, Gresham's "good citizens" costume themselves in "neat attire" and prepare to see and be seen by their customers. Gresham speaks of this audience in terms of "a girdle of chaste eyes, / And ... a globe of beauty round about." I would like to suggest that the imagery he uses – "girdle ... / ... globe ... round about" – invites comparison of the Exchange and London's public amphitheaters, many of which (like *the* Globe) were circular. On an amphitheater's stage an actor would have been surrounded by a girdle of eyes: Webster's "character" of an "excellent Actor" (1615) seems to say as much in suggesting: "sit in a full Theater, and you will think you see so many lines drawn from the circumference of so many ears, whiles the *Actor* is the *Center*."[14] Like the citizen merchant and his wife, actors apparelled themselves for the business of selling commodities. One of the commonplaces connected with shopowners in the drama, in fact, held that they calculatingly dimmed the light in their shops to set the stage for retailing shoddy goods.[15] The similarity of the two endeavors, selling goods and selling performances, evolves out of the gaze, display, and the way seeing anticipates and infuses buying.[16] Stephen Gosson, himself a playwright before becoming one of the theater's most vehement critics, drew strong connections between the theater and the market, in one place characterizing the Royal Exchange as an institution where transactions similar to those taking place in the theater could be found: "Mine eyes throughly behold the manner of Theaters, when I wrote plays myself, and found them to be the very markets of bawdry, where choice w[i]thout shame hath been as free as it is for your money in the Royal Exchang[e], to take a short stock, or a long, a falling band, or a French ruff."[17] Gosson's emphasis on "choice w[i]thout shame" stresses the commodity function of the Renaissance theater, a place where money can buy the fantasy of one's choosing.

Thomas Middleton would follow Gosson in using the Exchange as the ultimate metaphor of conspicuous display (and envious admiration) in Allwit's description of his pregnant wife in *A Chaste Maid in Cheapside* (1613):

> A lady lies not in like her; there's her embossings,
> Embroid'rings, spanglings, and I know not what,
> As if she lay with all the gaudy-shops
> In Gresham's Burse about her.

> (1.2.31–34)[18]

A few years earlier, in 1611, the relationship between business and theater had found articulation in Arthur Gorges' petition to King James for the founding of a "Public Register for General Commerce," a petition printed, significantly, at a shop in "Britain Bourse" – that is, the New Exchange. Gorges pleads for an institution which would centralize information about real estate and other financial matters so that, when forced to sell holdings for ready cash, members of the (decaying) gentry would be able to get a better price. One of the many ironies behind the proposal is that, at least in Gorges' argument, the Register would be more honest, ultimately, because of its secrecy. As Gorges suggests, the parties themselves that do either lend or borrow, buy or sell, may use it with as great security and secrecy as they shall think fit by using other men's names than their own, other places than their own houses, and other friends or Factors for themselves if they be so disposed. So as by this free, plain and easy course all men may rest satisfied, that there is no cunning intent by means of this Office, to defraud men, nor by the practice thereof to discover men's wealths or secret estates, futher than to themselves shall seem good.[19]

Theatricality, to Gorges, ensures complete honesty in these financial matters: "free, plain and easy." Others regretted the conflation. Slightly over four decades later John Hall would decry the theatrical basis of business and "gaudy-shops" in a passage in *The Advancement of Learning* (1649), where he stated that "Man in business is but a Theatrical person, and in a manner but personates himself, but in his retired and hid actions, he pulls off his disguise, and acts openly."[20] In a less critical manner Gresham's happy laud grounds the topography of the Exchange and the business of commerce in a theatrical phenomenology. That it does so in the context of a play, a play itself transacted in a "fair space," only highlights the deeper connections between the two institutions. Indeed, in retrospect this scene of Heywood's offers an almost incestuous paean to an institution similar to the playhouse itself.

Hence were the playhouses frequently characterized, by detractors and supporters alike, as markets in miniature. The typical Puritan animus toward the theater traditionally sprang from the ostensibly profane nature of the market and display generally. Not surprisingly, those who derived all or part of their living from the theater saw things differently. In *The Gull's Horn-Book* (1609), for instance, Thomas Dekker described playhouses in more favorable, although no less commercial, terms: "The theatre is your poets' Royal Exchange, upon which their Muses – that are now turned to merchants – meeting, barter away that light commodity of words for a lighter ware than words – plaudits and the breath of the great beast which, like the threatenings of two cowards, vanish all into air."[21] As markets, playhouses often brought a lucrative return on investments. If no one became wealthy *writing* plays, it was from the Renaissance theater, as Keynes noticed in *A Treatise on Money*, that Shakespeare did in fact become rich: his money came not from the genius of his dramatic compositions, but from the percentage he drew – through his control of shares in the acting company – of the Globe and Blackfriars' gate.

As Dekker's "commodity of words" might indicate, it was also during Shakespeare's lifetime that plays themselves were beginning to be described in terms of their exchange value. Sandra Clark characterizes this period as one in which "the demand-supply continuum between an expanding public and its reading matter was set up."[22] Playwrights assumed the lead in articulating this continuum, the beginnings (i.e. prologues, inductions, and preface epistles) and endings (epilogues) of plays forming the traditional loci in which to stress their commodity function as well as the contractual relationship between author, players, and audience. Addressing the readers of *The Roaring Girl* (1611), Middleton declared that "the fashion of play-making I can properly compare to nothing so naturally as the alteration in apparel," and followed this comparison with an extended parallel between the vagaries of taste in garments and drama.[23] Jonson took up the play-as-commodity conceit in the Prologue to *Bartholomew Fair* (1614) as well; there his Scrivener reads a lengthy "Articles of Agreement" between "the Spectators or Hearers, at the Hope on the Bankside, in the county of Surrey on the one party: and the Author of *Bartholomew Fair* in the said place, and county on the other part."[24] The anonymous epistle prefacing *Troilus and Cressida* (1602) suggests that "were but the vain names of comedies changed for the titles of Commodities," the drama's censurers would "flock to them," and that when its author "is gone, and his Comedies out of sale, you will scramble for them."

Play performances also drew this kind of description. The placelessness of the Renaissance platform stage worked to exoticize and commodify space, endowing the act of conflation itself with a sexual, fetishized value. In the words of the Prologue of *Henry V* (1599):

> Can this cockpit hold
> The vasty fields of France? Or may we cram
> Within this wooden O the very casques
> That did affright the air at Agincourt?
> O, pardon! since a crooked figure may
> Attest in little place a million,
> And let us, ciphers to this great accompt
> On your imaginary forces work.

> (11–18)

Shakespeare's understated bawdy here – "cockpit hold ... / ... may we cram / Within this wooden O" – is synthesized with a portrait of actors and playhouse engaged in a theatrical enterprise of rational accounting. By the time Shakespeare came to write this prologue, Gosson had already described an actor as being "like to a Merchant's finger, that stands sometime for a thousand, sometime for a cipher."[25] With the aid of such players who act as "ciphers" to the "great accompt" of English military adventures in France, geographic space becomes a reducible commodity – a commodity which could be (and was) sold to the audience of the "wooden O" itself. Providing dramatic commodities for public consumption, the Renaissance theater functioned as an institutionalized, profitable market.

In this way playhouses like the Rose, Swan, Globe, and Hope replicated the phenomenon which Jean-Christophe Agnew, in a recent study, explores in describing 1550–1750 as a period "when the residual boundaries separating market from other forms of exchange were rapidly dissolving."[26] Taking up the theater's relationship to the market, Agnew sees the English Renaissance stage as "a laboratory of and for the new social relations of agricultural and commercial capitalism."[27] Describing the "experimental, exploratory, and extraterritorial qualities" of the Renaissance theater, he suggests that these qualities "allowed the theater of that epoch to operate as a proxy form of the new and but partly fathomable relations of a nascent market society. The professional theater of the English Renaissance became in effect a 'physiognomic metaphor' for the mobile and polymorphous features of the market."[28]

Rather than a "proxy form" of the market, however (the word here implies substitution, and in doing so confers upon the stage a privileged position in relation to the "real" market), London's playhouses were, of course, actual markets. When discussing *Bartholomew Fair*, Agnew accedes to the fact that "the theater was itself a market," but this admission functions in the context of a study which most often sees "market" and "theater" as worlds apart – as discrete, if related, entities.[29]

Agnew's argument often emphasizes the marginality of the Renaissance playhouses, even speaking once of "the limbo of London's liberties."[30] In doing so, it participates in an understanding of the Renaissance theater most fully detailed by Steven Mullaney's influential study, *The Place of the Stage: License, Play, and Power in Renaissance England*. Mullaney's account locates what many see as subversive or destabilizing qualities in the *texts* of Renaissance drama in the cultural geography of London's Liberties themselves:

When popular drama moved out into the Liberties to appropriate their ambivalent terrain for its own purposes, it was able to do so only because the traditions that had shaped and maintained those Liberties were on the wane. A gap had opened in the social fabric, a temporary rift in the cultural landscape that provided the stage with a place on the ideological horizon, a marginal and anamorphic perspective on the cultural dynamics of its own time.[31]

To Mullaney, the "ambivalent terrain" of London's Liberties offered a form of critical haven for the Renaissance stage, one from which the playhouses explored the cultural milieu of Elizabethan and Jacobean England. This terrain thus gave the public playhouses a "liberty that was at once moral, ideological, and topological – a freedom to experiment with a wide range of available ideological perspectives and to realize, in dramatic form, the cultural contradictions of its age."[32]

My differences with Mullaney's position in the following study rise out of a belief that the playhouses were deeply implicated in a narrative of institutional development which transcended geographical boundaries. It is my argument that to posit a relatively stable and unchanging London against which the Liberties and certain plays seem rebelliously marginal is to underestimate the fluidity of existence and exchange in the early modern city. It may also recuperate the stance of the paternalistic "authorities" (puritan and governmental alike) whose often vituperative denunciations of the popular playhouses, as the above examples might suggest, form a large part of the contemporary comment on the English Renaissance theater. Against Mullaney's argument that "the place of the [Renaissance] stage was a marginal one, and in the world of early modern culture such marginality was in itself significant,"[33] I would posit that the theaters of Renaissance England (public and private alike) were both responsive and responsible to the desires of their playgoing publics, and were potentially no more marginal a part of London than their publics demanded. Places of business, they regularized and normalized carnival. And although the commercial in no way precludes the marginal or actively ideological, it seems undeniable that in Renaissance London the profit motive claimed a great, even predominant measure of the theaters' practical energy.[34] Certainly issues and elements such as the political tension between government and players, the aristocratic patronage of acting companies, and the folk and festive aspects of performance, among many others, must be included in any full understanding of the playhouses and their relationship to the larger social world of early modern England. But the economic foundation of the playhouses, I believe, established a map of interests that must be charted alongside, if not before, a similar sketch of more explicitly ideological concerns.

It is my intention in this study to begin with the premise that the theater was, a priori, a market, that it was, primarily, a place of business – and, as a business, part of a complex of centralizing institutions. This need not imply that the playhouses were without a social vision. Their market function, however, necessarily mediated, even directed, that vision. As sellers of dramatic literature, London's public and private playhouses came to stage scenarios which represented, reflexively, the market's extensive cultural implications; they responded with a felt, if complicit, urgency, I believe, to the ability of economic forces to shape urban society.

Thus, what should remain in the forefront of critical analysis of Renaissance drama is the theater as place of commercial exchange. Of cardinal importance to our understanding of the plays of Shakespeare's age – plays often retailed in concrete, textual form – are the fifty million visits paid to theaters during the period. In the social context of Tudor and Stuart

London, playgoing constituted a regular cultural activity, playhouses institutional participants in the cultural milieu of a commercial London. The plays people saw and heard spoke to them about their shared society, I would suggest, in ways more ordinary than radical. Rather than end at asking, "What did those in London's social world say about the stage?," then, I want to go on to ask "What did the plays which people attended say about London's social world?" And further, what does it mean that plays were, in the words of Kathleen McLuskie, "the products of an entertainment industry?"[35]

To answer these questions, ones which I have posed in relation to a wide range of Renaissance plays, I elaborate in the following study what I call a poetics of the market. Beginning with the premise that the Renaissance theater must be seen in the context of an early modern culture industry – an institutional participant in what Joan Thirsk has called the "scandalous phase" in "the development of a consumer society in early modern England"[36] – this examination works to show the social mythology and poetics of nascent capitalism in late-Tudor and early-Stuart London as expressed reflexively in English Renaissance drama.

2 Drama and the age

We were just in a financial position to afford Shakespeare when he presented himself.

J. M. Keynes, *A Treatise on Money*

During the late sixteenth and early seventeenth centuries, a combination of general historical factors coincided with special economic and demographic developments to mark the early modern era as the time social change began to become, for England generally and the city of London in particular, a phenomenological constant. Earlier, around the year 1500, according to Fernand Braudel, England could be aptly described as a "'backward' country, without a powerful navy, with a predominantly rural population and only two sources of wealth: huge wool production and a strong cloth industry."[1] During the course of the century, however, sustained forces began affecting England's economic foundations, ultimately transforming its society, as Margot Heinemann points out, from one "based on rank and status to one based more directly on wealth and property."[2] Figuring prominently among such influences were a continually high level of inflation; the extension and intensification of merchant adventurism and other speculative financial activity (including the increase in "projects" and "projectors"); the material implications of international trade expansion; the rapid growth of London's population and the subsequent complications of urban pressure; and, perhaps most important, the progressive, structural institutionalization of the market economy.

The cumulative effect of these socioeconomic changes forever altered the structure of English society. Stressing the radical character of change in the period, Agnes Heller describes the age in the following way:

the Renaissance was the first wave of the protracted process of transition from feudalism to capitalism. Engels rightly spoke of it as a "revolution." In that process of transformation a whole social and economic structure, an entire system of values and way of life were shaken. Everything became fluid; social upheavals succeeded one another with unbelievable speed, individuals situated "higher" and "lower" in the social hierarchy changed places rapidly.[3]

Although it is possible to overestimate the swiftness and scope of this change – especially after recent studies of the history and literature of the Middle Ages and post-Reformation England[4] – Heller's generalized summary of the period's changeful character exaggerates less than it might seem to. The period from 1580 to 1620 in particular became the focus of a variety of conflicting social pressures, constituting ultimately, in the words of Lawrence Stone, "the real watershed between medieval and modern England."[5] And while such a portrait finds support in both contemporary opinion and formal historical data, the socioeconomic transformation of early modern England is nowhere delineated so clearly or compellingly, perhaps, as in the literature of the period.

Indeed, so strong were the social forces at play in late Tudor and early Stuart England that, as a cultural distillation of historical pressures, the idea of change itself pervaded the literary imagination of the English Renaissance. Directly and indirectly, artists of the period continually responded to the phenomenon of change, often displacing the social onto the level of the personal. Significantly, Ovid's *Metamorphoses*, probably the most influential secular work of the Elizabethan period, held a powerful fascination for authors and audiences of the 1590s and early 1600s. A number of works paid homage to its thematic influence even as they testified by title to the period's concentrated interest in the process and implications of change; these include *Love's Metamorphosis* (1590), *The Metamorphosis of Ajax* (1596), *The Metamorphosis of Pygmalion's Image* (1598), *The Maid's Metamorphoses* (1600), *The Transformed Metamorphosis* (1600), *The Metamorphosis of Tobacco* (1602), Spenser's "Mutability Cantos" (159?; pub. 1609), *The Mask of the Metamorphosed Gypsies* (1621), and *The Changeling* (1622). The genesis of such interest displayed in these and other Renaissance texts, I would argue, resided in both the attractiveness of change as a model with which to enfigure the meaning (and instability) of personal relationships, and also in the authors' response to the real and perceived material transformation of English society, a reaction manifested in their thematizing of the very changes which would afford England its "Renaissance" in the first place. The distinctive character of Renaissance culture, in fact, traced its origin in large part to a unique, historically determined confluence of wealth, people, and material, a confluence which afforded England an unheralded period of artistic production. As Harry Levin indicates, "commercial prosperity was as much a precondition of the English Renaissance as were its responses to intellectual currents from the continent."[6]

Responsive to the ways such preconditions are embodied in the material bases of cultural production, modern literary critics have increasingly examined the literature of the English Renaissance alongside the growth and complexity of England's economy.[7] Since the Depression-era publication of L. C. Knights' *Drama and Society in the Age of Jonson* (1937) it has become a critical commonplace to point out that, concurrent with the escalating development of commerce and trade during the late-Elizabethan and early-Jacobean period, London's drama became intensively preoccupied with the moral and social connotations of what modern historians have retrospectively labeled "nascent capitalism" and the "market society."[8] Many of Shakespeare's own literary contemporaries – writers like Thomas Heywood, John Marston, and Ben Jonson – appear to have seen commercial exchange as the predominant force behind the alterations taking place in the extended city of London. As the pamphleteer Nicholas Breton held in 1600, in a work entitled *Pasquil's Madcap*,

> The market doth not serve to look on minds,
> 'Tis money makes the way with everything;
> Coin alters natures in a thousand kinds,
> And makes a beggar think himself a king,
> The carter whistle and the cobbler sing:
> Money, oh God, it carries such a grace
> That it dare meet the devil in the face.[9]

Money, in Breton's satiric lament, has a singularly transformative power, altering "natures in a thousand kinds" and leading to an illusory social mobility wherein a beggar might "think himself a king." Money also transgresses conventional moral boundaries: with its unflinching, Medusan gaze, it "carries such a grace / That it dare meet the devil in the face."

In a footnote to the first volume of *Capital*, Marx quoted a similar complaint from Shakespeare's *Timon of Athens* (1607), a passage in which Timon ascribes to "Yellow, glittering, precious gold" the power to "make / Black white, foul fair, wrong right / Base noble, old young, coward valiant" (4.3.26–30).[10] To Timon, as to Marx, money has the power to alter, even invert, reality. Its magic overturns the actual, alienating both physical and mental processes. For all its numinous transformative ability though, Timon's "precious gold" stood in an undeniably metonymic, even subordinate relationship to what Breton simply calls "The market." His diatribe, in fact, comes to us through a dramatic commodity, the text of a play – a fact Marx, preferring to see it as coextensive with Shakespeare's own sentiments, never acknowledged. Yet the myth of dangerous market forces had strong roots in reality. Within the bars of the city as well as in the suburbs, as Breton's lament intimates, the market seemed to gain increasingly powerful sway over the lives of Londoners in the 1590s and early 1600s. The idea of buying and selling, of exchange for profit and socially approved surplus value all took on heightened levels of sig-

nificance in the two decades surrounding the turn of the century. In
presenting commercial transaction as a natural, inescapable phenomenon, the market assumed an ever noticeable place in the foreground of
urban life.

The market

Yet what was the Renaissance market? In answering this question, problems of reference arise. Any definition aspiring to preciseness ("a market
is . . .") would undoubtedly fail to characterize the fluidity of the market's
operations. Perhaps more important, it would also obscure the fact that
few of Breton and Shakespeare's contemporaries could or did define it
with any level of certainty. For all of its attractiveness to Marx, Timon's
lament underscores the enormous differences between economic exegesis
in the early-modern and modern eras. What Marx would set forth with a
confident precision and technical vocabulary often constituted, for Elizabethan and Jacobean playwrights, a project of almost insurmountable
proportions.

For a general definition of market, then, I want to turn initially to the
Oxford English Dictionary's inflected chronology. There, "market" is
defined most usefully in the following ways. *MARKET*:

A public place, whether an open space or covered building, in which cattle,
provisions, etc. are exposed for sale . . .

The action or business of buying and selling; an instance of this, a commercial
transaction, a purchase or sale; a (good or bad) bargain.

Sale as controlled by supply and demand; hence, demand (for a commodity).

Opportunity for buying or selling.

Place, action, demand, opportunity. These four words provide a valuable
starting point from which to begin the project of defining the term. By
way of conditional characterization, I would offer that the Renaissance
market was as much concept as place. In this way action, demand,
opportunity, and the human actors who sponsor them constitute a
primary part of the business of commerce. The aggregate of the Renaissance market's effective power, then, transcended not only exact definition, but indeed the physical loci of exchange – a fair ground, a
commercial street, a room in a brothel. Assuming both physical and
idealized forms, the market – as if paraphrasing Marlowe's Mephisto-
pheles – went wherever Londoners went.

London's drama often encoded this placelessness in scenes showing an
acquisitive impulse that was quickly becoming characteristic of the

culture at large. When Trinculo stumbles across the "strange fish" called Caliban in *The Tempest* (1611), he exclaims:

Were I in England now (as once I was) and had but this fish painted, not a holiday fool there but would give a piece of silver. There would this monster make a man; any strange beast there makes a man. When they will not give a doit to relieve a lame beggar, they will lay out ten to see a dead Indian. (2.2.27–33)

A prospective exhibitor of the strange fish, Trinculo functions as the agent of English commercial voyeurism. His enthusiasm here springs from his expectation of how much Caliban, a live "Indian," would bring once placed on display in London. Even on his island home, then, Caliban finds his value calculated in relation to the demand for his patent exoticism.

Later in the play, after Ariel has driven Caliban, Stephano, and Trinculo on stage, Sebastian laughs at the trio, turning to Antonio with "Ha, ha! / What things are these, my Lord Antonio? / Will money buy 'em?" Significantly, Antonio's only line in the whole of the fifth act comes in response to this question. Presumably looking at Caliban (who has been called a "fish" by the English throughout the play) he remarks: "Very like; one of them / Is a plain fish, and no doubt marketable" (5.1.263–66). Like Trinculo, Antonio sees Caliban in terms of market value. However humorous the intent of his remark, Antonio's observation works to reveal the mercenary impulse uncomfortably latent in Elizabethan colonialism. The Europeans of *The Tempest* contribute, in fact, to a larger cultural endeavor, rendering the play, in the words of Paul Brown, "a limit text in which the characteristic operations of colonialist discourse may be discerned."[11] As illustrated in *The Tempest*, the market found agency through human actors who vivified and extended a commercial ideology.

Taken in the context of Trinculo's vision, Antonio's comment also underscores the fact that the process of commodity evaluation comprised a significant measure of the Renaissance market's instrumental dynamics. In such a way the power of the market depended as much on its placelessness as on any permanent or periodic physical status. Indeed, the market translated its force conceptually, acting as the annex through which monetary forces expressed – in Renaissance London and outside it – the energy of nascent capitalism. It did not do so without complications. To Breton and Shakespeare, as to many of their contemporaries, in allowing money an ostensibly unprecedented, unrestrained latitude in the determination and characterization of urban relations, London's market functioned not only as a site of opportunity for retailing their literary works, but also as a dynamic locus of dangerous social change.

In the late 1590s and early 1600s the playwrights of Renaissance

London began confronting the extent and implications of the market with what can only be described as an anxious urgency, a felt imperative to interpret the "new" intricacies of commercial exchange with a newly-constructed theatrical vocabulary of the urban marketplace. By no means a new activity, economic transaction in an expanding market *seemed* novel, if only because of the market's rapid evolution, geographic extension, and the increasing anonymity of exchanges performed there. During this period, roughly from *The Merchant of Venice* (1596) to *Bartholomew Fair* (1614), London's dramatists not only turned their attention to the relationship between sexual and monetary transaction in the city, the conceptual bases of labor and property, and the exigencies of urban life itself but, in a corollary move, came to erase traditional, referential boundaries separating stage and polis.

London's drama began to contribute in important ways to the manner in which playwrights and audiences thought through the relatively radical developments transforming their society. With the force of social perturbation infusing the lives of Londoners with an increasing insistence, English drama found itself actively inventing answers to questions of special social import. Individual incidents and events characterized this period as one in which the social implications of economic activity came to the fore. One might take as representative the manner in which the agricultural depression of the 1590s prompted a large rural migration to London (which in turn led to increased unemployment there); increased poverty and vagrancy, and the Poor Law of 1597/8 (reenacted, with slight alterations, 1601); the anger directed at the economic success of immigrants and foreigners living in London throughout the 1590s; the official founding of the East India Company in 1600; and the escalating, often notorious, activity surrounding monopolies and patents during James' reign. In his study of "Social Protest and Popular Disturbances in England, 1509–1640," Roger Manning points out that the last two decades of Elizabeth's reign witnessed a disproportionate amount of popular protest in London:

Between 1581 and 1602, the city was disturbed by no fewer than 35 outbreaks of disorder. Since there were at least 96 insurrections, riots, and unlawful assemblies in London between 1517 and 1640, this means that more than one third of the instances of popular disorder during that century-and-a-quarter were concentrated within a 20-year period.[12]

Manning ascribes this unrest in great part to "the effects of war and the extraordinarily rapid population growth."[13]

Issues and incidents like these proved of great interest to playwrights in the period. In response to them, a substantial portion of the drama served a primary, topical end. With their emphasis on and import for English characters and politics, plays like *Arden of Feversham* (1591), *A Larum for London, or The Siege of Antwerp* (1599), and *The Roaring Girl* (1611) work to substantiate Andrew Gurr's observation that, from the 1590s, "the popular playhouses began to tap that reservoir of curiosity about the real lives of living people which is now the chief refreshment in newspapers."[14] But it is instead the way the late-Elizabethan and early-Jacobean era became the focus of a variety of pressures, I believe, that most distinguished it as a time of heightened interdependency of the literary and the social. Most often the plays of Shakespeare's age seem to have responded to highly generalized historical forces, the influence of the material on the living surfacing primarily as the accumulation of additive, rather than abrupt, factors. Although pressures like the economic brought about, with sustained force and endurance, significant change across a broad spectrum of society, the traces of such pressures can be seen better in sum than in part. Correspondingly, the task of retrieval becomes more complicated, as one attempts to trace the indirect, often subtle ways the abstract pressures of social change manifested themselves in dramatic texts.

One of these forces was the high rate of economic inflation, surely a factor in the increase of social unrest and popular disturbance during the period from 1581–1602. Historians have pointed to this period, in fact, as a time of telling discrepancy between wages and buying power. Indexing the prices of six categories – farinaceous, meat and fish, butter and cheese, drink, fuel, and textiles – against the real income of builders in Southern England in the years 1264–1954, E. H. Phelps Brown and Sheila V. Hopkins find the early modern period to have been a time of great poverty for many: "A drastic fall set in about 1510: the level enjoyed at the accession of Henry VIII was not to be reached again until 1880; the lowest point we record in seven centuries was in 1597, the year of the *Midsummer Night's Dream*."[15] Literary scholars today would be more likely to locate *1 Henry IV* or *The Merry Wives of Windsor* in that year , but Brown and Hopkins' point still holds: during Shakespeare's lifetime – during the period he was producing English literature's most acclaimed work – the real incomes of many of his countrymen and women were the lowest they would be in seven centuries. As Peter Ramsey points out, in the later sixteenth century "the main victim of price changes was undoubtedly the urban labourer, producing none of his own food and perhaps suffering a fall in real wages of more than 50 per cent."[16] Ramsey goes on to notice that "Studies of urban communities in the late sixteenth and early seventeenth century suggest that perhaps half their populations lived in direst poverty and squalor, on the edge of total destitution and starvation."[17] While the poverty was real and pressing, however, in 1600 "there was less relief available for a larger population than in 1500, and a greater proportion of them were poorer than ever before."[18]

Another example of material change characterizing the period of 1590–1620 and its drama resides in the tremendous growth of London's population, an increase which exacerbated the problems of overcrowding already in existence and undoubtedly worsened the economic situation of the poor. Yet concentrating large numbers in a central urban place, it also enlarged the scope and extent of the market by enhancing economic activity with increased demand and opportunity for commercial exchange, legal and illegal alike. Certainly the problems of poverty led to an increase in crime and vagabondage: much literature of the 1590s and early 1600s is, in fact, obsessed with the liquidity of property and people. To define the Renaissance market in terms of place, action, demand, and opportunity is, again, to acknowledge the overwhelming importance of human agency in the schema: all four drew energy, I would argue, from the sustained concentration of people afforded by the historical process of urbanization. Population growth thus participated in a symbiotic relationship with the expansion and intensification of market activity, and formed one of the material bases of the Renaissance theater.

The people

London's population escalated in the hundred-year period from 1550 to 1650. While estimates of the real numbers vary, the following table provides an estimate of the growth of both London and England.

	England	London
1576	3,412,000	180,000
1603	4,156,000	250,000
1642	5,112,000	350,000[19]

These figures substantiate A. L. Beier and Roger Finlay's observation that the "sharpest increase in the capital's population came between 1580 and 1640."[20] As this table also reveals, London far outstripped England in terms of population growth rate. The significance of the disparity did not go unnoticed. A contemporary chronicler claimed that London "is going to eat up all England," and King James himself prophesied that, "With time England will be only London."[21] In a pamphlet entitled *A Good Speed to Virginia*, published in 1609, Robert Gray used overpopulation as an excuse for colonizing the New World:

Our multitudes, like too much blood in the body, do infect our country with plague and poverty; our land hath brought forth, but it hath not milk sufficient in the breast thereof to nourish all those children which it hath brought forth; it affordeth neither employment nor preferment for those that depend upon it.[22]

Gray's argument came when such an assertion was safe to make: by the turn of the century the extent of the problem of overpopulation in London had already become glaringly apparent. In a 1602 proclamation "Prohibiting Further Building or Subdividing of Houses in London," the Elizabethan authorities attempted to give new teeth to a phenomenally unsuccessful order of 1580 which had banned the building or subdividing of new houses in London. The 1602 proclamation detailed the problems – actual and potential – of urban crowding in the following way:

Whereas the Queen's most excellent majesty heretofore in her princely wisdom and providence foreseeing the great and manifold inconveniences and mischiefs which did then grow and were like more and more to increase unto the state of the city of London, and the suburbs and confines thereof, by the access and confluence of people to inhabit in the same, not only by reason that such multitudes could hardly be governed by ordinary justice to serve God and obey her majesty without constituting an addition of more officers, and enlarging of authorities and jurisdictions for that purpose, but also could hardly be provided of sustentation of victual, food, and other like necessaries for man's relief upon reasonable prices; and finally for that such great multitudes of people being brought to inhabit in small rooms, whereof a great part being poor and such as must live by begging or by worse means, and being heaped up together and in a sort smothered with many families of children and servants in one house or small tenement, it must needs follow if any plague or other universal sickness should by God's permission enter among those multitudes, that the same would not only spread itself and invade the whole city and confines but would be also dispersed through all other parts of the realm.[23]

For all its official rhetoric, the proclamation manages to paint a disturbing portrait of how the city's concentration of population had led, by 1602, to an inhuman "heap[ing] up" of its people. In his study of the plague's influence on Renaissance England, Paul Slack notes that the Recorder of London reported an instance in 1603 where "there were 800 cases of plague in a single building, formerly one of four large mansions which now together housed 8000 people."[24] As horrible as such living conditions must have been, however, they become historical "fact" only through the official mortality records. Formal chronicles typically capture the real only by accident – or, as in the case of the above plague deaths, by what appears accidental. Because of its nature as a graduated, ostensibly inexorable process, population increase stands in the background, rather than forefront, of the social reality encoded in literature. But it is precisely because of population growth's real and quotidian influence that it needs to be studied as a basis to the culture and cultural production of Renaissance England.

In a recent essay Lawrence Manley underscores the cultural response to population growth in describing a transformation in the character of London's "topographical writing," or cartography, during the seventeenth century. In the new city maps, according to Manley, "the cultural facts of urban life began to be conceptually opposed to nature, as the human status once claimed by the city began to be appropriated to individual observers situated in an unnaturally changeful, even monstrous, landscape."[25] Any study of Renaissance London's "monstrous" topography must focus on the material forces – in Manley's phrase, "cultural facts" – changing the way Londoners themselves perceived the city; these perceptions, as well as the material forces underlying them, emerged in the maps, pamphlets, and plays of Renaissance London: the city often encoded in its cultural self-representations what the population table gives in statistics.

I cite the example of population growth also because, even as it managed to fuel the already volatile workings of the urban market, the influx of people into London from other areas of England assumed a signal role in the construction of the Elizabethan and Jacobean drama. During the period in which London and England underwent a tremendous period of growth, both economic and demographic, an unprecedented number of plays, playwrights, and playhouses rose to fill the demand for popular entertainment. In one way, Keynes was correct in suggesting that "we" were "just in a financial position to afford Shakespeare at the moment when he presented himself."[26] Instead of "we," though, one might read "London," because the urban market for popular entertainment expanded dramatically in the years immediately preceding the turn of the century. Parts of the extended market itself, popular and private playhouses all depended on the regular attendance of Londoners to stay in business.

Beginning with the Red Lion in 1567, the Theater in 1576, and the Curtain in 1577, London audiences sponsored the construction (and conversion of existing structures into theaters) of the Rose in 1587, the Swan in 1595, the Second Blackfriars in 1597 (used from 1600), the Globe in 1599, the Fortune in 1600, the Boar's Head (from 1597 to) 1602, the Red Bull in 1604, the Whitefriars in 1608, the Hope in 1614, and the Cockpit (also known as the Phoenix) in 1616. One might note that nine of the twelve theaters began operations within the 1595–1616 period. In no way, of course, could so many theaters have existed in and around London without the financial support of a continually expanding playgoing populace. Thus the material conditions of English history – and

more specifically, of the city of London and its immediate environs –
worked toward a powerful concentration of artistic talent and popular
demand for entertainment. If William Empson was partly facetious in
suggesting that "the arts are produced by overcrowding,"[27] it is nevertheless evident that the "overcrowding" of the extended city of London –
something more remarkable then than now – produced a diverse group of
plays that contributed, individually and collectively, to the audience's
reflexive understanding of the nature and extent of the forces transforming their shared society.[28]

The playhouse

In some ways the playhouses for which the Renaissance dramatist wrote
can be seen as metaphors of the city and the urban experience generally.
Sometimes, in fact, the formal operations of city and playhouse struck
observers as being closely aligned. Each tended to be characterized by
crowding, and by the potential effects – both good and bad – of groups of
people in proximity. Satisfying these groups through the spectacle of
performance, whether political or theatrical, became the key to their
continuance. The publication, in 1532, of Machiavelli's *The Prince* provided Renaissance commentators with philosophical and practical connections betweeen appearance and achievement. As Jonas Barish points
out, Machiavelli "launched a theatrical conception of human behavior
upon the world. The essence of the numerous cautions and counsels urged
upon the prince ... was that he could acquire the power he sought, and
maintain it once he had acquired it, only by showing himself in a certain
light."[29] In a chapter entitled "What a Prince Should Do to Be Held in
Esteem," Machiavelli praises his contemporary, Ferdinand of Aragon,
the king of Spain, who has "always done and ordered great things, which
have always kept the minds of his subjects in suspense and admiration,
and occupied with their outcome."[30] Describing how Ferdinand has
committed various cruelties while "under this same cloak" (i.e. the cloak
of religious hypocrisy, which he has worn as though costumed),
Machiavelli makes clear the theatrical basis of the office of the modern
Prince, a ruler who keeps his subjects "in suspense and admiration, and
occupied with [the] outcome" of his theatricalized politics. His subjects,
like spectators at a play, watch him act.

In the manner of Machiavelli's Prince, theatrical rulers like Duke
Vincentio of Shakespeare's *Measure for Measure* (1604) make apparent,
with their speech as well as their behavior, the reasons why the words
"politic," "political," "policy," and "politician" held such pejorative
meanings in Renaissance usage.[31] Vincentio's metaphor for the busi-

ness of governing the polis of Vienna springs from the boards of the
stage:

> I love the people,
> But do not like to stage me to their eyes;
> Though it do well, I do not relish well
> Their loud applause and aves vehement ...

(1.1.67–70)

These "loud applause and aves vehement" resemble nothing so much as
the (intended) response to a dramatic production in one of London's
numerous playhouses. It is worth noting that the Duke's disavowal here
precedes his more thorough theatricalizing of his persona – his disguising
himself as the "duke of dark corners." Indeed, his patent separation of
playhouse and polis functions itself as a theatrical gesture, suggesting the
necessity of a ruler's maintenance and manipulation of illusion. In their
need for and dedication to the spectacular, the actor and politician shared
a similar goal.

Like politicians, playwrights need audiences. With up to or over 3,000
people filling an amphitheater playhouse like the Swan or the Globe,[32] the
physical conditions experienced during a production at a purpose-built
Renaissance theater must have replicated in telling ways those of the city
in large. To the actors on the open stage, the surrounding, Argus-eyed
audience probably seemed, as in the phrasing of the proclamation quoted
above, "heaped up together and in a sort smothered." Not surprisingly,
what one might call the theme of theatrical claustrophobia ran through
much of the self-representation of Renaissance plays, with dramatists and
other writers often expressing a (now familiar) resentment toward crowds
and crowding. "The beast multitude," for instance, was one of Jonson's
favorite ways of describing the audience.[33] Similarly, Shakespeare's
adjectival modification of "multitude" is nearly always pejorative. Characters in his plays use the following terms and phrases to qualify the word:
"still-discordant, wav'ring," "giddy," "rude," "ragged," "Lightly blown
to and fro," "many-headed," "distracted," "barbarous," and "differing"
(i.e. fickle).[34] Prejudice attributed to dramatic characters, such constant
animus may have had its roots in theatrical praxis. Aversion to the
playhouse masses surfaces clearly in the preface epistle to the second state
of the 1609 quarto of *Troilus and Cressida* (1602), where the anonymous
author promises the purchaser that it is a "new play, never stal'd with the
Stage, never clapper-clawed with the palms of the vulgar." The punning
on "clap" as applause in "clapper-clawed" looks upon the physicality of
the playhouse audience with disdain. Similarly, the Prologue of Jonson's
Poetaster (1601) expresses rhyming contempt for those "base detractors
and illiterate apes, / That fill up rooms in fair and formal shapes"

(Prologue, 9–10). Likewise, Cleopatra's trepidation over being displayed with Iras as "an Egyptian puppet" in Rome – where "Mechanic slaves / With greasy aprons, rules, and hammers shall / Uplift us to the view" (5.2.209–11) – underscores a continual uneasiness surrounding mass congregation and popular spectacle in the Renaissance theater. A modern parallel: after the opening of the new Swan playhouse at Stratford, Barry Russell noticed something of the same thing – even with the new Swan's much smaller (*c.* 430-seat) capacity – as I am arguing for in relation to the Renaissance playhouse. "The feel of the auditorium," he writes, "is surprisingly intimate ... I suspect that, from the actor's point of view, it may prove a daunting space to perform in. Certainly, some members of the company for *The Two Noble Kinsmen* (Russell later adds that many were "seasoned veterans") showed signs of feeling terribly exposed when they came more than halfway downstage." Russell continues: "It cruelly exposes any weakness of gesture or lack of physical intensity."[35] The "surprisingly intimate" atmosphere of the new Swan may give us a clue as to the kind of physical pressure actors underwent in the Renaissance playhouse.[36]

The problems of mass congregation, however, were not confined to the interiors of the playhouses themselves. When James Burbage attempted to open a new hall playhouse in Blackfriars in 1596 after having converted the old monastery especially for theatrical use, the generally affluent residents of the special City Liberty petitioned the Privy Council to bar the theater from beginning operations. Their reasoning reveals not only that London was becoming a much bigger – and, paradoxically, at the same time smaller – place, but also the fact that the playhouses of London functioned as a kind of city in miniature, focusing and elaborating the problems of London proper. "The said Burbage," the petition ran,

> is now altering and meaneth very shortly to convert and turn the same into a common playhouse, which will grow to be a very great annoyance and trouble, not only to all the noblemen and gentlemen thereabout inhabiting but also a general inconvenience to all the inhabitants of the same precinct, both by reason of the great resort and gathering together of all manner of vagrant and lewd persons that, under color of resorting to the plays, will come thither and work all manner of mischief, and also to the great pestering and filling up of the same precinct, if it should please God to send any visitation of sickness as heretofore hath been for that the same precinct is already grown very populous ...[37]

Burbage's commercial venture within the City walls prompted the signatories of the Blackfriars petition to claim, and apparently with good cause, that the City was too "populous" to bear a full-time professional theater. One might take the imagery underlying the petition – "which will grow ... great resort and gathering together ... great pestering and filling up ... already grown populous" – and compare it with the wording of the "Building or Subdividing" prohibition of 1602: "great multitudes ... in small rooms ... heaped up together and in a sort smothered." To the petition's signatories the proposed theater would only exacerbate the problem of overcrowding in their precinct.[38] This is likely to have been accepted as a legitimate complaint: it was, after all, as the embodied metaphors of London itself that the theaters bore the immediate economic burden of the bubonic plague. Whenever plague deaths in London exceeded a certain number, the authorities forced the playhouses to close their doors in an attempt to prevent the spread of the "pestilence." The Blackfriars petition makes capital of this in its bad faith expectation of providence sending "any visitation of sickness as heretofore hath been." It was partly as a malign trope of the precinct itself, then, that the proposed playhouse came to arouse such concerted opposition.

In conjunction with their urban symbolism, London's playhouses can also be described as practical examples of the market. The popular theater itself was, of course, entirely commercial. As Michael Bristol points out, "the public playhouses ... were a de facto element in the economic and social life of London," and "on a day-to-day basis, the professional companies conducted their affairs as a commercial enterprise."[39] From carpenters like Peter Street, responsible for the "erecting, building and setting up" of the Fortune in 1600, to any of the many shareholders in the acting companies and even watermen whose living depended on ferrying theatergoers across the Thames to the Bankside and back, the workings of the playhouses revolved around money. Before assenting to a special staging of *Richard II* (1595) at the Globe on the eve of the Essex rebellion in February of 1601, for instance, members of the Chamberlain's Men made certain they secured a bonus, expecting a low turnout for such an old play. In the official deposition given to the authorities during the subsequent inquiries, Augustine Phillips, one of the Chamberlain's Men and an original shareholder in the Globe, confessed to having performed the drama only after obtaining a special fee. Phillips, called the "Examinate" in the document, said that several of the men in Essex's faction

spoke to some of the players in the presence of the Examinate to have the play of the deposing and killing of King Richard the Second to be played the Saturday next ... Where this Examinate and his fellows were determined to have played some other play, holding that play of King Richard to be so old and so long out of use that they should have small or no company at it. But at their [the conspirators'] request this Examinate and his fellows were content to play it the Saturday and had their xl[s] more than their ordinary for it, and so played it accordingly.[40]

Whether Phillips and his companions sympathized with the conspirators (it seems safe to assume they were not entirely ignorant of the special production's potential political ramifications), their insistence upon the forty-shilling subsidy remains significant. If not actually as mercenary as it made them seem, the players might nonetheless have counted on the bonus payment to persuade the authorities to the contrary: a kind of cynical insurance policy. In a situation so fraught with danger, it may also have constituted a potential *reminder* to the authorities – rather than a new argument – of the theater's essential commercialism.

The mercenary part of the theater apparent from this anecdote surfaces nowhere so clearly, of course, as in the pages of Philip Henslowe's *Diary*. Henslowe, apprenticed to a London dyer, "made himself wealthy by the simple expedient of marrying his master's widow."[41] Calling Henslowe "a businessman, and not an over-scrupulous one," Peter Thomson points out that Henslowe was involved with mining, "the manufacture of starch, in real estate, in pawnbroking, and in money-lending."[42] We know that Henslowe was involved in the construction of the Rose playhouse in 1587, and later developed a strong financial interest in animal baiting. When, in 1592, his step-daughter Joan married Edward Alleyn, the preeminent actor of his day, Henslowe gained an invaluable contact in the acting profession. With Alleyn, Henslowe obtained a joint patent as Master of the Royal Game of Bears, Bulls, and Mastiff Dogs in 1604. With its clerical, obsessive concern over profit and commodity, Henslowe's *Diary* – a combination of notebook and ledger – stands as strong testament to the commercial basis of the Renaissance theater. His careful notations show a virtual web of financial relations, the seemingly endless list of entries like "Item paid for," "Item lent unto" and "Received of" connecting dramatists, carpenters, actors, and shareholders through strands of debt and credit. The following constitutes a typical entry in the *Diary*:

Memorandum that the 6 of October 1597 Thomas Downton came and bound himself unto me in forty pounds in covenant and assumpsit by the receiving of three pence of me before witness[es]. The covenant is this: that he should from the day above written until Shrovetide next come two years to play with me in my house and in no other about London publicly; if he do without my consent to forfeit unto me this sum of money above written witness to this

E Alleyn	Robert Shaw
William Borne	John Singer
Dick Jones[43]	

Henslowe's contract, based on the exchange of three pence and a promise for the security of forty pounds, reads more like an indenture. Apparent from this, and every page of the *Diary* concerning the theater, is the inescapable fact that the Renaissance stage was, primarily, a place of business. As businesses, playhouses operated with a logic of profit and loss; it is to such a logic, I believe, that we should look in order to understand their place in the cultural dynamics of Renaissance London.

Indeed, in addition to its implications for our understanding of the cultural situation of London's theaters, what the failure of Burbage's venture in the Blackfriars precinct also suggests is that the Renaissance amphitheaters might have been built in the outskirts of London not only to circumvent the City Fathers and Puritain detractors, but also in response to contemporary political and economic exigency. At the same time that it made some areas of the city unobtainable for and even hostile to theater operation, demographic pressure rendered the relatively open land of the Fields and Liberties surrounding London more attractive areas on which to construct new places of business. As many of the detail maps and engravings of Elizabethan London and its environs indicate, the Fields and Liberties offered the prospective theater-owner an open area for building.[44] Even the desire to avoid the political power of the City Fathers, however, can be seen as economic, rather than ideological, in origin. Jealous of their investments, investors probably thought of financial considerations before ideological ones. While we must not underestimate the importance of political opposition as a partial motivation for construction of the theaters in extramural London, it would appear that – at least economically – the owners and operators of the amphitheaters may have had little other choice: physically, as well as ideologically, the public theaters stood in direct competition with the business and businesses of the City. Among these, of course, was the business of housing the populace.

After the advent of the Civil War forced the closing of the theaters in 1642, for example, the Globe, Blackfriars, and Hope all succumbed to the pressures of population growth, giving way to new housing. As a manuscript continuation of John Stowe's *Annales of England* records:

The Globe playhouse on the Banks side in Southwark, was burnt down to the ground, in the year 1612. And now built up again in the year 1613, at the great charge of King James, and many Noblemen and others. And now pulled down to the ground, by Sir Matthew Brand, On Monday the 15 of April 1644, to make tenements in the room of it.

The Black Friars players playhouse in Black Friars, London, which had stood many years, was pulled down to the ground on Monday the 6 day of August 1655, and tenements built in the room ...

The Hope, on the Banks side in Southwark, commonly called the Bear Garden, a Play House for Stage Plays on Mondays, Wednesdays, Fridays, and Saturdays, and for the baiting of the Bears on Tuesdays and Thursdays, the stage being made to take up and down when they please. It was built in the year 1610, and now pulled down to make tenements, by Thomas Walker, a petticoat maker in Cannon Street, on Tuesday the 25 day of March 1656.[45]

A traditional characterization of the conversion of playhouses to tenements might describe the action as unfortunate, perhaps even "tragic," reading the process from a Friends of the Globe position: unscrupulous landlords (including "a petticoat maker") capitalize on political instability to the detriment of Art. Thus the genius of Tudor and Stuart drama falls victim to historical accident. Read from another perspective, however, the conversion of the theaters into tenements might not only seem an ethical one – possibly providing much-needed living space in an inhumanly crowded city – but indeed part of a historically inevitable process of urban concentration and expansion. Whatever its politics, such a perspective would return the Renaissance theater to a concrete place in the structure of the material world, acknowledging the primacy of the material over the ideal. Such an acknowledgment was made first by the dramatists of the Renaissance themselves.

3　"City comedy" and the materialist vision

Earlier in this study I argued against seeing the Renaissance playhouse as a marginal institution, suggesting that such a dichotomy misapprehends the fluidity of the market and the city, and overestimates the ideological difference of the Elizabethan and Jacobean playhouses. I posited, in its place, a material theater, a theater revolving around profit and closely connected with a dynamic market and the exigencies of urban life. A final objection to the idea of London as a stolid, unapproving entity whose Liberties are exploited by the playhouses might be lodged on the grounds that such a portrait engages the euphemistic sense of the phrase "taking liberties," calling up a paradigm in which the City, here gendered male (cf. "City Fathers"), is cuckolded in the (female) suburbs and outskirts by lawless (male) players and playhouses. Although poets of the period frequently employed these gendered topographies – here one might point to Rosalind's remark on dwelling "in the skirts of the forest, like fringe upon a petticoat" (*As You Like It* 3.2.335–37), or any of the many examples of the topoi of a city's sack as "rape" (the city here gendered female) – such anthropomorphic depictions, I would suggest, can limit our critical understanding of real social situations. In segmenting different areas of the city, I want to argue, conceptualizations like this tend to exaggerate the differences between margin and center – differences which, significantly enough, scenes and characters in the plays often work to contradict.

For instance, when, in *Measure for Measure* (1604), Pompey announces the Duke's new proclamation stipulating that "All houses in the suburbs of Vienna must be pluck'd down," Mistress Overdone replies immediately: "And what shall become of those in the city?" (1.2.95–97). Thematically, her query underscores the institutional hypocrisy of Vienna. Her question, however, also emphasizes the fact that, at least in relation to early-modern urban geography, clear-cut divisions are often more fictive than actual. As Emrys Jones points out,

One of the characteristics of the later, industrial city – and of our cities today – is that marked social segregation gives rise to homogeneous social areas, such as working-class estates, and middle-class suburbs: social separation is clearly reflected in spatial separation. The pre-industrial city is characterised by great social mixing for two reasons. Firstly streets of substantial houses often had lanes and alleyways of squalor immediately behind them ... The parish was more like a microcosm of the city as a whole than a social quarter. Secondly, social mix prevailed even within the prosperous houses, which often consisted of a shop or workroom on the ground floor, proprietor on the first, journeyman on the second and servants in the attic.[1]

Although Jones is referring here to London in 1638, his description of the mixture of social classes and the lack of spatial separation generally applies to the London of Elizabeth and James as well. In his study of the parish of Southwark in the seventeenth century, Jeremy Boulton argues that "Demographically Southwark and its component parts were very much part of the metropolitan whole," and that the social map of Renaissance London "may be conceived of more fruitfully as a mosaic of neighbourhoods than as one single amorphous community."[2] As we have seen, however, the temptation to replicate the received boundaries of "City" and "suburbs" has led many critics into an equally unwieldy "two Londons" position. In what follows, I mean to show how the practice of reading London as the City rather than the city has led to the modern formulation of the Renaissance subgenre of "city comedy," a literary category stressing the surface features and topical import of plays openly set in London.[3] It is my belief that, while having proved instrumental in beginning a project which focuses on the political and social aspects of Renaissance drama, the concept of "city comedy" has outlived its usefulness as an aid to understanding plays of the era. Because of its acceptance – even institutionalization – as a subgenre, however, and because of the role it has played (and promises to play) in shaping critical ideas about the theater's connections with London, it cannot be dismissed lightly. What follows is a brief analysis of the role "city comedy" has taken, and continues to take, in examinations of the drama's relationship to social life. I argue that the concept of *place*, once crucial to a social analysis of the plays, is ultimately less important in Renaissance drama than a concern with material life which underlies the themes and structures of the drama, a concern I call the materialist vision.

"City comedy"

Coming out of the same tumultuous decade which produced Keynes' observations and L. C. Knights' *Drama and Society in the Age of Jonson*, R. C. Bald's 1934 article, "The Sources of Middleton's City Comedies," appears to have used the term "city comedy" for the first time.[4] The recognition of a kind of protorealism in the topicality of Jacobean drama, of course, was anything but new. Felix Schelling, for instance, had already used the phrase "comedies of London life" to describe plays like Dekker's *The Shoemakers' Holiday* (1599).[5] Likewise in 1925 Wilbur Dunkel suggested that Thomas Middleton "chose realistic rather than romantic places with the intention of making the actions of the plays thoroughly convincing as photographic representations of London life."[6] And while Wilhelm Creizenach called such plays "realistic London Comedies,"[7] L. C. Knights, in *Drama and Society*, preferred the label of "social dramas." Despite these general characterizations, it was not until 1968, and Brian Gibbons' highly influential *Jacobean City Comedy*, that "city comedy" earned official status as a Renaissance subgenre. In this study Gibbons insists that "City Comedy may be seen as a distinct dramatic genre with a recognizable form and conventions of theme, setting, and characterization."[8] He suggests as definition that "the plays are all satiric and have urban settings, with characters and incident appropriate to such settings; they exclude material appropriate to romance, fairy tale, sentimental legend or patriotic chronicle."[9] Gibbons describes one of his primary goals in the study as "to show that the dramatists of Jacobean City Comedy articulated a radical critique of their Age."[10] For Gibbons, as for many other critics, the London plays of Thomas Middleton form the core of the subgenre.

Gibbons' work sponsored an intensive critical interest in the plays he called "City Comedies," with the concept becoming ever more solidified in the critical imagination. Centering on the belief that city comedy forms a special, if small subgenre, something like a city comedy canon, in fact, has taken form. To Susan Wells, for instance, city comedy is a compact literary kind that "flourished from 1605 to 1630. Its most accomplished writers – Jonson, Middleton, and Marston – produced a limited number of 'city' plays, distinct in tone and structure from older romantic treatments of the city, such as Dekker's *The Shoemaker's Holiday*."[11] Similarly, Gamini Salgado admitted that "the phrase 'Jacobean City Comedy,' like all such phrases, is no more than a convenient label for the editor and critic," in the introduction to an anthology entitled *Four Jacobean City Comedies*.[12] Wendy Griswold's recent study, devoted in large part to the theatrical and social legacy of English Renaissance city comedy, takes up thirteen plays which form part of the nucleus of what is generally considered city comedy: Jonson's *Every Man in His Humour* (1598), *Epicoene* (1609), *The Alchemist* (1610), *Bartholomew Fair* (1614), and *The Devil is an Ass* (1616); Marston's *The Dutch Courtesan* (1605); Middleton's *A Trick to Catch the Old One* (1605), *A Mad World, My Masters* (1606), and *A Chaste Maid in Cheapside* (1613); Chapman, Jonson, and Marston's *Eastward Ho!* (1605); Lording Barry's *Ram Alley*

(1608); Fletcher's *Wit Without Money* (1614); and Massinger's *A New Way to Pay Old Debts* (1625).[13] The thematic characteristics and main topics which Griswold distills from these plays – London setting; socially heterogeneous characters; trickery; money; social mobility; cynicism; moral ambiguity – are all commonly accepted earmarks of the subgenre; in informing the above plays with an apparently special kind of topical energy, they constitute the basis of what is commonly called "city comedy."

Yet even the apparently homogeneous dramas cited in the list above fail to make up a distinct or even loose subgenre. As Lee Bliss indicates, city comedy is "a notably slippery genre concept, and definitions vary: to some, it means satiric urban comedy of financial and sexual intrigue ... for others the parameters broaden to include another development in the public theaters' heartily optimistic, morally didactic citizen comedies."[14] Indeed, as I will argue, a major difficulty raised both by "city comedy" and the less prominent subgenre of "citizen comedy" is that of place, of defining the city itself. Alexander Leggatt acknowledged the nature of the problem when, attempting to deal only with "citizen" comedies set in England, he was forced to except Heywood's *Honest Whore* (1604, 1605, I and II) because "its Bedlam and Bridewell scenes give it a definite local reference despite its ostensibly Italian setting" and "the Cambridge comedy *Club Law* (1599), in which Athens is a very thin disguise for the English university town."[15] Legatt's difficulty with these plays comes from their refusal to stay abroad: cities described as foreign are actually familiar. But this, of course, is more often the rule than the exception in Renaissance drama, for London habitually – even relentlessly – slides into the "foreign" settings of plays.[16] One name for such topographical solecism is "anatopism," a word coined by Coleridge and defined by De Quincy as a "geographical blunder."[17] Geographical blundering, though, can be a limited way of characterizing the tendency of the Renaissance theaters to collapse distance and difference. One place to locate the origins of this tendency, of course, is in the theater itself, where the anatopical foundations of Renaissance drama derive from the possibilities afforded by the open space of the platform stage, a place where, as Sidney complained in his *Apology*, "you ... have Asia of the one side, and Afric of the other."[18] The Renaissance stage remained notorious for its ability to compress, mingle, alter, interchange, and disguise geographic places. It is this ability – surfacing in the geographical "blunders" of the Renaissance stage – which forms the chief stumbling block to the concept of "city comedy."

An illuminating example (and even discussion) of this phenomenon comes in the bizarre "widow Dido" episode in *The Tempest* (1611), a passage which has traditionally puzzled critics. Following Adrian's suggestion that "Tunis was never grac'd before with such a paragon to their queen," Gonzalo responds, "Not since widow Dido's time" (2.1.75–77). Gonzalo's apparent mistake draws the ridicule of his fellow characters:

> ADRIAN. She was of Carthage, not of Tunis.
> GONZALO. This Tunis, sir, was Carthage.
> ADRIAN. Carthage?
> GONZALO. I assure you, Carthage.
> ANTONIO. His word is more than the miraculous harp.
> SEBASTIAN. He hath rais'd the wall, and the houses too.
> ANTONIO. What impossible matter will he make easy next?
> SEBASTIAN. I think he will carry this island home in his pocket, and
> give it his son for an apple.
>
> (2.1.83–92)

Instead of helping his cause, Gonzalo's attempt to save face ("This Tunis, sir, was Carthage") elicits further derision from Antonio and Sebastian. Their joking rebuttals, however, stand in the long tradition of what one might call Shakespeare's dramatic innoculation, that is, his habit of foregrounding elements of his dramaturgical craft in the action of the drama itself. He ironically anticipates (even preempts) notice of his theatrical manipulations by having members of the dramatis personae supplement the audience's eventual responses to the play, thus giving *The Tempest* a temporary veneer of realism by capturing its fantasy in a theatrical *mise en abyme*. For Antonio to suggest that Gonzalo's anatopical mistake is a "word . . . more than the miraculous harp" (in mythology, Amphion's harp raised the walls of Thebes), for Sebastian to point out that "He hath rais'd the wall, and the houses too," and to foresee the time Gonzalo might "carry this island home in his pocket, and give it his son for an apple" – these are observations not only on Gonzalo's errors, and Shakespeare's own habit of deliberate, sometimes mischievous geographical solecism (Jonson's disdain of which, for instance, appears very clearly in the *Conversations* in his remarks on the Bohemian shipwreck of *The Winter's Tale* (1610)), but also on the anatopical praxis of the Renaissance theater itself. Thus, for critics to locate one group of plays in London and another elsewhere fails to acknowledge the temporary power of certain locative meaphors and themes in Renaissance drama, and fails to recognize the ultimate *slipperiness* of settings and locales.

When, for example, is Florence Florence, and when is Florence London? As issued in the 1601 Quarto, Ben Jonson's *Every Man in His Humour* patently occurs in Florence, its dramatis personae having Italianate names. When published in the 1616 Folio, however, the scene is clearly defined as "London," its characters bearing English names: Lorenzo Senior becomes old Kno'well, Prospero becomes Wellbred,

Thorello Kitely, Stephano Stephen, Bobadilla Bobadill, Musco Brain-worm, Matheo Matthew, while Cob remains Cob, and Tib Tib. J. W. Lever, editor of the Regents parallel-text edition, notes that the change Jonson effected in his plays was, in fact, merely cosmetic: "the Florence of the Quarto version was a purely conventional backcloth for English characters and manners. Cob and his wife were undisguised Cockneys, even references to the Exchange, the Mermaid Tavern, pence and shillings, intruded."[19] With slight alteration, then, one city becomes another. Such, after all, is standard comedic practice. As Harry Levin argues about the term "city comedy": "given the long and consistent association of the generic with the thematic in this mode of expression – that is to say, of comedies with cities – the compounded epithet might seem slightly redundant."[20] Levin bases his argument on the Classical and Renaissance perception that comedy was of and about the city, and often topical. "Comedy, more than tragedy," he says, "is a creature of its times."[21]

In acknowledging the intrusive energy of the urban present, that is, the way one aspect of what Leah Marcus calls the "local"[22] manages to make its way into the general, such anatopism dots the fabric of Renaissance drama. Generally, middle and lower-class characters – like *Every Man*'s "Cockney" couple – are responsible for these "slips." Late in Thomas Lodge's Roman history, *The Wounds of Civil War* (1588), for instance, Curtall, a burgher, walks on stage and uses London's best-known landmark – by Lodge's day having been struck and burned by lightning – in a metaphor: "O base mind, that being in the Paul's steeple of honor hast cast thyself into the sink of simplicity."[23] Likewise, Lear's Fool, with his riddling backwards-prophecy and its references to London and England's contemporary situation (3.2.81–94), slyly calls up the ghost of London future – or, for the Globe audience, of London present. Why should it be lower- and middle-class characters who make these references? Perhaps because their social status, connected with the genre of comedy, determines their observations. That is, unlike some of the idealized and idealizing figures of formal tragedy, characters closely associated with appetite and the exigencies of material life – for the burgher: money and commodities; for the Fool: food, drink, and shelter – are anchors grounding the drama in a quotidian, local reality defined by that material life.[24]

Critics have traditionally seen this kind of displacement as an embarrassment: John Hunter, for example, said of the clock striking in *Julius Caesar* (1599) (2.1.192–93) that "this is one of Shakespeare's anachronistic licenses or inadvertencies."[25] Such "inadvertency," however, is too common among the dramatists of Renaissance England to be seen as a lapse. Instead, it was a foundational element of the drama. Part of this derives, I have suggested, from the formal tendencies of comedy itself. Another factor – and something I will explore at greater length below – may have resided in the city's inescapable physicality. The material reality of London undoubtedly had a strong influence on the way playwrights thought about the cities they fictionalized: for a character to swear (however ironically) on a steeple that no longer existed suggests that structures and other physical objects could leave powerful traces in the cultural imagination. London Bridge, London Stone, London Wall, St. Paul's, Paul's Walk, the Pissing Conduit(s), Paris Garden, Cheapside, Thames Street, the Custom-House, Blackfriars, the Exchange(s), the China-Houses, Billingsgate, Lincoln's Inn, Goldsmith's Hall, Bedlam, the Mermaid, Cuckold's Haven, Long Lane, East Cheap, Westminster Abbey, Temple Bar, Savoy Palace, Ram Alley, Bethnall Green, the Boar's Head Tavern, the Merchant Taylors' Hall: these are just a few of the places and structures, in and around London, locating the plays of the period. They often provided dramatists with topographical building blocks for constructing the imaginative structures of their plays – regardless of whether these plays were "set" in contemporary London.

Another possible source of the bifurcated topography of the drama resided in the humanist project: for playwrights exposed to the classical curriculum's emphasis on transhistorically parallel lives, actions and events tended to have a universal significance. Thus when Gail Paster offers that "London is only one of many cities – ancient and modern, actual and mythic – represented on the Elizabethan-Jacobean stage," and that "dramatists set their plays in Venice, Verona, Paris, Athens, Thebes, Troy, and of course Rome," one could go on to suggest that, further, for the Renaissance dramatist these other, various cities – "ancient and modern, actual and mythic" – frequently owe some debt (often a significant one) to London for their compositional genesis.[26] Often, London appears in these cities the same way a character might make herself or himself apparent through the veil of a stage disguise. Through humanistic parallelism and the exploitation of urban likenesses, London often became Rome, even as Rome became London. The same holds, of course, for Florence, Venice, and Troy. It is thus more anomalous to encounter historical and geographic verisimilitude in the plays of the period, or even the attempt to attain such – one notable near-exception being Jonson's *Sejanus* (1603) – than it is to be confronted with a burgher swearing by Paul's steeple, or a clock marking the time, in the midst of imperial Rome.

The above difficulties reside with the definition of cities as related to theatrical place. What about a genre constructed along lines of character, like "citizen" comedy? Here too generic definition proves extremely problematic, especially in relation to social place. Leggatt seems right to relegate citizens to what he calls the middle class, although – especially since J. H. Hexter's work on the myth of the middle class – it is far from certain that such clearly stratified layers were significantly more than the product of social mythology.[27] Class demarcation has proved no less problematic for the literary critic than the historian. Even holding to a loose definition of "citizen" – Leggatt suggests "shopkeepers, merchants, and craftsmen who are rich enough to employ the labor of other men" and those who fall within "the fluid, often ill-defined area that lies between [the court and aristocracy] and the lowest class of worker, servants, rogues, and vagabonds"[28] – one runs into difficulties. What does one do with characters that think and act like citizens, yet are seemingly from another "class"? What about shifting social places? Contradictory class locations?

Here one could look to Sir Timothy Troublesome in Sharpham's *Cupid's Whirligig* (1607), who behaves in every way like the typical citizen of Leggatt's genre. Jealous to the point of ridiculousness, Troublesome behaves so ludicrously that he leads Wages, his servant, to observe that the knight "would willingly prove an accessory to the stealing of his own goods."[29] Citizens of the drama characteristically live in just such a purgatory of self-assumed cuckoldry. Troublesome proclaims early that he will trumpet his cuckoldry: "for I will be a Citizen, and so be a Subject for Poets, and a slave to my own wife."[30] Apparently a knight, Troublesome is actually a citizen in all but name. *Cupid's Whirligig*, in fact, features all the characters – a jealous citizen and his wife; an amorous, predatory gallant; a Welshman; a witty servant; schoolboys – and scenarios typical of the genre. Indeed, in some ways it would be difficult to produce a more representative example of a citizen comedy; as the genre is currently characterized, however, this play would not be grouped with others similar to it in style and content.

In *Cupid's Whirligig* I have deliberately chosen an ambiguous example to illustrate my thesis, for the play clearly dramatizes a common complaint surrounding the Jacobean court – that is, James' habit of knighting wealthy men for money, of selling titles. In one kind of interpretation, then, Troublesome can be explained away as always having been a citizen. However, the apparent contradiction between his title and station – even (or perhaps especially) when seen in this historical context – speaks to that confusion, the confusion between what should be and that which actually is, which underlies the problematic definition of place, both social and topographical, on the Renaissance stage. *Cupid's Whirligig* is not alone, however, in sharing the attributes of citizen comedy without directly assuming its appearance. Plays like Sharpham's own *The Fleer* (1606), John Day's *The Isle of Gulls* (1606) – even, in many ways, *Othello*

(1604) – are much like *Cupid's Whirligig* in their characters and themes, and, also like it, lack the cosmetic appearance of citizen comedy. "Citizen comedy," then, seems no less problematic for genre definition than "city comedy." I do not mean to deny that there was a loose subgenre of citizen comedy on the Renaissance stage: Beaumont's *The Knight of the Burning Pestle* (1607) – in which citizen comedy is parodied by the title of the "intended" production (*The London Merchant*) and by similar, parodic titles suggested by the Citizen (like *The Life and Death of Fat Drake, or the Repairing of Fleet-privies*) as well as by the Citizen and his Wife themselves – makes it apparent that to certain London audiences citizen comedy constituted a recognizable dramatic form. But for the modern reader closely to demarcate the literature of Renaissance London into subgenres like "citizen comedy," "city comedy," and even "bourgeois literature" is to establish potentially misleading categories of analysis – categories which, while closely treating exterior characteristics, can obscure the more complex ways literature manages to incorporate social content.

Where to look for this social content, though, and how to retrieve it? The rapid growth of the city and the ever-intensifying process of change characterizing life in early-modern London led to social pressures finding their outlet not only in urban dramas like Middleton's *Michaelmas Term* (1606) and Jonson's *The Alchemist*, but also in plays as diverse as Shakespeare's *Coriolanus* (1607) and (?) Middleton's *The Revenger's Tragedy* (1606).[31] Correspondingly, much of the drama's own evaluation of the socioeconomic transformation of Renaissance culture was accomplished metaphorically, meditating on subjects of both immediate and perennial concern with a logic of its own construction. In assimilating and mediating the topical energy of the urban market, plays functioned as what one might call social dreams, collective fantasies in the form of popular and private theatrical productions with which English society worked through issues and anxieties irresolvable by non-ludic means. To the modern literary critic, the play-as-social-dream model affords analysis of the "irrational" side of cultural production, a form of textual exegesis aimed at what has been called the "absolute horizon of all reading and all interpretation" – that is, the political.[32] By definition, generic analysis tends to place its emphasis on the manifest – rather than latent – content and thoughts of the drama. Grouping plays together by surface forms, it can pass over deeper concerns and issues. Thus to look only – even initially – to that writing which makes obvious its topicality is to perceive the appearance, and not the submerged reality, of a culture's literary dream work. To address this critical inadequacy, part of the analytical project of the following study is dedicated to exploring the latent social content of Renaissance plays; I intend to do this not through genre, but in terms of what I see as a central preoccupation fusing them together.

The materialist vision

Underlying the thematic and symbolic structures of much of the period's drama is a historically determined pattern of concern with the social order and its relationship to material life, a concern referred to in the following study as the "materialist vision" of the English Renaissance. By this term I mean the collective focus of many dramatists on the essence of the physical world and its often demanding claims upon the foundations of urban existence. Seemingly an oxymoron, the "materialist vision" in fact describes the literary practice of a period which itself yoked material and ideal opposites with remarkable facility. Indeed, much of what is traditionally thought of as the "high" or elevated poetry of the Renaissance almost invariably depends on a rhetorical dialectic of the conceptual and the real.

Critics have described this dialectic in various ways. Eric Auerbach, noting the importance of the physical to some of Shakespeare's tragic characters, calls it a "mixed style," medieval and creatural at base and ultimately related to what he refers to elsewhere as *sermo humilis*.[33] Glossing Bakhtin's theory of Carnival, Michael Bristol speaks of a general "transformation downward and reinterpretation" of reality on the "material, bodily level," a phenomenon he describes in terms of *Hamlet* (1601) as affirming "ordinary productive life," "concrete experience," and "the material principle."[34] Susan Wells draws on Lukács in formulating what she refers to as the "typical" register of texts. To Wells, this register is built on parts of texts which "suggest a connection with the world" and help establish its "referential power," its ability to engage the reader in terms of lived, shared experience.[35] *Sermo humilis*, the material principle, the typical. What these three descriptive terms have in common is their concern with identifying the tension between the ideal and the material, a tension manifest in the praxis of Renaissance literature. They also isolate a central, socially grounded impetus behind this literature, an impetus to found the ideal and the conceptual on the fullness of the real; in brief, "to say what is." In many ways the materialist vision can be seen as the archetypal anticipation of such an injunction, for, by saying "what is" – or, at the very least, wanting to say "what is" – it readily lent itself to the description of physical forces, their effect on everyday life, and the ideational forms invented to make sense of an increasingly complex world.

It is commonly recognized that the themes and language of satire – so prevalent in both Jacobean comedy and tragedy – took firm hold of the dramatic imagination in the late 1590s. Critics usually attribute this development to the restraining order issued by the Archbishop of Canterbury and the Bishop of London on the first of June, 1599, an order which entailed the collection and burning of certain non-dramatic satires and prohibited the future publication of "*Satyres*" and "*Epigrams*." The traditional account of the rise of satire in drama suggests an almost hydraulic transference of satiric energy from pamphlet to playhouse, with the authors of verse satires pushed toward the stage by a governmental decree.[36] Such an explanation, I believe, underestimates the complexity of cultural production, of why writers write as they do when they do. Less important here than any causal explanation of this putative transference, however, is the basic *receptivity* of late Elizabethan and early Jacobean audiences to the satiric strain as expressed in the materialist vision. For the formal qualities of satire alone fail to account for the alteration of tone, style, and content of the drama of the 1590s and early 1600s.

Indeed, apart from the growing popularity of satire, the late 1590s also witnessed the solidification of what critics have come to call the comedy of humours. George Chapman's *An Humourous Day's Mirth* (1597) and Ben Jonson's *Every Man* plays (1598; 1599) portray individual characters as ridiculous types locked into a conceit or pattern of behavior from which deviance is all but impossible. Madeleine Doran refers to this phenomenon in describing the late Elizabethan tendency of "physiological psychology" which, in the construction of dramatic humours, "starts with the person and makes an individual excess, sometimes a vice or passion, but more commonly a mere eccentricity of behavior, the essence of character."[37] Doran points to a *locus classicus* of humours theory in the Induction of *Every Man Out of His Humour*, where Asper (Latin: "rough, uneven") provides a definition of the term:

> Now thus far
> It may, by metaphor, apply itself
> Unto the general disposition:
> As when some one peculiar quality
> Doth so possess a man that it doth draw
> All his affects, his spirits, and his powers,
> In their confluctions, all to run one way;
> This may be truly said to be a humour.

Asper continues:

> But that a rook, in wearing a pied feather,
> The cable hatband, or the three-piled ruff,
> A yard of shoetie, or the Switzer's knot

On his French garters, should affect a humour!
Oh, 'tis more than most ridiculous.

(Induction, 102–14)

Having set out the "true" basis of humours in a disproportion of "choler, melancholy, phlegm, [or] blood" (99) – thought to be material components of the body – Asper rails against the pretender ("rook") who affects humours through items of apparel. Where many critics choose to focus on the psychological structures behind the conceit, what interests me most about such plays and characters is the physical object of the "humour." Like the rook's clothing, Malvolio's yellow stockings and cross garters in *Twelfth Night* (1601) fall into a category Asper finds affected, and form part of a general commodity pattern which, in the thematics of Renaissance drama, is continually related to abnormal behavior and mental processes. Whether seen in terms of physiological psychology or an external, object-centered behavior pattern, humours as they appear in late-Elizabethan and early-Jacobean comedy almost inevitably posit a social world in which subject and object seek new relationships. This development appears to have had its ultimate roots in the market. So much is suggested, perhaps, by the "pied feather," the "cable hatband," the "three-piled ruff," the "yard of shoetie," and the "French garters" of Asper's satirical catalogue: all artificial items of fashion lending themselves to an invidious distinguishing (however accurate) of monied from moneyless. Like "city comedy" and dramatic satire, the comedy of humours constituted a concerted attempt to map out a new paradigm for the material relations of the social world of late-Tudor and early-Stuart England.

But why did this collected impulse occur when it did? We saw in the previous chapter how London's escalating population created, for many, new anxieties and pressures and rendered urban life an increasingly physical experience. Manipulated in London's expanding market, money, credit, and commodity also required an increased vacillation between the abstract (for example, a coin or commodity's socially-posited value) and the physical (the coin or commodity itself): Hamlet's "Hyperion to a satyr". Because intensified economic exchange necessitated new patterns of social understanding and activity, London's dramatists attempted to ground its operations in more recognizable terms in their plays. Looking to the *contemptus mundi* tradition inherited from the Middle Ages (and evident in the tone and subject of Renaissance satire) as one of the primary components of an attempted synthesis with idealism, playwrights sought to reconcile the social tensions inherent in the economic base of England's evolving society through an explication of the new forms of social transaction.

Deriving its force from the rising energy of the city and the pressures of social change, the materialist vision was characterized primarily by an obsession with the integrity of commodity and the seemingly inevitable hazards of ownership. This obsession revealed itself in the cultural life of London and the constellation of aesthetic objects produced there. The residents of London during this period appear to have become more intimately concerned with possessions: coin, cloth, spices, and commodities in general seized the collective imagination of the populace. Marlowe captured the late-Elizabethan preoccupation with luxurious objects most clearly, of course, in *Doctor Faustus* (1592), where he cloaks pure production – as did so often the theater itself – in the folds of black magic. Faustus' material desires are answered almost immediately with the stage version of valuable commodities. The following decades rendered Marlowe's play socially prophetic. In his *Discoveries* (published in 1640, but recorded earlier), Jonson saw English society as one obsessed with material wealth:

What petty things they are, we wonder at? like children, that esteem every trifle; and prefer a Fairing before their Fathers: what difference is between us, and them? but that we are dearer Fools, Cockscombs, at a higher rate? They are pleas'd with Cockleshells, Whistles, Hobby-horses, and such like: we with Statues, marble Pillars, Pictures, gilded Roofs ...[38]

Jonson's lament over the childish enthusiasm or "humours" of his society for the luxurious appears – at least in the context of the world described by his contemporaries in plays and pamphlets – to have captured the general perception of a social reality.

During this period the word "commodity" itself – once connoting something like "convenience," a meaning now obsolete – referred instead with more frequency to *concrete* things, exchangeable goods and wares like food and drink, cloth, paper, and string. As John Wheeler pointed out in 1601, in a frequently quoted passage,

The Prince with his subjects, the Master with his servants, one friend and acquaintance with another, the Captain with his soldiers, the Husband with his wife, Women with and among themselves, and in a word, all the world choppeth and changeth, runneth and raveth after Marts, Markets and Merchandising, so that all things come into Commerce, and pass into traffic (in a manner) in all times, and in all places: not only that, which nature bringeth forth, as the fruits of the earth, the beasts, and living creatures, with their spoils, skins and cases, the metals, minerals, and such like things, but further also, this man maketh merchandise of the works of his own hands, this man of another man's labor, one selleth words, another maketh t[r]affic of the skins and blood of other men, yea there are some found so subtle and cunning merchants, that they persuade and induce men to suffer themselves to be bought and sold ...[39]

This passage in Wheeler's *Treatise of Commerce* foregrounds a side of English society that many of his contemporaries emphasized as well, and constitutes a central observation of its kind and time. To Wheeler, everything – natural and artificial – passes "into traffic."

One reason for this might have been that – notwithstanding the aggravated poverty afflicting a great number of people during this period – there may have been more of this "everything" passing into and around in commercial circulation. As Joan Thirsk points out, there was a remarkable rise in domestically-manufactured commodities in England in the later sixteenth and early seventeenth centuries:

Whereas cloth had dominated exports in the sixteenth century, it had to share a place in the seventeenth century not only with re-exports from the colonies, but with miscellaneous home-produced wares, originally designed for the home market, such as knitted woolen stockings, knitted caps, felt hats, iron cooking pots, iron frying pans, knives, sword blades, daggers, nails pins, glass bottles, gloves, earthen pots, and copper wares, not to mention some of the specialized products of farms and market gardens, such as saffron and hops. These articles represented occupations which had blossomed in the later sixteenth and seventeenth centuries as projects, sometimes very humble projects, but were now finding a sale abroad as well.[40]

Thirsk's "articles" – and, perhaps more important, the social and historical impulse behind their production – sponsored an interest in commodities in the literature of Renaissance London. A general fascination with the objective world was widespread, and growing. Discussing the intellectual background of Renaissance England, A. D. Nuttall argues that "in seventeenth-century England the harder heads were all in favor of putting notions on one side and attending firmly to *things* in themselves."[41] And although harder heads like that of Francis Bacon may have been distant from the working-day world of urban London, something similar to the objectivism underlying the empiricist impulse seems to have been in general operation on the social plane at this time.[42] Manifest in the complexity of commodity function, this impulse underwrote the market-oriented ascription of unreal and inordinate value to material objects, something we have come to call the fetishization of commodities. The "Age of Shakespeare," in fact, could well be characterized as the Age of Commodity Fetishism, as the time the expanding market lent rededicated power to property, rendering operative and even concretizing such concepts as fetishism, reification, and personification to an extent as unprecedented as it was alarming.[43]

The commodification of the personal marked the drama of this period with new energy. Women were more often portrayed as commodities, with marriage frequently seen as a middle-class transaction, one which could remain financially profitable well after the ceremony and the exchange of dowry. As Richard Horwich says of marriage in Middleton's drama, it "becomes not an alternative to or an escape from the predatory marketplaces but a marketplace itself."[44] The logic behind such a transition held women as social tokens. In a foundational essay on Shakespeare's *The Rape of Lucrece* (1593–94), Coppélia Kahn notes that the "biological importance of female chastity is . . . inseparable from its social importance."[45] The importance placed on chastity worked, of course, to the detriment of women's social mobility. Alongside Kahn's observation, one could bring to bear Lawrence Stone's thesis about the diminished status of women in sixteenth- and seventeenth-century England. Stone argues that, during this period, "power flowed increasingly to the husband over the wife and to the father over the children."[46] Both would support what is only too clear in the drama: that wives are frequently considered and treated as objects. A commonplace allegation of the time – one that I explore at length in the following chapter – held that citizens often used their wives' sexual favors for financial gain. In fact, many aspects of commercial exchange were figured in terms of natural reproduction and the marriage relationship. As the Bastard makes apparent with his diatribe in Shakespeare's *King John* (1591), the word "commodity" also functioned as a *double-entendre* for the female genitals.[47]

Property also received new emphasis conceptually, the idea of chattel – and the self's relation to property – coming to assume a cardinal role in the theatrical construction of an early-modern, bourgeois subjectivity. In the transition from Elizabethan to Jacobean farce, for example, one can trace an intensification of the practice of inscribing identity into dramatic props. Rings, moneybags, and other chattel served as the tabulae rasae on which plays literally wrote the personal, subjectivity thus becoming tightly involved in the cultural status of property. The drama shows a related interest in, even an obsession with, the personal side of loss and gain. Where the Morality play emphasized the abstract side of loss and its general implications for the hereafter, the secular drama highlights its effects on individual consciousness and urban existence. The movement (representational and referential) from universal to particular, from communal purpose to individual advantage can be seen even in the progression of titles from the late 15th-century Morality *Everyman* to the more specific *Every Man in His Humour*, and *Every Woman in Her Humour* (1607) of the early seventeenth century, to Bulwer-Lytton's *Walpole: or Every Man Has His Price* (1869) and the Depression-era handbook, *Everyman and His Common Stocks* (1931). Suggested in this brief rehearsal of titles, perhaps, is that the concept of "Everyman" became less representative and more individualistic in Anglo-American cultural representations during the transition from early to modern capitalism. As Auden noted: "take away Everyman, substitute for him as the hero one of the seven deadly sins, set the other six in league to profit from it, and one has the basic pattern of the Jonsonian comedy of humours."[48]

Of course, acquisition and individuality were by no means inventions of the Renaissance. During this period, however, a new emphasis came to be placed on their extensive social implications, an emphasis anticipatory of later historical developments. Correspondingly, one encounters in the drama of this period an increased emphasis on unmediated competition in an urban setting. It has been argued that much of the drama of Renaissance London used and developed a materialist philosophy. To Brian Gibbons, "there are striking likenesses between the world brought alive in City Comedy and that formulated by Machiavelli in *The Prince* and by Hobbes in *Leviathan*."[49] For Lauro Martines, "a sense of inner worth (traditional, static, hierarchical: the stamp of an earlier society) gives way to a sense of self in terms of use or market value, a notion fully articulated by Thomas Hobbes two generations later."[50] Similarly, I would argue, in Middleton and Dekker's *The Roaring Girl*, Moll anticipates a crude form of Darwinism by several centuries in describing "fish that must needs bite or themselves be bitten" (3.1.94), a sentiment echoed by Curtleax when he claims "all that live in the world are but great fish and little fish, and feed upon one another" (3.3.135–36).[51] Often this kind of cynical (if realistic) complaint was directed toward the market and market forces. In John Day's *The Isle of Gulls*, for instance, Hippolita complains that "covetous wealth pursues / The trembling state of their inferiors."[52] The "naturalness" of such proverbs, like the rural qualities of the cony-catching and cuckold myths, helped playwrights gloss the brutality of urban experience: nature endorsed the triumph of strong over weak. The Elizabethan and Jacobean drama differed from earlier drama in that it more forcefully enacted such proverbs. Struggle and predation – whether sexual, financial, generational, military, domestic, or a combination of these – became its keynotes.

Part of the market's energy found mercantile and imperialist outlets as England strengthened its commercial ties with parts of Europe and began extending links with Asia and the Americas, seeking all the time new avenues of profit and exchange. The colonial impulse, of course, surfaces very obviously in Marlowe's plays, where characters like Tamburlaine seem to emblematize England's own imperialistic ambitions. The appetite for this kind of dramatic commodity struck Thomas Platter, a German traveler who attended productions at several of London's theaters in the early fall of 1599, as characteristically English. Describing both playgoing and animal baiting, Platter observes:

With such and many other pastimes besides the English spend their time; in the comedies they learn what is going on in other lands, and this happens without alarm, husband and wife together in a familiar place, since for the most part the English do not much use to travel, but are content ever to learn of foreign matters at home, and ever to take their pastime.[53]

Here we return to the central problem of *place* (in this case, topographical) taken up in the preceding remarks. The English, Platter suggests, prefer to learn of "foreign matters" in the context of their "home." Plays "about" foreign countries and exotic cities provided Londoners a view – and almost always a fantastic or sentimental one (see "familiar place") – of what English expeditions might encounter abroad. London, with its expressive, international nature, functioned as a gate to the fictions, as well as the realities, of distant worlds; like the Thames, playhouses and plays provided a key to that gate. Through action and metaphor plays like *Englishmen for My Money, or A Woman Will Have Her Will* (1598), Day's *The Travels of the Three English Brothers* (1607), and Heywood's *The Fair Maid of the West, or A Girl Worth Gold* (1604) explored London's tendency to adventurism while describing its "foreign" exploits, and helped persuade Londoners that they were learning "what is going on in other lands."

At the same time the English were exploring the world, they also began recognizing the diversity of their own island's hinterlands. In *Poly-Olbion*, for instance, written between 1598 and 1622, Michael Drayton charted the topography of England, detailing its rivers and streams and carefully enumerating the surface features of the countryside. Plays of this time similarly stress the diversity of London itself, representing the city as a melting pot of dialect and habit. Italian, French, Dutch, Spanish, Welsh, Scottish, Irish – characters from every conceivable location make their appearance in London's churning cauldron as represented on the stage. London had grown to the point where it expressed diversity not only of national, but indeed of almost international scope: as suggested above, the plays of Jonson and Middleton (both of whom lived in London from an early age), among others, enthusiastically catalogue the maze of taverns, streets, shops, and districts a rapidly unfolding London was to offer. As the Vice Iniquity in Jonson's *The Devil is an Ass* (1616) boasts to an impressed Pug:

> I will fetch thee a leap
> From the top of Paul's steeple to the Standard in Cheap
> And lead thee a dance through the streets without fail,
> Like a needle of Spain, with a thread at my tail.
> We will survey the suburbs, and make forth our sallies
> Down Petticoat Lane, and up the Smock-alleys,

To Shoreditch, Whitechapel, and so to Saint Kather'n's,
To drink with the Dutch there, and take forth their patterns ...
I will bring thee to the bawds, and the roysters
At Billingsgate, feasting with claret-wine and oysters;
From thence shoot the Bridge, child, to the Cranes i' the Vintry ...

(1.1.55–70)

A century before Jonson's play, such a rhyming travelogue might have been considerably shorter and much less rich in diversity of detail – one could contrast the above passage, for example, with a fifteenth-century ballad like "London Lickpenny." By the end of Elizabeth's reign, as John Stowe's massive and detailed *Survey of London* (1598; 1603) indicates, London had nearly become a nation unto itself.

4   Horns of plenty: cuckoldry and capital

Plenty's horn is always full in the City.

Dekker and Ford, The Sun's Darling

Down the Thames from Renaissance London, approximately three miles east of St. Paul's and on the Surrey shore, in a location which came to be known, variously, as Cuckold's Haven or Cuckold's Point, stood a monument to the ostensibly unavoidable consequences of marrying a woman. Though some distance from the City proper, the priapic marker of Cuckold's Haven – a makeshift arrangement of wooden pole topped by animal horns – participated in an odd form of literary engagement with the drama of early Jacobean London, coming to serve, paradoxically, as an urban icon. From its earliest recorded appearance in the diary of Henry Machyn in 1562, Cuckold's Haven provided London's playwrights with a popular local reference point.[1] Edward Sugden's dictionary of topographic allusions in English Renaissance drama cites over a dozen references to the locale, most of them in comedies directly concerned with London or London characters.[2] In plays like *The London Prodigal* (1604), *Northward Ho!* (1605), *The Isle of Gulls* (1606), and *The Travels of the Three English Brothers* (1607), Cuckold's Haven constitutes the equivalent of a geographical punch line. In *Eastward Ho!* (1605), for example, Security, Winifred, and Quicksilver – a trio of unscrupulous city adventurers who have set out for Virginia – wash ashore at that humiliating location. Ford, Rowley, and Dekker's *The Witch of Edmonton* (1621) refers to it almost proverbially: "that confidence is a wind, that has blown many a married Man ashore at Cuckold's Haven, I can tell you" (2.2.29–30).[3]

Only two years later, however, the marker at Cuckold's Haven seems to have disappeared. The Water Poet John Taylor, in "A Discovery by Sea, from London to Salisbury" (1623), lamented the absence of both horn and pole:

> For there old *Time* had such confusion wrought,
> That of that ancient place remained nought.

No monumental memorable Horn,
Or tree or Post, which hath those Trophies born,
Was left, whereby Posterity may know
Where their forefathers' Crests did grow, or show.[4]

However accurate Taylor's chronicle of the marker's vanishing, it should be pointed out that London had two myths of origin for Cuckold's Haven, both supported by a similar model of social interaction. One account revolves around the sexual indiscretions of the last Angevin monarch:

The Miller of Charlton, having discovered K[ing] John kissing his wife, demanded compensation, and was granted all the land he could see from his door. He therefore claimed all as far as this point, which was thereafter called C[uckold's] P[oint]. The king, however, added this condition, that he should walk every 18th of October (St. Luke's Day) to the point with a pair of buck's horns on his head.[5]

An alternate version of the foundation story appears in Nicholas Breton's 1612 pamphlet *Cornu-copiae* (subtitled *Pasquil's Nightcap: or, Antidote for the Headache*), where the cuckold's pole has been erected in honor of Lady Fortune for her role in the simultaneous creation of marriage and cuckoldry. The official establishment of Cuckold's Haven, Breton relates, came about when "certain *London* butchers" consented

That they sufficient horns should still provide,
For to repair the post when it should need:
   And for reward the neighbouring fields should be
   Theirs and their heirs' to hold eternally:
   Provided still, that horns did never want,
   For then they made a forfeit of their grant.[6]

Even as John demanded of the Miller a ritual of debasement before the community in return for granting him special property rights, the London butchers agree to continuous maintenance of the pole and horns in exchange for title to "the neighbouring fields" in perpetuity.

Like the anecdote of John's infidelity, Breton's account of the origin of Cuckold's Haven describes a pageant of contractual obligation. Indeed a large part of what these two pieces of folkloric mythology have in common is an imaginative explanation of cuckoldry based on a delineation of exchange in which women like the Miller's wife are used, in a system of male-to-male transaction, as the literalized, objectified version of what Pierre Bourdieu calls "symbolic capital:" "a transformed and thereby *disguised* form of physical 'economic' capital."[7] The native fabliau had traditionally represented women as helpless counters signifying loss (to the cuckold) and victory (to the one who cuckolds) in ludic struggles between men: witness, for example, the narrative and intra-narrative role of another Miller's wife (and daughter) in *The Reeve's Tale*.[8] Yet what was in medieval literature "disguised" capital became for Shakespeare's London an overwhelmingly explicit doubling of the monetary on the plane of the personal, an articulation on the comedic level of the new intricacies and extensions of the economic. In the middle of his narrative, in fact, Breton foregrounds the commercial implications of Cuckold's Haven in observing "That cuckolds often are the wealthiest men" and that "*Profit and pleasure both spring from the horn.*"[9]

During the two decades before the publication of Breton's pamphlet in 1612 the myth of cuckoldry came to play a cardinal role in London's drama. Katharine Eisaman Maus points out that "not only does jealousy dominate the plots of many plays, but songs about the cuckolded and the abandoned, jokes and saws about the unreliability of wives and lovers, turn up in other plays on the slightest of pretexts."[10] Indeed it is difficult to overestimate the predominance of cuckoldry in the popular drama of the period. I say "popular" drama because, although cuckoldry and the fear of cuckoldry pervades many private theater tragedies, for the most part cuckoldry remains inextricably linked with the populace, with images of fertility and, further (through its association with the cornucopia and horned animal ritual), with the countryside: see, for instance, the climactic scene of *The Merry Wives of Windsor* (1597). As C. L. Barber pointed out,

During Shakespeare's lifetime, England became conscious of holiday custom as it had not been before, in the very period when in many areas the keeping of holidays was on the decline. Festivals which worked within the rhythm of an agricultural calendar, in village or market town, did not fit the way of living of the urban groups whose energies were beginning to find expression through what Tawney has called the Puritan ethic.[11]

Like the myth of "cony catching," which gave the pamphleteers of the nineties a popular, rural conceit with which to interpret urban confidence games, cuckoldry acted as a portal trope between country and city, a figure with which the playwrights of the English Renaissance projected their economic vision of London's intensifying social dynamics. In the remarks that follow, I will delineate the structural logic of cuckoldry as a metaphor of gendered labor and economic relations, offering an understanding of the myth's role as a central constituent in London's theatrical grammar of cultural change.

Cuckoldry and the Good Husband

Cuckoldry (which is in literature at least as old as the Greek Anthology) made its first explicit appearance as a trope for labor in a passage in

Horace's *Satires*, where mimicry of the cuckoo appears as an aggressive taunt:

> *tum Praenestinus salso multoque fluenti*
> *expressa arbusto regerit convicia, durus*
> *vindemiator et invinctus, cui saepe viator*
> *cessisset magna compellans voce cuculum.*

> Then in answer to this torrent of wit
> the Praenestine returned the real squeezings,
> like a vine dresser, tough and unbeatable, to
> whom the vanquished wayfarer had often shouted "cuckoo."[12]

Appropriately opposing the antagonistic pair – "*vindemiator . . . viator*" – at opposite ends of his line, Horace describes the *vindemiator*, "vine dresser" as *durus et invinctus*, both "tough and unbeatable:" indeed, his point revolves around the word *cuculus* as a challenge, an insulting taunt. Also important is the antagonists' status, for their occupations define their narrative personalities as well as their social roles. The *viator*, "traveler" or "wayfarer," heckles the industrious vine dresser, implying that he has been late in pruning his vines – something that should be completed before the cuckoo appears in the spring. Pliny provided the background information for this puzzling incident in his discussion of the farmer's springtime duties:

In this space of time the farmer must hurry on during the first fortnight with work which he has not had time to finish before the equinox, while realising that this is the origin of the rude habit of jeering at people pruning their vines by imitating the note of the visiting bird called the cuckoo, as it is considered disgraceful and deserving of reproach for that bird to find the pruning-hook being used on the vine; and consequently wanton jokes . . .[13]

The "consequently" (*et ob id*) of Pliny's last line bridges the gap between labor and sexuality; for the cuckoo to find a man at work testifies symbolically to that man's inadequacy, partly because being caught in such a position implies tardiness, even impotence, and partly because it focuses public ridicule (or at least poses the threat of public scrutiny) upon the laborer. The "wanton jokes" (*petulantiae sales*) probably find their source in the castration threat implied by the business of pruning and in the implicit argument – one which Renaissance drama would continually suggest – that sexual intercourse itself is a kind of physical labor.

This archetypal struggle between *viator* and *vindemiator*, predator and husband, underlies the long history of the cuckold myth. The patiently productive husband – vine dresser, blacksmith, moneylender, tobacconist, farmer – is robbed and mocked by a picaresque opportunist.

Methods of labor constitute the crux of the struggle in a seemingly transcultural archetype. On one side lies craft as intellectual expression – that is, "guile" – on the other craft meaning occupation, or steady employment at a trade. Out of these polarities, from different and competitive conceptions of labor and production, came a social tension resolved by cuckoldry.

What led to the association of cuckoldry with labor? I suggest that the connection has its source in the historical gendering of patient production as feminine, in at least partial relation to the notion of pregnancy and "labor" as primary production. Although the effort associated with childbirth had long been described as "labor," only around 1610 does Shakespeare use the word specifically for a woman in labor.[14] Likewise in the various English editions of the Bible it is not until the Douai (1609) and the King James (1611) that "labour" is used to describe Rachel's mortal delivery (Genesis 35:16).[15] The word "husband" itself enjoyed in Renaissance usage both its current meaning of "man joined to a woman by marriage" (*OED* I.2), and also "one who tills and cultivates the soil" (II.3), "the manager of a household or establishment" (II.4), or more specifically "one who manages his household, or his affairs in business in general, well or ill, profitably or wastefully" (II.4). Thomas Tusser's didactic poem in praise of thrift, *Five Hundred Points of Good Husbandry* (adapted from his own *Hundred Good Points of Husbandry* (1557) and appearing in at least ten editions between 1573 and 1672) provides a succinct, rhyming definition: "The husband is he that to labor doth fall, / the labor of him I do husbandry call."[16] Husbandry is labor. Schmidt cites instances of Shakespeare using the term in each of the above meanings, many of them emphasizing the word's connections with property and labor.[17] In *The Taming of the Shrew* (1592), for instance, the father/cuckold Vincentio provides an early, figurative example of what would shortly become concrete: "O, I am undone, I am undone! While I play the good husband at home, my son and servant spend all at the university" (5.1.68–70). In this (almost parodically) typical comedic lament, the *senex iratus* decries the traditional profligacy of his son and servant, an indiscretion only exacerbated in light of his patient labor as a "good husband." If the twin marital and economic meanings of "husband" underscored the social implications of cuckoldry, so did the Renaissance "huswife" (or "housewife"), meaning both "a woman skilled in female business and superintending the concerns of a family" *and* "a hussy."[18] A woman who controlled the household economy, who "wore the breeches," seemed more likely to control her own sexual economy. In the misogynistic words of Iago to Emilia, women are

> pictures out a' doors,
> Bells in your parlors, wild-cats in your kitchens,
> Saints in your injuries, devils being offended,
> Players in your huswifery, and huswives in your beds.

> (2.1.109–12).

His last line connects the dual meanings of "huswife": the domestic manager and the unrestrained sexual wanton. Iago leaves it strategically unclear whether by "you," the governing subject of his insult, he means women like his wife and Desdemona or women in general. He avoids clarifying his slur immediately thereafter when claiming "You rise to play, and go to bed to work" (2.1.115), again conflating sexuality with labor. Iago gives the connection its clearest expression, however, in describing Bianca, a prostitute of Cyprus, as "A huswife that by selling her desires / Buys herself bread and clothes" (4.1.94–95).

The Drudgery of Labor

I alluded above to the concluding scene of *The Merry Wives of Windsor*, where Falstaff becomes a literal scapegoat, the bourgeois community of Windsor diluting through concerted ridicule the threat of his predatory priapism. In this way Shakespeare's play, a "city comedy" in every aspect save locale, functionally endorses middle-class husbandry. More often in the drama of the period the cuckold is not the predator, but the practitioner of husbandry. Cuckoldry's metaphoric origins in the drudgery of the husband appear clearly in the parade of animals associated with the image. The horned ox is frequently described as the cuckold's emblem, hence King John's legendary request that the Miller perform his cuckold walk on St. Luke's day – the enduring ox being Luke's iconographic symbol.[19] The camel and snail, both harmless drudges, were frequently portrayed as cuckolds as well; perhaps more to the point, the snail was customarily described in proverbs as a householder, one that bore his domicile atop his own back.[20] Foremost among the cuckold animals, of course, is the ass, the traditional beast of burden. Accutus, in *Every Woman in Her Humour* (1607), literalizes the correspondence between the ass's ears and the cuckold's horns when he taunts "thou hast long ears, and thinkest them horns, thy conceits cuckolds thee" (5.1.197–98).[21] The transformation of Bottom into an ass in *A Midsummer Night's Dream* (1596), like that of Midas and Lucius, Apuleius' protagonist, takes this form for social ridicule.

Bottom, the butt of much of the play's humor, is the lucky agent of Oberon's wittolry, or self-cuckoldry. Modern productions of the comedy tend to make explicit potential jokes about Bottom's enlarged genitals and the intercourse he engages in with Titania. What goes relatively unexamined in modern critical discourse on the play, however, is the rationale for Bottom's agency in the cuckold plot. Why is it necessary for the royal Oberon to employ Bottom in the ostensible "punishment" of his wife? Is it because Bottom comes, as his name suggests, from the lowest possible rank of the social ladder? I would argue that it evolves out of Bottom's status as a laborer and as an Athenian, a mechanical belonging to the city. Bottom acts out, even personifies, the dialectic between country and city, a tension set up by modes of labor. His "use" to Oberon parallels the manner in which Cuckold's Haven traditionally drew city types. Yet Bottom is a user himself. His insistence on reducing Titania's four Fairies to their use value, in fact, reflects a larger scheme of social behavior, a pattern of activity in which Oberon, Theseus, and the rest of the "upper class" of the drama participate: "Good Master Mustardseed, I know your patience well. That same cowardly, giant-like ox-beef hath devour'd many a gentleman of your house. I promise you your kindred hath made my eyes water ere now. I desire you of more acquaintance, good Master Mustardseed" (3.1.191–96).

In passages like this, *A Midsummer Night's Dream* anticipates the protorealistic dramas of the early Jacobean era even as it begins to close the door on the pastoral possibilities of Lyly's drama. The city bears responsibility for this change. Bottom's manipulation at the hands of Oberon enacts a rural version of what would shortly become a standard dramatic scenario (the cuckolding of a citizen by a gallant), for although Bottom is, symbolically at least, made a priapic cuckold figure, he is enlisted in a labor that will at once reinitiate Titania into the adult sphere of heterosexuality, enact Oberon's desires toward Titania – or rather, his desires concerning *her* desires – and prove to her the dangers of "her" excess. Bottom thus wins and loses: as an urban pawn in cuckolding Oberon, he sensually redeems with sexual labor his own role as cuckold and comic scapegoat.

Indeed, the concept of "drudgery" permeates the dramatic construction of labor in the work of Shakespeare and his dramatic contemporaries. Frequently it refers to the work required during sexual intercourse. In describing his escape from the stupendous bulk of Nell, who "would have [him] as a beast," the Syracusan Dromio calls her a "drudge," apparently displacing his own fears of bond-slavery (3.2.140). Angelica, Juliet's Nurse, chortles how "I am the drudge, and toil in your delight; / But you shall bear the burthen soon at night" (2.5.75–76). Mouldy, about to be "pricked" for military service in *2 Henry IV* (1598), complains that "I was prick'd well enough before, and you could have let me alone. My old dame will be undone now for one to do her husbandry and her drudgery"

(3.2.111–13). One might look as well at Firk in *The Shoemakers' Holiday*
(1599) – his name a crude euphemism for "to copulate" – who pleads with
Rowland Lacy, an impressment officer, to allow a young married couple,
Jane and Rafe, to stay together. Firk claims that Rafe is "as good a
workman at a prick and an awl, as any is in our trade" (1.1.139–40). If
Rafe goes to the wars, Jane "shall be laid at one side like a pair of old
shoes else, and be occupied for no use" (1.1.142–43). Thus "occupation,"
meaning both to work on shoes with a prick and an awl, and to occupy –
or not to occupy – one's wife, embraces both sex and industry. Othello
plays on the senses of "occupation" as both coitus and livelihood (adding
also the sense of military "occupation") in his line "Othello's occupation's
gone."[22] "Occupy" alone constituted an extremely common sexual pun in
Renaissance drama.[23] Underlying Mouldy's claim, however, and not
present in Firk's or Othello's, is a slight trepidation, almost the proverbial
Shakespearean "sex nausea." In Mouldy's description, sex is toil.

   Lavatch, the clown in *All's Well That Ends Well* (1602), jests with the
Countess of Rossillion about his intended marriage, suggesting "I hope to
have friends for my wive's sake." When the Countess retorts "Such
friends are thine enemies, knave," Lavatch launches into an extended
syllogism, a sorites, on the benefits of wittolry:

Y'are shallow, madam – in great friends, for the knaves come to do that for me
which I am a-weary of. He that ears my land spares my team, and gives me leave to
inn the crop. If I be his cuckold, he's my drudge. He that comforts my wife is the
cherisher of my flesh and blood; he that cherishes my flesh and blood loves my
flesh and blood; he that loves my flesh and blood is my friend: *ergo*, he that kisses
my wife is my friend. (1.3.39–50)

At the beginning of his utterance Lavatch uses the traditional metaphor
for sexuality and childbirth which occurs so memorably in *Antony and
Cleopatra* (1607) – Agrippa, speaking of Caesar and Cleopatra, tells
Enobarbus "He ploughed her, and she cropp'd" (2.2.228). Lavatch,
however, speaks finally of sexuality with the air of reluctance lurking
behind Mouldy's metaphor. Lavatch pictures procreation as a form of
labor, and expresses his delight at the exchange: "If I be his cuckold, he's
my drudge."

   The close of this speech plays on the wedded unification of husband
and wife claimed by Ephesians, "So ought men to love their wives, as their
own bodies: he that loveth his wife, loveth himself" (5:28) and hints at the
homosocial bonding frequently seen in the wittol relationship: "He that
kisses my wife is my friend."[24] The wittol often admires some aspect of the
cuckolder's personality or station, perhaps explaining why, in the drama
of the period, the wittol is so often a social-climbing citizen, the cuckolder
so often an aristocrat; "class," in its modern sense of "prestige," is what

seeks and is sought by money. Linda Woodbridge cautions against reading such literary scenarios as history, suggesting that "it is unlikely that young aristocrats cuckolded prosperous merchants with such regularity in real life: gallants would have had little motive for patronizing a drama based on such wish-fulfillment fantasies if they were getting their own social revenge by cuckolding real citizens."[25] I would maintain, however, that the import of the cuckold scenario in English Renaissance drama does not depend on its realistically reflecting the social scene, but on the urgency and consistency of pattern to the merchant/cuckold thematic – that is, in what it tells us about how London's playwrights expounded their sense of the relations in question.

Merchants and the Fruitful Horn

Why are merchants so often cuckolds, and cuckolds so often merchants? I have argued above that part of the explanation lies in the predator/husband rivalry, where cuckoldry is a carnivalesque celebration of what seems an older and more fertile way of existence. Another reason lies in the reception of methodical labor as effeminate. There are other, related, causes. Money typically has been portrayed as an impediment to the body physical and procreation.[26] Stephen Hannaford goes so far even to state that "it is a commonplace of the English Renaissance stage that he who enjoys fortune rarely enjoys sex."[27] Such fears perhaps derive from money's anthropomorphic nature, for coins, merely in their aesthetic aspect, multiply an individual's visage almost beyond accounting. Interest and profit are frequently understood as reproductive, generative acts, and thus compete with natural fertility. As the goddess of Shakespeare's *Venus and Adonis* puts it: "gold that's put to use more gold begets" (line 768). Flamineo's famous image from Webster's *The White Devil* (1612) tellingly illustrates the extent to which anxiety infused the reproductive aesthetic. In an insincere attempt to assuage Camillo's fears, he relates:

It seems you are jealous; I'll show you the error of it by a familiar example: I have seen a pair of spectacles fashioned with such perspective art, that lay down but one twelve-pence o'th'board, 'twill appear as if there were twenty; now should you wear a pair of these spectacles, and see your wife tying her shoe, you would imagine twenty hands were taking up your wife's clothes. (1.2.95–101)[28]

Flamineo's spectacles show a world engaged in uncontrolled and uncontrollable reproduction. Multiple perspective combines with undiscriminating fertility to produce, for the householding "husband" Camillo, a nightmare of generation.

The merchant must also accustom himself to allowing wealth and commodity to pass from his hands into those of another. The connection

with marriage and cuckoldry resides, at root, in the problems of ownership. The anxiety latent within the concept of property itself is nowhere
better described than by Antonio's fellow merchants in *The Merchant of
Venice* (1596), who respond to the drama's opening line – "In sooth, I
know not why I am so sad" – with what can only be described as
archetypally bourgeois analysis. Salerio suggests: "Your mind is tossing
on the ocean, / There where your argosies with portly sail / Like signiors
and rich burghers on the flood" (1.1.8–10). Solanio echoes the conceit,
agreeing

> Believe me, sir, had I such venture forth,
> The better part of my affections would
> Be with my hopes abroad. I should be still
> Plucking the grass to know where sits the wind,
> Piring in maps for ports and piers and roads;
> And every object that might make me fear
> Misfortune to my ventures, out of doubt
> Would make me sad.
>
> (1.1.15–22)

Indeed he gives further hypothetical anecdotes, concluding for them: "I
know Antonio / Is sad to think upon his merchandise" (1.139–40).[29]
Because to be a merchant is to risk loss, to render commodity up to
chance, the business of commerce produces inescapable anxiety.

The first part of Thomas Dekker's *The Honest Whore* (1604), subtitled
"with the Humours of the Patient Man and the Longing Wife," offers a
provocative example of how the cuckold/merchant's patience may trans-
late into profit. In this play Fustigo and Viola, wife of Candido, an
unbelievably patient merchant, attempt to devise methods of shaking
Candido's seemingly unswayable patience:

> FUSTIGO. ... make him a cuckold.
> WIFE. Puh, he would count such a cut no unkindness.
> FUSTIGO. The honester Citizen he.
>
> (1.2.92–95)[30]

Candido receives the following praise from Fluello – "Thou art a blest
man, and with peace doest deal, / Such a meek spirit can bless a common-
weal" (1.5.228–29) – and it soon becomes apparent that, in Dekker's
bourgeois world view, the cuckold merchant is a kind of Christ figure with
almost supernatural endurance.[31] Instead of an object of derision,
Candido serves as role model. Castruchio, aptly named in that he
attempts to castrate Candido symbolically by cutting a penny's-worth of
linen precisely from the center of the bolt (thus ruining the piece), reacts
with amazement at the hermaphroditic patience of the merchant: "is't
possible that *Homo*, / Should be nor man, nor woman: not once moov'd; –
/ No not at such an injury, at all!" (1.5.106–08). The "cut" he insists upon

plays both on Viola's "he would count such a cut no unkindness" and the contemporary bawdy reference of the term to the pudendum.[32] Candido allows Castruchio to do what he likes with his cut, claiming that "We are set here to please all customers" (1.5.121). For Candido, symbolic cuckoldry is good business. Dekker's portrayal of the admirable, hermaphroditic cuckold goes hand in hand with his admiration for patient endurance – this is the author, after all, of *Patient Grissel* (1600) – and with his support of commercial activity generally: *The Shoemakers' Holiday* stands as the strongest voice in a choir of proindustry literary works.

Merchants were often portrayed as brokers of their wives' sexuality. It is to this commonplace of characterization which Corvino alludes when, in the midst of attempting to use his wife for financial gain in *Volpone* (1606), he calls jealousy a "poor, unprofitable humor" (2.7.7).[33] The Country Wench of Middleton's *Michaelmas Term* (1606) plays on this as well in asking "Is not wholesale the chiefest merchandise? Do you think some merchants could keep their wives so brave, but for their wholesale? You're foully deceiv'd and you think so" (4.2.13–16).[34] Wholesale here is actually prostitution: her *double-entendre* was more obvious in the first and second quartos of the play, which read "hole-sale." The idea of marriage as "hole-sale," as prostitution, dogged merchants throughout late Elizabethan and early Jacobean drama. Purge, the jealous apothecary of Middleton's *The Family of Love* (1603), opens the second act with a notice: "'Tis time for tradesmen to be in their shops; for he that tends well his shop, and hath an alluring wife with a graceful 'what d'ye lack?' shall be sure to have good doings, and good doings is that that crowns so many citizens with the horns of abundance" (2.1.2–6).[35] Doll, in *The Book of Sir Thomas More* (1595), rebukes the presumption of Francis de Barde with the following speech: "Compel me, ye dog's face! thou thinkst thou hast the goldsmith's wife in hand, whom thou enticedst from her husband with all his plate, and when thou turndst her home to him again, madste him, like an ass, pay for his wife's board" (1.1.11–16).[36] Security, the Usurer of *Eastward Ho!*, attributes cuckoldry to his profession in a song:

> O Master Touchstone, /
> My heart is full of woe!
> Alas, I am a Cuckold;
> And why should it be so?
> Because I was a usurer
> And bawd, as all you know.
>
> (5.5.133–38)[37]

Jonson echoes what seems to have been his own conceit in his fifty-seventh Epigram, "On Bawds, and Usurers": "If, as their ends, their fruits were so, the same, / Bawdry, and usury were one kind of game."[38] If, as Jonson argues, money and sexuality have the same ends, then patient servility is required of the retailer as well as the wholesaler, for patience produces profit.

To some, the effect of market relations – combined with the proximity of persons afforded by urban crowding – left cuckoldry an inevitable part of commercial life. In *The Counter's Commonwealth* (1617), for instance, William Fennor speaks of "unconscionable citizens" whose

usurious dealings make so many cornutos in the City as there are; for, when young gentlemen have been beggared by their extortion, they have no other means than to fall in with their wives and seek to them for supply.[39]

Fennor's lament ascribes "so many cornutos" to the high rate of interest involved in financial transactions in contemporary London. The gallants' "fall[ing] in with their wives" is, in this version of urban relations, so that they might "seek to them [i.e., the citizens' wives]" for the "supply" to pay back their loans.

The Covenant of the Horn

If the role of cuckoldry as an economic metaphor in the drama of Renaissance London derived in part from the social gendering of labor, so too did cuckoldry operate in what one might call a religious context, as both an emblem of original sin and as a ritual of attaining faith. The "faith" referred to above in conjunction with the uncertainty of capitalistic investment found its parallel in the evolution of a Protestant, mercantile covenant. The *locus classicus* of this labor/religion conjunction in Western culture comes, of course, in the book of Genesis with God's angry reaction to Adam and Eve's first disobedience, the fruit thereof being the beginnings of work: "In the sweat of thy face shalt thou eat bread, til thou return to the earth: for out of it wast thou taken, because thou art dust, and to dust shalt thou return" (3:19). Heywood might have recalled this passage when, in *The Brazen Age* (1611), his Mars seduces Venus by saying:

> Come: shall we now, whilst Vulcan plies his forge
> Sweats at his Anvil, chokes himself with dust,
> And labours at his bellows, kiss and toy?[40]

Antagonistic to unrestrained eroticism, toil derives from the sins of knowledge and sexuality. Vulcan is cuckolded because he labors, and labors because he is cuckolded.

Dramatic cuckoldry foregrounded the links between paternalism, faith, and the economic, especially in its manifestation as wittolry – that is, where the cuckold is aware of and content with his lot, *mari cocu et complaisant*. As the servant Wages in *Cupid's Whirligig* (1607) says of Sir Timothy Troublesome, "I see he would willingly prove an accessory to the stealing of his own goods."[41] Wittols are not only rightly certain of their cuckoldry, but indeed content with it. Most often the wittol endures this relationship for economic reasons.[42] Freevil, in Marston's *The Dutch Courtesan* (1605), describes the logic of this relationship in recounting a tavern transaction: "The drawer, for female privateness' sake, is nodded out, who, knowing that whosoever will hit the mark of profit must, like those that shoot in stone-bows, wink with one eye, grows blind o' the right side and departs" (1.1.19–22).[43] I have mentioned above that marriage was frequently portrayed as an institution which committed the husband to a life of servitude. Money was also described as this kind of servant, the "pale and common drudge / 'Tween man and men," as Bassanio calls silver during the Casket Choice in *The Merchant of Venice* (3.2.103–04). The economic often drew its literary formulation from the familial and domestic. Reciprocally, cuckoldry acted as a kind of metonymic double for the cash marketplace, a symbol that, like money, worked to eradicate the distance and difference between the sexual and economic terms. Such an eradication, then as now, necessitated a mystificatory mythology. In delineating the social construction of this mythology, the dramatists of Renaissance London located cuckoldry's economic force within the religioerotic bases of wittolry.

Here I offer a representative passage from Middleton's *A Chaste Maid in Cheapside* (1613), where the householding "husband" Allwit (a transposition of "Witall") celebrates his own cuckoldry. Alerted that Sir Walter Whorehound, his wife's lover and his provider, has come to town, Allwit gives vent to an extended encomium:

> The founder's come to town: I am like a man
> Finding a table furnish'd to his hand,
> As mine is still to me, prays for the founder, –
> "Bless the right worshipful the good founder's life."
> I thank him, 'has maintain'd my house this ten years,
> Not only keeps my wife, but a keeps me
> And all my family: I am at his table;
> He gets me all my children, and pays the nurse
> Monthly or weekly; puts me to nothing,
> Rent, nor church-duties, not so much as the scavenger:
> The happiest state that ever man was born to!
> I walk out in a morning; come to breakfast,
> Find excellent cheer; a good fire in winter;
> . . .
> O, two miraculous blessings! 'Tis the knight

Hath took that labour all out of my hands:
I may sit still and play; he's jealous for me,
Watches her steps, sets spies; I live at ease,
He has both the cost and torment: when the strings
Of his heart frets, I feed, laugh, or sing:
[*Sings*] *La dildo, dildo la dildo, la dildo dildo de dildo.*

(1.2.11–56)[44]

Allwit's speech stands as a dramatic thesaurus of the Renaissance theater's commercial mythology, a mythology centering upon the horn of plenty. He appears to revel in the material accommodation of the wittol relationship. The "livestock" he keeps – "she's even upon the point of grunting;" "My wife's as great as she can wallow" – ensures that he is kept like livestock himself: "[he] not only keeps my wife, but a keeps me." Note the passage's relation to the biblical side of cuckoldry discussed earlier. It contains, throughout, a strong resemblance to the phrasing and themes of the Psalms. The King James version of the twenty-third Psalm's fifth verse – "Thou preparest a table before me" – may have provided Middleton with a model for his first two lines.[45] Allwit's choice of individual words is no less suggestive, balancing out "hell" and "torments" with "paradise" (in the lacuna) and "miraculous blessings." "Jealous" as a word and a concept dominates the passage. Displacing his jealousy onto a strong paternal godhead who provides material comforts and many offspring, Allwit derives comfort from a (pre-oedipal) freedom of servitude. It is no great extension of analysis to trace in this relationship a parody of the Hebrews' covenant with Jehovah. It is also easy to see the bearing of this passage on the historical narratives drawn by Weber and Tawney, both of whom connected the structures of religious belief with early capitalism and the rise of the bourgeois individual.[46] Yet the preceding remarks on cuckoldry suggests that it was the paternalistic – and not, as Weber argues, the ascetic – nature of religion that the Renaissance associated with commerce.

Also meaningful here is the fact that the father-founder, a knight of the countryside, is "come to town," that is, makes the rural to urban passage evidenced (and reversed) in so many cuckold stories. Allwit brags that this father-founder "took that labour all out of my hands: / I may sit still and play; he's jealous for me." "That labor," clearly, is the labor of intercourse: as house "husband" Allwit would rather be one of his wife's children than her spouse. He finishes the speech with a bawdy refrain celebrating the phallus: "*La dildo, dildo la dildo, la dildo dildo de dildo.*" Suited to the infantile state to which he has regressed, the displaced "dildo" stands highly similar – in terms of mythological symbolization –

to the cuckold's horn. As Coppélia Kahn points out, "Regarded endo-psychically, from the cuckold's point of view, horns are a defense formed through denial, compensation, and upward displacement."[47] Here, I would argue, Allwit's "dildo" functions as a transitional object in an erotic project pointed *back* to the mother, instead of away from her. In this way the cuckold's horn, used in an attempt to deny active female participation in the literary scenarios of nascent capitalism, makes manifest the overwhelming importance of the myth of female fertility underlying the fictive rhetoric of London's market.

London's drama seized upon the cuckold myth as a dialectical meta-phor capable of reconciling – however uneasily – evolving tensions between country and city, production and reproduction, female and male. As is evident in play after play, the cuckold's patience translated readily into images of commercial investment. Attempting to associate fertility with the bounty of a paternalistic deity, the dramatists of Renaissance London saw cuckoldry as not only *a* natural but perhaps *the* natural collective metaphor with which to gloss a thematics of nascent capitalism. An enormous sculptured transitional object representing the social erotics of economic mythology, the symbolic horn of plenty at Cuckold's Haven appears to have functioned as a marker of historical transition as well, providing the playwrights in the first decade of James' rule with an element of topographical meaning that, already carved into the folklore of the city's immediate environs, could be inscribed as well in the popular urban imagination.

The myth of cuckoldry came to form an indispensable part of the London theaters' rhetoric of social and economic relationships, a cultural grammar which, as I have indicated, developed rapidly during the late Elizabethan and early Jacobean period. As London increasingly came to resemble a nation in miniature, confident in its ostensible self-sufficiency, it ultimately required less of the countryside for interpretive mythology. Hence the "confusion" wrought by Time in Taylor's account, hence the end of the "monumental memorable Horn." The myth of cuckoldry, however, continued to serve England's chief city as a powerful economic trope. London so incorporated and institutionalized the cuckold myth, in fact, that throughout a large part of the eighteenth century the play regularly produced on Lord Mayor's day – the day when London dutifully celebrated its own civil and commercial splendor – was Edward Ravenscroft's *The London Cuckolds* (1681).[48] And, according to *New Remarks of London*, collected by the Company of Parish Clerks and published in 1732, early eighteenth-century London also boasted both a "Cuckold's Court" and "Cuckold's Alley."[49] The "passing" of Cuckold's

Haven decried by Taylor can be construed, then, not so much as an indication that cuckoldry had lost its symbolic potency for the English Renaissance, but as evidence of the fact that, by 1623, London had so assimilated the myth into its literary vocabulary that actual, physical testament – the pole with its animal horns – became unnecessary.

5 The objects of farce: identity and commodity, Elizabethan to Jacobean

sic parvis componere magna solebam

thus it was my habit to compare great things to small ones

Vergil, *Eclogues*

Comedy generally, and farce in particular, often feature a misplaced object or objects, the finding of which leads to a recognition and brings on, finally, the story's dénouement. Movable objects like rings, letters, and articles of clothing come to be invested with a narrative value replicating itself uncannily in the larger world of reading and interpretation. Powerful centers of desire, such objects may function as tokens of identity, or parts thereof, dramatically substantiating Georg Simmel's belief that "every possession is an extension of the self, a phenomenon within subjective life, and its whole meaning lies in the conscious and emotional reflexes that are the mind's response to the self's relations to objects."[1] Objects of this kind can also configure interpersonal relations: frequently signifying the means of resuming a bond between separated characters, sometimes they symbolize and qualify the reason for separation itself. Calling upon the multiple valences that physical symbols can possess for various characters, such objects may emblematize any or all these relations. One of these many valences, of course, is the literal. As Stanley Cavell argues about the "intercostal clavicle" and the phallic punning which revolves around this bone in Howard Hawks' *Bringing Up Baby* (1938), "if it is undeniable that we are invited by these events to read them as sexual allegory, it is equally undeniable that what Hepburn says, as she opens the box and looks inside, is true: 'It's just an old bone'."[2]

English Renaissance drama – in particular, its comedy and farce – is rife with old bones of this polyvalent nature, props which, passed from hand to hand, possess an almost totemic significance. That the plays of this period should manifest such a heightened, fetishistic interest in commodity only replicates a larger social fascination with the material: Jonson's "petty things" and Wheeler's "merchandise." The theater's

63

commercial basis – that is, its construction of spectacle as commodity – made such a link almost inescapable. Indeed, because of its spectacular nature – its dependence upon the visual embodiment of the material plane – the theater has traditionally stressed the similarities between the human and the objective. Jiří Veltruský's structuralist analysis of "man and object" in the theater sees such as inherent in the representational mode of drama itself:

> The function of each component in the individual system (and in the drama as a whole) is the resultant of the constant tension between activity and passivity in terms of the action, which manifests itself in a constant flow back and forth between the individual components, people and things. It is therefore impossible to draw a line between subject and object, since each component is potentially either. We have seen various examples of how thing and man can change places, how a man can become a thing and a thing a living being. We can thus not speak of two mutually delimited spheres; the relation of man to object in the theater can be characterized as a *dialectic antinomy*.[3]

While useful for a transhistorical model of theatrical praxis, Veltruský's "dialectic antinomy" can be historicized for English Renaissance drama, I believe, through an examination that takes into account (and, in doing so, attempts to explain) the increased emphasis on commodity – and the relationship between materiality and subjectivity – in the plays of the period. Such an examination would explore what Veltruský calls the "constant flow back and forth between . . . people and things," explicating this flow in terms of the market, and the playhouses' relationship to the social function of commodity exchange.

   In its institutional function as part of an early modern culture industry, the Renaissance theater functioned as what one might call the dream screen of nascent capitalism, a ludic platform upon which London explored the social implications of the market. Mimetically glossing a growing cultural preoccupation with commodity and materiality – a preoccupation developing out of a complex constellation of socio-historical developments – the role assumed by movable objects in the drama from (roughly) 1590 to 1620 progresses to the point where stage "properties" not only serve as floating signifiers between individuals – signs, for example, of chastity, marriage, and social position – but become a focus of interest in themselves. Whereas through most of the Eliza-bethan drama, in plays such as *Gammer Gurton's Needle* (1553), *The Comedy of Errors* (1592), and *The Two Gentlemen of Verona* (1593), for instance, dramatic commodities like needles, chains, and rings were important for what could be called their locative signification – that is, where the stage property *was* implied certain things in relation to theme, character, and characters' personal or social relationships – in the late Elizabethan and early Jacobean drama commodities would come to be a source of interest in their own right, as the center of a purity discourse which worked to equate subject and object on the material plane. Shifting its attention from semiosis to subjectivity, the drama began to explore the reified basis of personal relations even as it tended, with more and more frequency, to personify commodities, according them a life of their own. Identity thus came to be inscribed *in*, instead of *by*, these objects.

Far from incidental, such a shift reproduces dramatically a significant historical alteration in the social unconscious of Shakespeare's London. Here the theatrical sense and physical presence of the stage property intersected with the socially constructed *concept* of property. As C. B. Macpherson points out, with the rise of capitalism in the seventeenth century "the idea of common property drops virtually out of sight and property is equated with private property ... whereas in pre-capitalist society a man's property had generally been seen as a right to a revenue, with capitalism property comes to be seen as a right in or to material things, or even as the things themselves."[4] Macpherson's observation found powerful expression in the intricate performative dynamics of the Renaissance theater. In the objective tendency of Renaissance comedy and farce, as in the commodification of the cuckold scenario, male subjectivity reveals its absolute dependence upon an invidious gender tension, a powerful and historically determined project of identity construction based in the market and directed toward objectifying the female (and objectifying male identity in "feminized" objects)[5] through a process I will refer to as "commercial inscription." I use the term to describe a reifying process that, like much comedy and farce, marks objects with human identity, and qualifies subjectivity with characteristics of and reliance upon the objective.

Renaissance drama depended on a crude form of reification for glossing social change and interpreting the changeful implications of commodity exchange. In an effort to delineate the dramatic response to this property-centered social transformation, I intend to explore in the following remarks the cultural and historical implications of these "things themselves," the properties or "props" associated with identity in the transition from the Elizabethan to the Jacobean drama. To trace the dramatic development of the commercial inscription of identity, I take up, in this chapter, principally *Jack Juggler* (1555), Shakespeare's *The Comedy of Errors* and *Twelfth Night* (1601), and Dekker's *The Shoemakers' Holiday* (1599). And although these plays are not only about objects, the physical props of Elizabethan and Jacobean farce nonetheless composed an important constituent of the drama's cultural grammar: to follow them, as I hope to show, is to follow a narrative concerned with the theatrically cathected status of things in Renaissance England.

Farce

Because dramatic farce has appeared in so many theatrical guises during its history, from Aristophanes and Molière to Lubitsch, the Marx Brothers, and beyond, a brief definition – however general – forms a necessary preface to the following argument. In accomplishing this project I follow Barbara Freedman, who, in an influential psychoanalytic treatment of *The Comedy of Errors*, addresses the task in concluding that "a survey of definitions of farce in dictionaries, encyclopedias, and literary and theatrical glossaries ... provides us with three basic structural elements."[6] For Freedman, these are (1) An Absurd Situation; (2) Normally Unacceptable Libidinal Action; and (3) Flat, Surrealistic Characters. Admitting that "farce is a negating force, hard, if not impossible, to trap and pin down," Albert Bermel, in a recent study entitled *Farce*, none the less echoes several of Freedman's categories in noting that "farces share several family traits: unreality ... brutality, and objectivity."[7] Although his trio of characteristics parallels Freedman's closely, Bermel's analysis of farce becomes essential to the following argument when he suggests that "objects ... behave like characters in certain plays and most farces."[8] "Farce," he points out, "shrinks the difference in consciousness between objects and people;" these objects "are thematic and wind into and out of the action, much as the characters do."[9] Like Simmel's theory of the subjective's relation to the concrete, Bermel's reading of the manner in which farce vivifies the objective centers on a functional slipperiness between two patently disparate planes. In farce, as elsewhere, Bermel stresses, "objects are would-be actors."[10] To Freedman's trio of characteristics generally ascribed to farce, then, one might add a fourth, taken from Bermel: (4) Lively Objects.

This phenomenon has been noticed by other critics as well. Bergson's well-known theory of the risible, for example, centers upon the image of "something mechanical encrusted on the living."[11] He posited that the "attitudes, gestures and movements of the human body are laughable in exact proportion as that body reminds us of a mere machine."[12] The converse of this, I would suggest, the assumption of "human" qualities by the mechanical or objective, can function similarly for literary praxis and the business of reception. Recently Cavell has pointed out that, in his essay "The Uncanny," "Freud denies, no fewer than four times, that the inability to distinguish the animate from the inanimate is what causes the sense of the uncanny."[13] Cavell's interest in the metaphysical importance of denial leads him to ask, in cases like this, what lies behind the felt need to deny. The answer, I believe, may have to do with the way conflation of apparent unlikes fuels the uncanny, that is, how repressed similarities between "different" objects and experiences (e.g. human and material agents, human and mechanical activities) manage to intrude into lived experience. Here Launce's "This shoe is my father" soliloquy in *The Two Gentlemen of Verona* (2.3.1–32) remains a *locus classicus* of the phenomenon. Perhaps not coincidentally, it was the uncanniness of capitalism's valuation system, a system that promotes eradication of boundaries between the subjective and objective – a shoe, a father – even as it claims to protect their difference, that came to dominate the thematics and action of London's farce in the period from 1590 to 1620. Historically, the rise of the market during the English Renaissance contributed to a sustained interest in the intersection of these chiastically-related phenomena. From the 1590s onward London's drama became increasingly concerned with the uncanny facility of transference between the subjective and the objective, and with the implications of their interchangeability.

Speaking of the drama of confused identity in sixteenth- and seventeenth-century England, Stephen Greenblatt maintains that farce's object tendency is closely related to its interest in identity: "It is no accident ... that in virtually all of these plays ... the intrigue that arises from the willed or accidental mistaking of one person for another centers on property and proper names: purse and person are here inseparably linked."[14] "Property" and "proper," of course, both trace their etymology through Middle English *propre*, "one's own, distinctive," to Latin *proprius*, "one's own, personal, particular." The point is, in relation to Greenblatt's observation, that purse and person could be said *always* to be, and to have been, "inseparably linked." Simmel, again, noticed that "Ownership, however comprehensive and unlimited, can do with things nothing other than provide an opportunity for the will of the Ego to find its expression in them."[15] As I have suggested is the case with the Renaissance cuckold scenario, merchants and citizens – because of their ownership of and connection with property – gained, in literary representations, a special reputation for anxiety. In its dramatic portrait of loss and gain, Elizabethan and Jacobean farce enacts this anxiety, foregrounding farce's urban dynamics and its corollary phenomenon: the symbiotic interrelation of objects and identity.

In exploring the physical reenactment of such anxiety, one of Freud's anecdotal histories provides an important conceptual metaphor for the following discussion of Renaissance farce. In a famous passage in *Beyond the Pleasure Principle*, Freud chronicled the childhood pastime of a boy age one and a half (actually his own grandson) in the habit of "taking any small objects he could get hold of and throwing them away from him into a corner, under the bed, and so on, so that hunting for his toys and picking them up was often quite a business."[16] The little boy accompanied the throwing and finding of these objects with the German words *fort* ("gone") and *da* ("there"), using the game, in Freud's understanding, to compensate for his mother's absences:

The interpretation of the game then became obvious. It was related to the child's great cultural achievement – the instinctual renunciation (that is, the renunciation of instinctual satisfaction) which he had made in allowing his mother to go away without protesting. He compensated himself for this, as it were, by himself staging the disappearance and return of the objects within his reach.[17]

Freud proceeds to discuss the game as a device for learning:

At the outset he was in a *passive* situation – he was overpowered by the experience; but, by repeating it, unpleasurable though it was, as a game, he took on an *active* part. These efforts might be put down to an instinct for mastery that was acting independently of whether the memory was in itself pleasurable or not.[18]

By using objects to represent lapsed and potential relationships, farce operates formally much like this child's game of *fort-da*. More than repetition-compulsion mastery over loss, however, the dichotomy of *fort-da* can describe also the construction of a character's individuality through a temporary loss of identity and alienation from community. Indeed, farce employs this loss, paradoxically, to build identity.

Here I depart from classical materialist formulations of commodity fetishism and the objective alienation and estrangement of the self in favor of a *constructive* paradigm of the relationship between individuation and property. Thorstein Veblen's dictum that "esteem is awarded only on evidence" is, to me, a more apt means of understanding how London's drama portrayed the creation of the early modern, bourgeois subject.[19] Such evidence comes as property which reinforces and substantiates the "individual's" subject position. "Possessive individualism," then, becomes conceptually tautologous, a redundancy of what Guy Debord calls "the domination of the economy over social life." This domination, in Debord's critique, brings "into the definition of all human realization the obvious degradation of *being* into *having*."[20] The drama of early modern London demonstrated the evolution of this relationship in its emphasis on the inner life of property. Acknowledging the social dependency of the self, Renaissance farce makes manifest again and again the objective basis of subjectivity, proving that only that which can be lost (or stolen) can be possessed.

D. W. Winnicott's remarks on the "transitional object," the "not-me" possession that an infant finds/creates "in the sense of finding externality itself"[21] provide the final blocks in the theoretical understructure for what I have called the commercial inscription of identity, a culturally and historically determined process by which identity is constructed by being "written" into or onto objects. Winnicott suggested that between what he called the "relating" and "use" phases of object relations, the subject must "destroy" the object – and see it survive the destruction – to attain individuation. At the same time, however, "the object develops its own autonomy and life, and (if it survives) contributes-in to the subject, according to its own properties. ... In other words, because of the survival of the object, the subject may now have started to live a life in the world of objects."[22] This "world of objects," I suggest, and the employment of the objective in identity construction had their simulacra in the dream world of the Renaissance theater – a cultural institution both developing and developing with the nascent period of English capitalism in London. Freud's *fort-da* paradigm most exactly describes the general structure of Elizabethan farce, whereas the Jacobean drama, placing more emphasis on the objects of farce themselves, constructed identity through the practical subjectivity of the objective world.

The individual in history

The escalating importance of the self in the literature of the English Renaissance has become, in the past decade, the focus of a considerable body of critical commentary. Studies by Joel Fineman, Anne Ferry, Jonathan Dollimore, Stephen Greenblatt, and Catherine Belsey, among others, have explored the changing, resonant concept of the individual and self-consciousness in the literature of Tudor and Stuart England.[23] However generalized, Jacob Burckhardt's historical argument about the "development of the individual" appears to have had substantial literary confirmation in the English drama of the turn of the century. None of Shakespeare's or Chapman's tragedic soliloquies, for instance, with their interest in depth psychology and the subterranean currents of the mental process, would have made sense in the context of the late medieval Morality Play and its holistic, God-centered thematic. Speaking of the Greek playwrights, Werner Jaeger held that "Euripides was the first *psychologist* ... He created the pathology of the mind."[24] While I would wish to separate any playwright from this degree of agency, it is none the less tempting to describe Marlowe, Chapman, and Shakespeare as England's equivalents. It would be misleading, obviously, to contrast the soliloquies of plays like *Doctor Faustus* (1592), *Bussy D'Ambois* (1604), and *Hamlet* (1601) with those of *Gorboduc* (1562) or *The Misfortunes of*

Arthur (1588), and, on the basis of their disparate rhetorical and psychological content, offer conclusions about the rise of the individual in England in the latter part of the sixteenth century.[25] But it *is* apparent that during the very period in which religious struggle made it more likely that the individual would think about spirituality in personal, rather than institutional, terms, the Elizabethan drama – and literature of the period generally – displayed a rising interest in the individual, grew ever more sophisticated at portraying the individual's consciousness, and became increasingly concerned with the effects of such individualism on the social order – and, correspondingly, the effects of the social order on the individual. Marlowe's supermen, Chapman's Bussy, and Shakespeare's tragic figures, for example, particularly exemplify this tendency. That farces such as *Jack Juggler*, Gascoigne's *Supposes* (1566), and *The Comedy of Errors* preceded these tragedies in first posing and answering questions about the self stands Marx's dictum on its head: the literary history of the individual occurred here first as farce, then as tragedy.

I would like to suggest at this point that the new emphasis on the "self" evident in the early Tudor farce evolved in absolute conjunction with material concerns and the vagaries of urban life. The growth of London brought new and problematic complexities to London's citizens, chief among them the construction of subjectivity in the increasingly anonymous center of English commerce; as Sicinius observes in *Coriolanus*: "What is the city but the people?" (3.1.198). The paradox of isolation in the midst of an urban environment is expressed most memorably, perhaps, by Antipholus of Syracuse in *The Comedy of Errors*. A stranger to Ephesus, he reflects on his present state of estrangement and his past adventures in one of the drama's more elaborate images:

> I to the world am like a drop of water,
> That in the ocean seeks another drop,
> Who, failing there to find his fellow forth
> (Unseen, inquisitive), confounds himself.
> So I, to find a mother and a brother,
> In quest of them (unhappy), ah, lose myself.

(1.2.35–40)

Antipholus' quest for familial reunion begins in the classical mode of romance (that is, with a sea voyage and shipwreck), yet ends in the whirl of confused identity and coincidental meeting of urban farce. He must lose himself to find himself: the paradox is both Christian and civic, for to build an urban persona is to accept the necessary tension between isolation as an individual and the identity provided through anonymous membership in the crowd. With its emphasis on proximity, possession of commodity, and anonymous exchange, the city was to farce a natural center for plots based on the misplacing of (stage) properties and its corollary, the loss of identity. Standing midway between the community of comedy and the isolating brutality of tragedy, farce enjoyed great popularity throughout the sixteenth century, plays such as *Johan Johan* (1520), *Ralph Roister Doister* (1552), and *The Bugbears* (1564) contributing considerably to the era's dramatic heritage. Why did farce attain such popularity at this time? Much of farce's popularity during this period seems to have resulted from the subgenre's adaptability to the growing, post-Reformation discourse of consciousness and the self.[26] Transferred from the countryside to the buzzing rush of the city street, farce served as the literary mode through which dramatists of the Renaissance, emphasizing the importance of the city to the individual, exploring the place of the individual in the early modern city. From *Jack Juggler* and *The Comedy of Errors* to *The Shoemakers' Holiday* and *Bartholomew Fair*, the city acts as the centrifugal force behind this tension, a site where the construction of the individual is accomplished through material possession and loss.

Jack Juggler and transubstantiation

Jack Juggler came at a transitional moment in the history of English drama and society. Baldly stated, that transition marked the post-Reformation emergence, in literature, of the bourgeois subject. Addressing the emergence of the individual during the Renaissance, Richard Marienstras holds that "the author of *Jack Juggler* has given his character a dimension alien to previous plays: the consciousness of the 'self'."[27] In *Jack Juggler*, mind and material, purse and person, reveal their absolute interdependence, a relationship fostered by the city. Marienstras' "self," phrased topically as part of a religious equation, looks in fact to the dynamics of urban existence for its foundational energy.

A short way into the play the audience learns that Jenkin is "as foolish a knave withall / as any is now within London wall" (116–17).[28] Indeed, an urban location is essential to the confusion of identity in the play, for so much of its action hinges on the proximity of characters and the conflict of motivations afforded by city crowding. The play's plot is relatively straightforward: Jack Juggler, a roguish Vice figure, encounters the prodigal servant Jenkin Careaway as Jenkin returns home from a dissolutely spent afternoon. Jack mischievously plots to impersonate him, making Jenkin believe "That he is not himself but another man!" (179). For this purpose he has imitated Jenkin's dress and memorized what Jenkin has said in monologue about the events of his day. Jack meets Jenkin at the door and refuses him entry, claiming that he (Jack) is the real Jenkin

Careaway. A farcical conclusion follows, with Careaway becoming more and more frustrated at his inability to prove who he is. Although he asserts "And beat on me till I stink and till I die, / And yet will I still say that I am I!" (496–97),[29] ultimately he has no means of proving this: Juggler has appropriated his identity.

Of *Jack Juggler*, B. J. Whiting observed some time ago that "it is with surprise, and almost with fascinated horror, that the reader of this thoroughly derivative farce comes gradually to realize that he is engaged with a clever, though not very subtle, attack on transubstantiation."[30] Marie Axton echoes Whiting's interpretation of the play in arguing that "the play's action presents a comic paradigm of the crisis of personal identity which was a common experience for those who lived through the Henrican break with Rome, the Edwardian reformation and Marian counter-reformation."[31] The Prologue to *Jack Juggler* punningly raises the matter in warning the audience "that no man look to hear of matters substantial" (73), a promise Careaway breaks in vowing to "use a substantial premeditation" (730), that various characters allude to in their debate over whether it was really Careaway or, instead, his "shadow" (822; 880), and that the Epilogue (probably an Elizabethan, Protestant addition)[32] reaffirms in its assertion that "simple innocents" in the world must subscribe to a litany of ridiculous tenets: "He must say the crow is white, if he be so commanded, / Ye, and that he himself is into another body changed" (1019–20). Careaway's master, Boungrace, makes this explicit earlier in the play when he expresses his amazement at Jenkin's audacity in granting credence to

> That which was never seen nor hereafter shall be –
> That one man may have two bodies and two faces,
> And that one man at one time may be in two places

(785–87)

The religious turmoil of the sixteenth century and the vehemence of post-Reformation discourse generally intensified the debate over the legitimacy of transubstantiation to the degree where the doctrine represented a crucial site of religious contestation.[33] As Charles and Katherine George point out, "In regard to the sacramental system, the most significant aspect of the Protestant break from Roman Catholicism is the reevaluation of the nature and efficacy of that key sacrament in all Christianity, the Eucharist."[34] Arguing that the Protestant position in England was "defined first and most importantly by its decisive and unqualified repudiation of the doctrine of transubstantiation," they go on to cite Richard Hooker's statement that "The real presence of Christ's most blessed body and blood is not therefore to be sought for in the sacrament, but in the worthy receiver of the sacrament."[35]

The Moral drama frequently enacted this controversy. In Nathaniel Woodes' *The Conflict of Conscience* (1572), for instance, the "heretic" Philologus is put on trial for his Protestant views, his claims that "the bread remaineth still." James Bryant notes that, when the prosecuting Cardinal demands "In what sense said Christ, *Hoc est corpus meum?*" and Philologus replies "Even in the same sense that he said before: / *Vos estis sal terrae, Vos estis lux mundi,* / *Ego sum ostium,* and a hundred such more," it "shows how different Renaissance hermeneutics were from the medieval."[36] More precisely, perhaps, it shows how different post-Reformation hermeneutics were from Catholic modes of interpretation. As Christopher Sutton argued in 1604, "Religion is become nothing less than Religion, to wit, a matter of mere talk: such politizing is there on all parts, as a man cannot tell, who is who."[37] Instead of the potential "what is what," Sutton phrases his uncertainty in terms of identity. The debate, on one level, concerns the metaphorical status of identity. On another, it asks who can define that identity.

Some three centuries later Marx would repeat this move when, in the first volume of *Capital,* discussing the protean malleability of commodity in the price determination process, he hit on the celebration of the Eucharist as an illustrative figure: "it must quit its bodily shape, must transform itself from mere imaginary into real gold, although to the commodity such transubstantiation may be ... difficult."[38] For the human actor, as well as for Marx's "commodity," such transubstantiation proved (and continues to prove) difficult. Indeed, *Jack Juggler* succeeds mainly in outlining the questions of identity which would perplex later dramatists. Unlike with *The Conflict of Conscience,* it is never easy to tell exactly where *Jack Juggler* stands on the doctrinal debate over Christ's presence in the ritual of Communion. During the very time Tudor England was struggling to sever the objective from the subjective in matters of doctrine, however, *Jack Juggler* clearly used farce's uncanny predilection for free-floating identity to comment on the issue.

The binding chain

Like the ceremony of Communion itself, individual identity in *Jack Juggler* is bound up in the relationship between spirit and substance. It is the social import of such a relationship which underlies a good part of *The Comedy of Errors* – a farce, like *Jack Juggler,* of the city. Indeed, the city itself functions as a character in Shakespeare's drama. As Gail Paster maintains about the trio of plays she calls Shakespearean "city comedies" – *The Comedy of Errors, The Merchant of Venice,* and *Measure for Measure* (1604): "in each play, the city experiences a crisis of its own being which grows out of and is parallel to the experiences of its characters. The comic crisis that the characters must resolve interlocks with the crisis of an entire social order."[39] Paster also stresses "the noticeable tension between social identity and individual experience" in the dramatic action of these plays.[40] This tension is, literally, embodied by the farcical objects of *The Comedy of Errors*. As in one of its source plays, Plautus' *Amphitruo*, identity in Shakespeare's play is connected with gold: more specifically, with a chain and a sack of coins. Soon after giving his money to his servant Dromio for safekeeping, the Syracusan Antipholus meets the Ephesian Dromio, and becomes anxious about the safety of his gold. Four times in twenty-four lines –

> Where have you left the money that I gave you?
>
> Tell me, and dally not, where is the money?
>
> Where is the gold I gave in charge to thee?
>
> Now, as I am a Christian, answer me,
> In what safe place you have bestowed my money –
>
> (1.2.54; 59; 70; 77–78)

he demands to know its whereabouts. When Dromio, baffled by this stranger's mad discourse, flees the resultant beating, the Syracusan Antipholus gives voice to his fears:

> Upon my life, by some device or other
> The villain is o'erraught of all my money.
> They say this town is full of cozenage:
> As nimble jugglers that deceive the eye,
> Dark working sorcerers that change the mind,
> Soul-killing witches that deform the body,
> Disguised cheaters, prating mountebanks,
> And many such like liberties of sin:
> If it prove so, I will be gone the sooner.
> I'll to the Centaur to go seek this slave;
> I greatly fear my money is not safe.
>
> (1.2.95–105)

Of special interest here is the way Antipholus structures his complaint, framing his trepidation over magicians "that change the mind" and "deform the body" between the first two and the last lines of the passage, where he expresses his fear of monetary loss. Indeed, thinking of his money appears to lead him to suspect witchcraft's power over his mind, and from witchcraft he returns to his coins. To this Antipholus, money is connected with transformation, inextricably linking identity with property: Antonio's "my purse, my person" (*MV*, 1.1.138). One could see the loss and finding of Antipholus' money, in fact, like a dramatic game of *fort-da*, the money here symbolizing his own identity. In the essay I referred to above, Barbara Freedman offers an ingenious reading of the play, arguing that the brothers Antipholi act as symbolic halves of Egeon's fragmented consciousness, twin characters "serving as symbolic representatives of their father."[41] She continues: "the play, then, is not simply about the payments of debts or the physical division and reunion of a family, but about the psychic division and integration of a personality."[42] It is my argument that this "psychic division and integration" is not separate from, but instead connected inseparably to the "payment of debts," and that mental union is carried out first on the material level of society.

Adriana, wife of the Ephesian Antipholus, has been promised a golden chain – a "carcanet" – which to her represents not individual identity, but the binding love within the marital bond of which she so often speaks (cf. 2.1.106–15). In a reading of the thematic significance of this ornament, Richard Henze argues that "the chain is an image of the golden bonds [of marriage]; the misplacement of the chain and weakening of the bonds brings distrust, confusion, loss of social stability."[43] This loss of social stability comes about when, denied admittance to his own household (as Marjorie Garber points out, the door is a symbol for sexual access throughout *The Comedy of Errors*),[44] Adriana's husband gives this symbol of affection to a courtesan of Ephesus, relating to Angelo, the goldsmith whom he has contracted to make the chain:

> Get you home
> And fetch the chain; by this I know 'tis made.
> Bring it, I pray you, to the Porpentine,
> For there's the house. That chain will I bestow
> (Be it for nothing but to spite my wife)
> Upon mine hostess there. Good sir, make haste.
> Since mine own doors refuse to entertain me,
> I'll knock elsewhere, to see if they'll disdain me.
>
> (3.1.114–21)

Replaced as husband, Antipholus spitefully uses the chain in an attempt to substitute another woman for his wife. So much is close to the action of Plautus' *Menaechmi*. But Shakespeare goes beyond his model in using the chain to complicate an additional relationship, illustrating the powerful connections among personal and public, domestic and commercial.

As mentioned above, the Ephesian Antipholus has contracted for the chain with Angelo, a goldsmith of Ephesus, but not yet paid for the service. Goldsmiths in Shakespeare's age, of course, were more than craftsmen. In the vacuum of formal financial establishments in the fifteenth and sixteenth centuries they frequently assumed the role of bankers. As R. H. Tawney described it, "They provide[d] ready money against the deposit of valuables, [lent] money to finance merchants engaged in foreign trade or to needy gentlemen, and [stood] as security for the repayment of large sums borrowed by fellow tradesmen."[45] In agreeing to fashion the chain, and in delivering it to the man he thinks is the Ephesian Antipholus, Angelo makes a form of loan; the breaking of this obligation violates a civil agreement. Shakespeare intensifies the chain's significance as a symbol of civic and professional responsibility, however, by constructing another social obligation, that of Angelo's debt to the Second Merchant of Ephesus. With the wind and tide pending, the Second Merchant demands payment of a debt from Angelo:

> You know since Pentecost the sum is due,
> And since I have not much importun'd you,
> Nor now I had not, but that I am bound
> To Persia, and want guilders for my voyage:
> Therefore make present satisfaction,
> Or I'll attach you by this officer.

(4.1.1–6)

Angelo replies:

> Even just the sum that I do owe to you
> Is growing to me by Antipholus,
> And in the instant that I met with you
> He had of me a chain. At five a' clock
> I shall receive money for the same:
> Pleaseth you walk with me down to his house,
> I will discharge my bond ...

(4.1.7–13)

Because Angelo has given the chain to the wrong Antipholus, the gentleman he asks for payment refuses his request. Where Plautus was satisfied with what one might call "simple" dramatic confusion, Shakespeare multiplies the line of dependency, suggesting (in an argument which would later become standard among some of his characters) that discord on one level of society – that is, the familial and marital – translates into the breakdown of convention along others: here, the professional / commercial. But where the political discourse of characters like Canterbury, Ulysses, and Menenius focuses on a vertical hierarchy, the dramatic praxis of urban farce stresses a horizontal obligation, one kept level, in fact, by capital – that is, relationships have more to do with *external* properties (chattel, etc.) than with patently internal properties (e.g. grace, *noblesse*) and the abstractions of social station. As shown in Renaissance drama, money wields an almost vortical power in urban society, attaining an authority that mingles, reduces, doubles, and inverts.

Even the lowest common denominators of existence find expression and summation in commercial valuation. Just as this scene, with its temporal urgency and confusion of identity, goes a significant distance toward encapsulating the action of the play itself, so is the golden chain – in its concatenation of wife, courtesan, goldsmith, merchant, and brother – a piece of dramaturgical currency emblematic of larger issues in the drama.

Dekker's shoes

In a perceptive essay on the relationship between work and play, commerce and commodity in Thomas Dekker's *The Shoemakers' Holiday*, David Scott Kastan argues against the traditional critical tendency of interpreting the play as either harmless mirth or "a realistic portrait of Elizabethan middle-class life."[46] To Kastan, *The Shoemakers' Holiday* "is a realistic portrait only of Elizabethan middle-class dreams – a fantasy of class fulfillment that would erase the tensions and contradictions created by the nascent capitalism of the late sixteenth-century."[47] Dekker thus "idealizes the actual atomization of the culture" of Renaissance London.[48] This "atomization," I would argue, occurs most forcefully on the level of commodified subjectivity.

The incident in *The Shoemakers' Holiday* which bears most importance to the present argument is, like the play itself, sentimental: the presentation of a pair of shoes by Ralph, a journeyman shoemaker, to Jane, his wife. Ralph and his fellow craftsmen fashion these shoes especially for her:

> Thou know'st our trade makes rings for women's heels:
> Here, take this pair of shoes cut out by Hodge,
> Stitched by my fellow Firk, seamed by myself,
> Made up and pinked with letters for thy name.
>
> (1.1.233–36)[49]

The production is collective, Jane's identity emblem created through the craft's division of labor. The "ring" which the group has crafted for Jane is inscribed with her name, "pinked with letters" through which the shoe is laced. Jane's identity, and the collective identity of this guild subgroup, is concentrated through the writing of Jane's name into the shoes. Even as this commercial inscription of identity enforces a discursive relation between Jane and the material world, so does the very act of production here bind the men of the "gentle craft" together through the individuality of their separate but interdependent tasks of labor. Hodge cuts the forms from the leather, Firk stitches them together, and Ralph seams them. Like the *blazons* of the Petrarchan sonneteers, the male construction of female identity here depends on violent *building* of the woman. This production in turn constructs a collective (male) identity. As Durkheim argued, "mechanical solidarity does not bind men together with the same strength as does the division of labour."[50]

Ralph's perforation of the leather with the marks of Jane's identity is a sexually symbolic action resonating in an atmosphere of bawdy jokes already surrounding the shoemakers' "tools." Ralph continues with a plea:

> Wear them, my dear Jane, for thy husband's sake,
> And every morning, when thou pull'st them on,
> Remember me, and pray for my return.
> Make much of them, for I have made them so,
> That I can know them from a thousand mo.

(1.1.237–41)

The specification of identity in the last line here recalls Antipholus of Syracuse's "drop of water" lament in *The Comedy of Errors*. *Hamlet* is anticipated (or, perhaps, recalled) as well in Ralph's injunction, "Remember me." Inscribed with Jane's own name, the gift functions not as a memento of Ralph, but instead as a male-constructed reminder to her of their relationship. Possibly no drama affords a better example of the Renaissance market's tendency toward the commercial inscription of identity. The shoes themselves, as the shoemakers claim, are like rings for women's heels. They differ in import from the potentially abstract symbolism of the wedding ring,[51] however, in that Ralph and his fellow workers have inscribed Jane's identity into them in large letters: in the context of the shoemakers' shop she is what they have made her; literally, what she wears.

Hindsight reveals the appropriateness of the gift. Separated from Jane, Ralph has almost abandoned hope of finding her when one day he is surprised by a strange serving man who offers him one of Jane's special shoes as a model. Feeling that he has been presented evidence of his cuckoldry, Ralph exclaims:

> this shoe, I durst be sworn,
> Once covered the instep of my Jane.
> This is her size, her breadth; thus trod my love;
> These true-love knots I pricked ...

(4.3.44–47)

Ralph's seemingly unconscious quibble on "pricked" joins a number of other "occupation" jokes in *The Shoemakers' Holiday* in emphasizing the erotics of labor generally and the sexual nature of their trade in particular.

Malvolio as the letter "c"

In its stress on commercial inscription, the "shoe" passage in Dekker's play stands similar to another Shakespearean moment: Malvolio's punning on the handwriting he believes to be Olivia's – "Her c's, her u's, and her t's" (2.5.87) – and his remark, concerning the cryptic M O A I, that "every one of these letters are in my name" (2.5.141). It is by now a critical commonplace to describe Malvolio as an exemplar of class ambition in the English Renaissance. His ambitious attempt to promote himself socially through marrying above himself marks Malvolio as the scapegoat of the drama's political, as well as theatrical, society. In addition to his relationship to the commercial interests of contemporary Puritanism, however, what is important to me here is the way Malvolio literally *inscribes* part of Olivia's sexual identity – "c . . u . . ['n] . . t" – into a missive that (as, again, critics are fond of noting) contains none of those letters. As Terry Eagleton points out, *Twelfth Night* frequently endows objects "with a constant human existence: Belch wishes that his boots should 'hang themselves in their own straps' (1.3.[12–13])," and "Malvolio, at the moment he is endowing the symbolic shapes of written language with life, begs leave of the wax of the letter for breaking it."[52] "By your leave, wax" (2.5.91–92), is the passage to which Eagleton refers. In reading and interpreting the letter, however, Malvolio adds another stratum of objectification to the play. Malvolio's process of inscription is commercial, I would argue, in its materialist basis – commerce here taking place on a level of social manipulation. Not only does he attempt to write Olivia's identity into the physical text of the forged letter, but also foresees himself using it as a form of currency for self-advancement, attaining the physical luxury of the "branch'd velvet gown," winding up his new watch and playing with "some rich jewel" (2.5.47–48; 60).

Malvolio's mention of this fantasized "jewel" comes in an important context:

I frown the while, and perchance wind up my watch, or play with my – some rich jewel. (2.5.59–60)

His hesitation here is significant. As the Riverside editor suggests, in changing verbal directions Malvolio seems to be "on the verge of saying 'my chain' (his insignia of office as steward) but catches himself in time." Indeed, it is probable that the actor playing Malvolio would be stroking his chain as he delivers the line. The easy transition between "chain" and "jewel" here marks, of course, the facility of transference between objects, but also suggests an erotic context in which Malvolio satisfies himself by stroking a luxurious commodity – the "rich jewel" – which has displaced the symbol of his occupational status. This stroking connotes an auto-erotic project, one which finds itself replicated in the inscribing of Olivia's genitalia onto the letter which Malvolio so unwittingly glosses.

Maria, who has written these "obscure epistles of love" (2.3.155–56), functions as what the drama of the period might call a counterfeit bawd, substituting her "hand" for her lady's (2.3.159–61), as she appropriates Olivia's cunt for graphic presentation – and thus leaves Malvolio the tool or butt of a tendentious joke. The "hand" here becomes the transitional device between the individual (Malvolio, Maria) and the genital (Malvolio's "rich jewel" and Olivia's cunt). In thwarting the erotic plans of an ambitious figure (here one might compare Falstaff in *The Merry Wives of Windsor* (1597) and Angelo in *Measure for Measure*) Maria literally writes a symbolic version of Olivia's genitalia onto a letter for Malvolio's perusal, inscribing one socially suggested telos or end to the steward's marital plans (an end for which, significantly enough, Malvolio shows no special enthusiasm) onto a document that Malvolio believes offers a contractual promise of his rising in society: "in this she manifests herself to my love, and with a kind of injunction drives me to these habits of her liking" (2.5.167–69). In forging this sexualized contract, Maria and the "box-tree" gang found a suitable trap for Malvolio's ambition. As in *The Shoemakers' Holiday*, female sexuality is reified and manipulated in a process of identity construction.[53] The energy of labor and material ambition finds expression in the reduction and objectification of the female. If Malvolio is indeed a member the "rising" middle class, like the shoemakers of Dekker's sentimental play he eventually needs, in order to rise, something – or someone – to step on.

6   The farce of objects: *Othello* to *Bartholomew Fair*

The handkerchief which Othello gives Desdemona as a "token" of their love forges a *fort-da* link between the two in much the same way as Antipholus' chain eventually bound him to Adriana, and in the way Jane was connected to Ralph through her shoes. As I will argue, the handkerchief retains a social significance that depends on English society's growing commercialism. Yet in communicating the sense and signs of identity, the handkerchief also possesses a kind of internal significance characteristic of the Jacobean drama and its tendency toward the commercial inscription of identity. In this way it remains both part of a historical narrative driven by a developing market, and part of a literary narrative itself drawing power from and responding to this market-centered energy.

The strange importance of the handkerchief to the drama's action has long been noted. Thomas Rymer's well-known characterization of *Othello* (1604) as a "Bloody Farce" in his "Short View of Tragedy," for instance, springs from the neoclassical view that Shakespeare violated the rules of decorum by making, in Rymer's words, "a Tragedy of this Trifle."[1] Rymer regretted the disparity between cause and effect in *Othello*, thinking the handkerchief too trivial an object to excite such passion in the Moor:

Had it been Desdemona's Garter, the Sagacious Moor might have smelt a Rat: but the Handkerchief is so remote a trifle, no Booby, on this side Mauritania, cou'd make any consequence from it.[2]

"So much ado, so much stress, so much passion and repetition about an Handkerchief!" Rymer lamented, "Why was not this call'd the *Tragedy of the Handkerchief*?"[3]

Yet Rymer tacitly answers his own question in alluding to the handkerchief's sexual aura at two moments in his essay: first when he suggests, as one of the morals to be drawn from *Othello*, that "this may be a warning to all good Wives, that they look well to their Linen"[4] and second when, hypothesizing a different outcome for the play, he suggests that

"Desdemona dropt the Handkerchief, and missed it that very day after her Marriage; it might have been rumpl'd up with her Wedding sheets."[5] The handkerchief is embroidered, "spotted with strawberries" (3.3.435), and many critics have suggested that in this it symbolizes wedding sheets stained with the evidence of virginity. Lynda Boose, for example, notes its relation to the folk custom of displaying these stained sheets publicly for communal approval of the marriage.[6] Edward Snow goes further in offering that the blood might connote menstruation as well, "thereby facilitating an identification between virginal and menstrual blood in the male subconscious." "The handkerchief," he continues, "is thus a nexus for the three aspects of woman – chaste bride, sexual object, and maternal threat – which the institution it represents seeks to separate."[7] And in a more recent essay, Karen Newman argues for an enlargement of the object's significance, holding that "the handkerchief in *Othello* is what we might term a snowballing signifier, for as it passes from hand to hand, both literal and critical, it accumulates myriad associations and meanings."[8]

Indeed, in attempting to add to the "associations and meanings" accorded the handkerchief by literary criticism, Newman's valuable essay works against many psychoanalytic readings that have tended to occlude the social valance of the handkerchief's signifying process. For although, as Rymer noticed, the handkerchief has a signal, horrifying role in prompting and fueling Othello's jealousy, it also possesses a wide range of meanings for those in the drama itself. One of its more compelling meanings issues directly from the manner in which the handkerchief encodes, through the matrix of its "work," the erotic basis of labor and makes manifest, through the dramatic enactment of this eroticism, subjectivity's dependence on the objective.

The handkerchief comes into direct play first when Othello, suspecting himself a cuckold, complains allusively that "I have a pain upon my forehead, here"(3.3.284). Desdemona's reply carries an unwitting pun dependent on cuckoldry's ties to voyeurism: "Faith, that's with watching" (3.3.285). At this point, presumably, she takes out the handkerchief which Othello has given her as a sign of affection, offering to bind his forehead with it. Perhaps feeling that his invisible horns are too large to be encompassed by the handkerchief, Othello rudely brushes it aside – "Your napkin is too little" – and orders her to "Let it alone," the pair departing and leaving the handkerchief on stage. Emilia finds it, and in a soliloquy remarks:

> I am glad I have found this napkin;
> This was her first remembrance from the Moor.
> My wayward husband hath a hundred times

Woo'd me to steal it; but she so loves the token
That she reserves it evermore about her
To kiss and talk to. I'll have the work ta'en out,
And give't Iago. What he will do with it
Heaven knows, not I;
I nothing but to please his fantasy.

                                                            (3.3.290–99)

Several themes developed later in the play make themselves apparent in
Emilia's speech. First is the handkerchief's role as link between Othello
and Desdemona: a "token" which Desdemona keeps close to her, "To kiss
and talk to." Second is its desirability: even as it later becomes an object
of contention between Othello and Desdemona – he demanding to see it,
she wanting to recover it – one discovers here that Iago has long desired to
obtain it, his "fantasy" seducing Emilia into theft. Third is the theme of
stolen identity.

   Immediately after acquiring the handkerchief, Emilia says that she will
"have the work ta'en out." Editors usually gloss this passage with something like "pattern copied," a reading supported by a later line in the play
(3.4.190) and other examples of its usage during the period.[9] In copying
this pattern – or at least by implying that it *can* be copied – Emilia
articulates a rationale for Othello's anxiety: the fear that he can be
replaced sexually. Suggesting a historical parallel, Karen Newman refers
to a scandal of *cinquecento* Venice in demonstrating how handkerchiefs
could symbolize personal relations. One Tomaso, enamored of a married
woman, "presumed to follow the said lady and on this public street took
from her hands a handkerchief, carrying it off with him. As a result of this
deed the said Tomaso entered the home of Roberto many times during the
day and night and committed many dishonesties with this lady with the
highest dishonor for ser Roberto."[10] This story, as Newman notes, bears
special relevance for *Othello*: in both narratives the identity unfolds
subordinately from the physical, the handkerchiefs pure examples of
personal property and – through malign inversion – coming to stand for
the property of the person. Above all, handkerchiefs are easy to take and
conceal. As Peachum says of his linen booty in *The Beggar's Opera*
(1728): "In the meantime, wife, rip out the coronets and marks of these
dozen cambric handkerchiefs, for I can dispose of them this afternoon to
a chap in the City."[11] The "coronets and marks" are identifying symbols
embroidered on the handkerchiefs: to remove them is to erase the possession of the handkerchief, rendering it useful for another owner.[12] What
The Beggar's Opera enunciates in a readily recognizable criminal dialect,
however, *Othello* formulates in terms of tragic jealousy. Working on this
jealousy, Iago hints at the sexual nature of *Othello*'s handkerchief when

he goads the Moor, "if I give my wife a handkerchief – / She may, I think, bestow't on any man" (4.1.10–13).

The word "work" itself constituted a euphemism for coitus in Shakespeare: Othello later indicates as much with "She did gratify his amorous works" (5.2.213).[13] When Cassio encounters Bianca, a once-dependent prostitute whom he has jilted, he gives her the handkerchief (having found it where Iago left it in his chamber) and bids her, "Take me this work out" (3.4.180). Immediately jealous, she demands to know the identity of its owner. Cassio cannot know, of course, that it has passed from Othello's parents to Othello, from Othello to Desdemona, from Desdemona to Emilia, and finally from Emilia to Iago before it has reached him. Indeed, one might compare this extended chain of gift transference with the line of financial dependency in *The Comedy of Errors* (1592), and with the group production of the shoemakers in Dekker's play: in all three cases, an uncanniness arises as the result of an extended social order. An unwitting pawn of this uncanny order, Cassio only says once more: "I like the work well; ere it be demanded / (As like enough it will) I would have it copied" (3.4.189–90). When they meet again, however, he discovers that Bianca's jealousy has dissuaded her from copying the "work:"

Let the devil and his dam haunt you! What did you mean by that same handkerchief you gave me even now? I was a fine fool to take it. I must *take out the work*? A likely *piece of work*, that you should find it in your chamber, and know not who left it there! This is some minx's token, and I must *take out the work*? There, give it your hobby horse. Wheresoever you had it, I'll take out *no work on't*. (4.1.148–55, emphasis mine)

I have emphasized the manner in which "work" permeates her speech: incantational, like Iago's "put money in thy purse" and Othello's demonic "cause," its repetition emphasizes the extent to which the idea of copying, and general use, haunts Bianca.[14] One could say that this moment marks the emergence, in *Othello*, of a social unconscious, for the sexual sense of "work" finds itself connected with the more formal meaning of "work" as commercial or industrial labor in the occupation which fuses the two: prostitution.

Othello describes the uncanny magic of the handkerchief to Desdemona in his ornate but frightening recollection of the process by which witchcraft, Egypt, fate, a sibyl, sacred silkworms, and dye distilled from maidens' hearts all combine in the weave of a handkerchief that "an Egyptian to my mother [did] give" (3.4.55–75; 56). Perhaps this tale itself, however, functions as a kind of ghost story, for later, in a (seemingly) disinterested moment, Othello relates "It was a handkerchief, an antique token / My father gave my mother" (5.2.216–17). It is difficult not to agree here with Steevens, who suspected early that "the first account of the handkerchief, as given by Othello, was purposely ostentatious, in order to alarm his wife the more."[15] Preceding Bianca's emphasis on "work," Othello passes on his anxieties to Desdemona by ascribing magical properties to the weave of the handkerchief. Cloth, magical and otherwise, had of course long been connected with normalizing concepts of female sexuality and domestic conduct. Engels thought it an example of the severity of the monogamous family among the Greeks "how Telemachus in the *Odyssey* silences his mother:"

Go therefore back into the house, and take up your own work, the loom and the distaff, and see to it that your handmaidens ply their work also ... For mine is the power in this household.[16]

Spinning as a correct and desirable household activity appears, for instance, in the Argument of Shakespeare's "The Rape of Lucrece," where, as part of a symbolic chastity test, spinning is contrasted with female freedom:

In that pleasant humor they all posted to Rome, and intending by their secret and sudden arrival to make trial of that which every one had before avouched, only Collatinus finds his wife (though it were late in the night) spinning amongst her maids; the other ladies were all found dancing and revelling. (13–19)

Here, as in the *Odyssey*, domestic industry emblematizes chastity. Lucrece demonstrates her marital fidelity by expending her (potentially erotic) energy on non-sexual production.

Yet clothworking and many other forms of handicrafts also stood as metaphors for sexual supplementation in Renaissance literature. The act of spinning, for example, frequently carried with it the innuendo of copulation. In John Florio's *Second Frutes* (1591), Caesar tells Tiberia how their neighbors' daughter has cuckolded her new spouse: "She spins crooked spindles for her husband, and sends him into Cornwall without ship or boat."[17] Cornwall – through the Latin *cornu*, "horn" – is a pun here on "cuckold-land." Eric Partridge points to Sir Toby's rebuke of Sir Andrew, a character ridiculously proud of his hair: "Excellent, it hangs like flax on a distaff; and I hope to see a huswif take thee between her legs, and spin it off" (1.3.102- 04).[18] Vindice in *The Revenger's Tragedy* (1606) rails against the "careful sisters" who "spin that thread i' th' night / That does maintain them and their bawds i' th' day."[19] Taking up Vindice's image, James Henke explicates its basis as a sexual metaphor with the following:

The imaginative analog may be based on the operation of a spinning wheel – i.e., as the woman sits with the wheel between her legs to spin thread from flax, so, too, the prostitute, with her male customer between her legs, "spins" his flax (i.e., semen) to produce "thread" (i.e., money) to maintain herself and her bawd. There is also an analogy here between the rhythmic hip movements during copulation and the turning of the spinning wheel.[20]

In its correlation of the human and the mechanical, Henke's reading – basically a joke analysis – recalls Bergson. What Henke describes here with such scientific precision, however, subserved uneasily characters like Vindice (and playwrights like Middleton); it reconciled metaphorically the ostensibly feminine qualities of patient production with the ordinarily competitive (hence patently masculine) arena of the market. A basic fear of transaction, sexual and commercial alike, underlies the metaphor.

Desdemona's handkerchief remains integral to Othello and *Othello* in part because it demonstrates the irony of commercial transaction and assent: a participatory phenomenon, desire in the early modern world becomes communal, even as value is privatized.[21] Like the handkerchief, clothing becomes the body, in both senses of the verb. Renaissance plays frequently explored the connection. Disguised as Slack, a scholar, the young Lord Nonsuch of *Cupid's Whirligig* (1607) anticipated Freud by over three centuries in his explicitly sexual analysis of clothing:

True sir, there is nothing done, but there's reason for it, (if a man could find it) for what's the reason your Citizen's wives continually wear hats, but to show the desire they have always to be covered. Or why do your Sempsters spend their time in pricking, and your Ladies in poking of ruffes; but only to show they do as they would be done unto?[22]

In Slack's reading, the "Citizen's wives" and "Sempsters" express their sexuality both *through* and *in* clothing. Parodying the golden rule with this last line, "as they would be done unto," Slack indicates why clothing, intimately connected to the body and bodily functions, so frequently became a symbol of sexuality in the literature of the period. As both a labor-intensive product and a virtual second skin, cloth encapsulated work even as it lay next to the body. In this way it functioned as a material, chiastic nexus of social and personal activity. Likewise the "work" of Desdemona's handkerchief, a patently personal object composed of and defined by social valuation – a process which Shakespeare delineates through the tragic action of *Othello* – traces its fetishistic roots to the dynamics of the Renaissance market.

Sharking vintners

Othello's handkerchief and the chain of *The Comedy of Errors* are just two of the many objects in Shakespeare's plays which take on a higher importance for subjectivity. The moneybags of *The Merchant of Venice*,[23] the glove and the sleeve of *Troilus and Cressida* (1602), the ring in

Cymbeline (1609) – such carry more meaning than is usual for stage props, and can, in their genital symbolism, represent concepts like virility, fertility, and chastity. Shylock's "bags" and "stones," Troilus' "sleeve," Portia, Bertram, and Imogen's rings are all powerful in their signification: their importance centers on their bodily *and* narrative displacement and relocation. Beginning in the late 1590s, however, Renaissance drama began to place different emphasis on the method of object symbolization. In the space that remains I would like to explore the object relations of such props and commodities in two non-Shakespearean plays: John Marston's *The Dutch Courtesan* (1605) and Ben Jonson's *Bartholomew Fair* (1614).

The short Argument printed before *The Dutch Courtesan*, its "*Fabulae Argumentum*," offers an explicit (if obviously underdetermined) account of its major theme:

The difference betwixt the love of a courtesan and a wife is the full scope of the play, which, intermixed with the deceits of a witty city jester, fills up the comedy.[24]

Much of Marston's dramatic project seems devoted to illustrating these polarities. Unlike Middleton in *The Changeling* (1622) (witness, for example, both the behavior and nominal significance of Beatrice-Joanna), Marston, with *The Dutch Courtesan*, borrows from the psychomachia tradition of the Moralities in keeping his female characters cosmetically distinct, associating with the play's wife – aptly named Beatrice, or "one who blesses" – chastity, faithfulness, unselfish love, and purity, and with Franceschina, the Dutch Courtesan, libido, betrayal, self-interest, and disease. Although no one commits adultery in *The Dutch Courtesan*, and nowhere, even, is it threatened, the *idea* of adultery, through adulteration of commodity, figures prominently in this play. Commodity substitutes for and encodes the bodily.

The play opens with members of both plots congregated in a discussion of Cocledemoy's latest endeavor: "Cogging Cocledemoy," Freevill waxes incredulously, "is run away with a nest of goblets? True, what then? They will be hammer'd out well enough, I warrant you" (1.1.4–6). This last line calls up a fear seated deeply in Mulligrub: "*Hic finis Priami!*" he cries, lamenting that, in Freevill's words, "the nest of goblets were flown away" (1.1.38; 34), and that their shape is subject to mutation – "They will be hammer'd out well enough."[25] Objects like these mutable goblets appear in great numbers in *The Dutch Courtesan*. Two rings figure importantly in the main plot, symbolizing in the standard way fidelity (or lack thereof) between two pairs of lovers. But the subplot is replete with different props, duplicating in a way a Brueghel painting's emphasis on material life: goblets, a bowl, a moneybag, a purse, a cloak – even a salmon takes an important role in Cocledemoy's cony-catching.

In logic of the play, this "city jester" justifiably appropriates these tokens from the Mulligrubs, for the vintner and his wife are adulterers of commodity – "mangonists," to use Malheureux's term. He describes this idea in a puritanical diatribe beginning with the consumer and ending with the provider:

> Know, sir, the strongest argument that speaks
> Against the soul's eternity is lust,
> That wise man's folly and the fool's wisdom:
> But to grow wild in loose lasciviousness,
> Given up to heat and sensual appetite,
> Nay, to expose your health and strength and name,
> Your precious time, and with that time the hope
> Of due preferment, advantageous means
> Of any worthy end, to the stale use,
> The common bosom, of a money-creature,
> One that sells human flesh, a mangonist!
>
> (1.1.81–91)

Randle Cotgrave glossed "mangonism" in his *Dictionarie of the French and English Tongues* (1611) as "the craft of pampering, trimming, or setting out of saleable things."[26] Following Cotgrave's lead, the *OED* defines a mangonist as "one who furbishes up inferior wares for sale." In English Renaissance drama, this adulteration of commodity, "mangonism," doubled for sexual adultery; similarly, disquietude centering on the anonymity of a commodity's source and history enfigured anxieties over identity in marriage and society. The fear of adulterated commodity distinguishes much of the drama after 1598, although the pamphleteers and satirists of the 1590s had anticipated the concern. In *Pierce Peniless* (1592), for example, Nashe speaks of

Brewers, that, by retailing filthy Thames water, come in a few years to be worth forty or fifty thousand pound: others by dead wine, as little flying worms; and so the Vintners in like case: others by slime, as frogs, which may be alluded to Mother Bunch's slimy ale, that hath made her and some other of her fill-pot faculty so wealthy.[27]

The Host of the Garter in the Quarto of *The Merry Wives of Windsor* (1597) tells Bardolph "Let me see thee froth and lime" (1.3.14) – lime being added to the ale to disguise its flatness or impure state – something which does not escape the notice of Falstaff: "You rogue, here's lime in this sack too" (2.4.124).[28] Significantly, Helen, the archetype of female adultery, is described as a "flat, tamed piece" (4.1.63) in *Troilus and Cressida*. Merecraft, the ruthless projector of Jonson's *The Devil is an Ass* (1616), relates how he will frighten a potential customer by describing "what diseases / And putrefactions in the gums are bred, / By those are made of adult'rate and false wood" (4.1.104–06). A classical borrowing (from Latin *mango*, meaning salesman, especially a slave dealer), "mangonism" provided Marston both with a nonce word satirizing Malheureux's puritan cant and, simultaneously, with a term accurately descriptive of the Mulligrubs' practice of adulterating their commodities. Through "mangonism" the adultery of the Dutch Courtesan and the adulteration of the Mulligrubs' stock of libations are joined.

Mulligrub is continually described as a dishonest vintner. The play opens with Freevill addressing him as "my good host" (1.1.1), whereupon Malheureux adds "most hardly-honest Mulligrub" (1.1.3). Tysefew, a gallant, later calls Mulligrub "A sharking vintner" (5.2.107). None of these characters separates Mulligrub's religious beliefs from his mercantile practices. In fact, the constant punning throughout *The Dutch Courtesan* on the conflicting tenets of Catholic, Protestant, and Puritan faiths often comes in a commercial context, recalling the manner in which *Jack Juggler* (1555) used transubstantiation to explore the physical basis of identity. Cocledemoy, for example, responds to the bawd Mary Faugh's fear that he will "play the knave and restore [the goblets]" with "no, by the Lord, aunt, restitution is Catholic" (1.2.6–8), and the drama jokes almost incessantly on ostensible connections between prostitution and the "Family of Love," the Familist sect then notorious as a free love organization. In a parody of puritan admonishment, Freevill warns Mulligrub: "remember the sins of the cellar, and repent, repent!" (1.1.40–41). "Cellar" is a modern emendation: the quarto of 1605 read "sellar" and the 1633 edition "seller." Either way – cellar or seller – the pun is obvious to the ear: Mulligrub's sins are commercial.

Mistress Mulligrub testifies to as much in her confession: "we do wink at the sins of our people, our wines are Protestants" (2.3.8–9). Later Cocledemoy delivers a long and parodic harangue on Mulligrub's seller / cellar sins:

brother, brother, you must think of your sins and iniquities. You have been a broacher of profane vessels; you have made us drink of the juice of the whore of Babylon. For whereas good ale, perrys, braggets, ciders, and metheglins was the true ancient British and Troyan drinks, you ha' brought in Popish wines, Spanish wines, French wines, *tam Marti quam Mercurio*, both muscadine and malmsey, to the subversion, staggering, and sometimes overthrow of many a good Christian. You ha' been a great jumbler. Oh, remember the sins of your nights! for your night works ha' been unsavory in the taste of your customers. (5.3.103–12)

In a recent edition of the play, MacDonald Jackson and Michael Neill explain the wine/religion connection with the following note: "in both cases the implication is that the wines are adulterated, like the religions with which they are associated."[29] At least since the closing tale in

Skelton's *Merry Tales* (published 1558/1567), in which Skelton uses a story about receiving Communion at mass to fool a dishonest alewife into admitting that she has adulterated the wine, the religious import of wine's purity had been used comedically, in a commercial context.[30] Cocledemoy characteristically adds sexual innuendo to the combination with bawdy quibble on "juice of the whore of Babylon" and "jumbler," upon which Jackson and Neill comment as follows: "*jumbler*: adulterator of wine; but 'to jumble' is also 'to have intercourse'; Cocledemoy continues his bawdy quibbling through 'overthrow ... jumbler ... sins of your nights ... night works ... customers'." By stealing the valuables of the Mulligrubs, Cocledemoy repays the vintner duo for what he comically portrays as their adulteration of pure British ale, here a symbol of religion and nationalism. The focus is not merely on the whereabouts of the wine, but on its integrity. The process of reification so common to farce is, in *The Dutch Courtesan*, carried to its logical conclusion. The inscription of identity into objects is followed by an admission that the subjective then shares the properties of the material world. *The Dutch Courtesan*'s dual emphasis on (marital) chastity and (commercial) honesty thus conjoins in a dialectic of purity discourse.

Adulterous women

Jonson's *Bartholomew Fair* shares *The Dutch Courtesan*'s puritanical concern with ritual pollution and cleanliness. Like Marston's play, *Bartholomew Fair* produces a world of objects, a world where loss and gain, possession and theft, predominate thought and activity. Setting up real puritans for ridicule – here the infamous Zeal-of-the-Land Busy and the misnamed Dame Purecraft – Jonson's drama, as Marston's, nevertheless endorses a *version* of these miasmic concerns.[31] A temporary model of the city itself, Bartholomew Fair is a swirling collection of dishonest tradesmen and gullible customers.

Jonson foregrounds the commercial universe of the Fair to follow when, in the closing lines of the Induction, the Scrivener delivers a message from the playwright:

he prays you to believe, his ware is still the same, else you will make him justly suspect that he that is so loth to look on a baby, or an hobby-horse here, would be glad to take up a commodity of them, at any laughter, or loss, in another place. (Induction, 141–44)

In his edition of the play, G. R. Hibbard gives a brief explanation of the practice of "taking up on commodities," and glosses the passage with the following: "Jonson is saying, in effect, that the spectator who is not willing to pay with laughter for the excellent play he is being offered will be forced into buying very inferior wares elsewhere and will expose himself to derision as a consequence."[32] For Jonson to figure his drama as merely another commodity in a mercantile world only too fittingly anticipates the frenzy of acquisition and theft characterizing the world of Bartholomew Fair. As Bartholomew Cokes puts it at one point: "but I do want such a number o' things" (3.4.80–81).

Fetishistic desire propels the play from its beginning. To gain permission to visit the pagan world of the fair, Littlewit urges Win, his wife, to feign morning-sickness and to "long to eat of a pig ... i' the Fair" (1.5.137–38). Arriving at the Fair, Littlewit desires his wife to continue her wishes:

we shall never see any sights i' the Fair, Win, except you long still, Win, good Win, sweet Win, long to see some hobby-horses, and some drums, and rattles, and dogs, and fine devices, Win. The bull with the five legs, Win; and the great hog: now you ha' begun with pig, you may long for anything, Win. (3.6.4–8)

The play illustrates this uncanny habit of dislocating desire when Littlewit greets Win by ridiculously fetishizing her apparel:

Now you look finely indeed, Win! This cap does convince! You'd not ha' worn it, Win, nor ha' had it velvet, but a rough country beaver, with a copper-band, like the coney-skin woman of Budge Row? Sweet Win, let me kiss it! And her fine high shoes, like the Spanish lady! Good Win, go a little, I would fain see thee pace, pretty Win! By this fine cap, I could never leave kissing on't. (1.1.17–23)

Nothing stands desirable in and for itself: only in its displacement, or mimetic presentation, when it is in fact desired by others. Win's velvet hat, an item of apparel marking her as a citizen's wife, excites her husband sexually: like Nick Stuff, the tailor of Jonson's *The New Inn* (1629), Littlewit becomes aroused primarily by luxurious clothing. The sexual problematics of objects like this hat pervade *Bartholomew Fair*, as when, for example, Joan Trash, the gingerbread seller, quibbles "I hope my ware lies as open as another's; I may show my ware as well as you yours" (3.4.90–92) and Cokes asks, rhetorically, "Cannot a man's purse be at quiet for you, i' the master's pocket, but you must entice it forth, and debauch it?" (3.5.199–200).

Cokes, like Littlewit, seems to plead for the theft of his own property. In the cony-catching scene which precedes the above outburst, he boasts again and again about the care he takes with his purse, holding it up for display – wishing, it appears, for someone to steal it. "I am an ass, I cannot keep my purse" (3.5.137), he says, and Wasp advises him "Come, do not make a stir, and cry yourself an ass through the Fair afore your time" (3.5.167–68). The bestial side of the cuckold myth surfaces in their speeches, and Quarlous, echoing this sentiment, suggests that Coke is a willing cuckold: "Of all beasts, I love the serious ass. He that takes pains to be one, and plays the fool, with the greatest diligence that can be" (3.5.246–48). Littlewit's wittolry is not nearly so figurative. One first learns of his secret desires when Quarlous hints at a promise sealed during a drinking bout with "Proctor John" Littlewit the past night:

We were all a little stained last night, sprinkled with a cup or two, and I agreed with Proctor John here to come and do somewhat with Win (I know not what 'twas) today; and he puts me in mind on't now; he says he was coming to fetch me ... (1.3.25–28)

Proctor John is a wittol. Because Quarlous is a suitor to Win's wealthy mother, Dame Purecraft, Littlewit looks the other way when Quarlous begins kissing his wife. Though Win protests – "Look you! Help me, John" – Littlewit approves of the action, responding to Quarlous's suggestion that he and Win "kiss again and fall in" with an imprecation to his wife: "Yes, do, good Win" (1.3.33–44). Once in the Fair, Littlewit leaves his impressionable wife with two "honest gentlemen," Knockem and Whit, both of whom are panders. The impulse to ingratiate himself with Dame Purecraft's future husband leads Littlewit to use his wife as symbolic capital – capital to invest. Littlewit fails to realize, however, that the market has an energy and aims of its own. As it does with all desires, the world of the Fair pushes this one to its logical conclusion: the two "honest gentlemen" recruit Win as a prostitute.

Bartholomew Fair misogynistically ironizes Dame Purecraft's "purity" and suggests that the threat of adulteration is as real as that of adultery. The issue of mangonism is defined first in *Bartholomew Fair*, as it is defined in *The Dutch Courtesan*, through puritanical, Old Testament insistence on ritual purity. As Dame Purecraft urges Win, pushing her to reveal the demon who has tempted her: "what polluted one was it, that named first the unclean beast, pig, to you, child?" (1.6.7–8). Littlewit plays on this obsession with cleanliness in a remark concerning Zeal-of-the-Land Busy's preoccupation: Busy will join the rest of the characters on stage, Littlewit says, "as soon as he has cleansed his beard. I found him, fast by the teeth, i' the cold turkey-pie, i' the cupboard" (1.6.30–31). Then, when Busy enters: "Here he is now, purified, Mother" (1.6.35). The irony here – Busy the glutton/Busy the railer against appetite – is the selfsame irony surrounding Malheureux in *The Dutch Courtesan* and Puritans in the drama generally. Thus when Busy cites moral codes prohibiting the eating of the unclean beast, pig – "in the Fair, and as a Bartholomew pig, it cannot be eaten, for the very calling it a Bartholomew pig, and to eat it so, is a spice of idolatry" – it is not surprising to see him changing his mind – "we may be religious in midst of the profane, so it be eaten with a reformed mouth, with sobriety, and humbleness" (1.6.47–49; 64–66). Like Dame Purecraft, Malheureux, Malvolio, and other aggressive moralists in the plays of the period, Busy is a hypocrite.

Adam Overdo, the disguised justice who surveys the underworld of the Fair from the inside, takes up Busy's puritanical obsession in a series of speeches in act two, scene six. He warns his fellow company to beware "the fruits of bottle-ale and tobacco!" (2.6.1) with the following rationale:

Thirst not after that frothy liquor, ale: for who knows when he openeth the stopple what may be in the bottle? Hath not a snail, a spider, yea, a neuft [i.e. newt] been found there? Thirst not after it, youth: thirst not after it (9–12)

Neither do thou lust after that tawny weed, tobacco (19)

who can tell if before the gathering and making up thereof, the alligator hath not pissed thereon? (23–24)

The creeping venom of which subtle serpent, as some late writers affirm; neither the cutting of the perilous plant, nor the drying of it, nor the lighting, or burning, can any way persway, or assuage (32–35)

Overdo's "some late writers" encompasses most notably, of course, King James himself and the monarch's own *A Counterblast to Tobacco*, published in 1604. A fierce piece of invective against the novel but extremely popular practice of smoking (or "drinking," as it was often put) tobacco, James' *Counterblast* characterizes the weed with satirical adjectives like "vile," "stinking," "unsavory," "filthy," "infecting," "oily," and "corrupted."[33] James argues that the pollution of the body with tobacco leads, correspondingly, to the corruption of the body politic: "surely in my opinion, there cannot be a more base, and yet hurtful, corruption in a Country, than is the vile use (or rather abuse) of taking *Tobacco* in this Kingdom."[34] Comparing its corrosive powers to those of syphilis (for which tobacco smoking was held a cure), James explains that tobacco corrupts on the domestic level as well: "moreover, which is a great iniquity, and against all humanity, the husband shall not be ashamed, to reduce thereby his delicate, wholesome, and clean complexioned wife, to that extremity, that either she must also corrupt her sweet breath therewith, or else resolve to live in a perpetual stinking torment."[35]

If our text of *Bartholomew Fair* faithfully represents the version performed before James on the first of November, 1614 – and it is by no means clear if it did – one can wonder how Overdo's rhetorical extravagances sat with the monarch, or whether James *would* have seen them as extravagances. Like the King, Overdo alludes to the contemporary belief that smoking darkened the interior of the body cavity (2.6.37–40), and, like James, he compares tobacco's corrosive effects with those of syphilis:

Nay, the hole in the nose here, of some tobacco-takers, or the third nostril (if I may so call it) which makes, that they can vent the tobacco out, like the ace of clubs, or rather the flower-de-lys, is caused from the tobacco, the mere tobacco! When the poor innocent pox, having nothing to do there, is miserably, and most unconscionably slandered. (2.6.43–48)

Certainly Overdo's speeches contain a strong vein of parody – and in this, danger to the habitually reckless Jonson if performed before James – but the play itself prevents such diatribes from becoming burlesques. Like *The Dutch Courtesan*, *Bartholomew Fair* sets out in a quintessentially "Jacobean" manner to demonstrate that reason exists for this kind of satirical lament. One sees in the two farces an increasing concern with, on the one hand, the nature of identity and, on the other, with the manner in which objects and commodities can create as well as corrupt that identity.

At one point in the drama Leatherhead, a "hobby-horse-seller," and Joan Trash, a dealer in gingerbread, compete for the most favorable location in the Fair. Leatherhead warns Joan Trash to "Sit farther with your gingerbread-progeny there, and hinder not the prospect of my shop, or I'll ha' it proclaimed i' the Fair what stuff they are made on" (2.2.3–5). When Joan argues that her ware is "Nothing but what's wholesome," Leatherhead replies: "Yes, stale bread, rotten eggs, musty ginger, and dead honey" (2.2.7–8). Both of Joan's names signify baseness: Middleton, as indicated above, was to use "Joanna" as the corrupted opposite of the holy "Beatrice," Joan an Elizabethan commonplace for "peasant girl;"[36] "Trash" described the ingredients of her gingerbread – ware called "progeny" and fashioned into human shape.

Ursla, "pig woman" and general bawd of the Fair, also adulterates her vendibles. Calling her "the agent of the transformation of others," Peter Stallybrass and Allon White point out that, "Around her tent, food, drink, sex, urine and even property in the form of Edgeworth's stolen goods, constantly circulate."[37] During this circulation, however, these material goods themselves are transformed. "Threepence a pipeful," Ursla brags, "I will ha' made, of all my whole half pound of tobacco, and a quarter of a pound of coltsfoot, mixed with it too, to itch it out" (2.2.81–83). From there she (re)instructs her tapsters "how to raise" the ale:

Froth your cans well i' the filling, at length, rogue, and jog your bottles o' the buttock, sirrah, then skink out the first glass, ever, and drink with all companies, though you be sure to be drunk; you'll misreckon the better, and be less ashamed on't. But your true trick, rascal, must be, to be ever busy, and mis-take away the bottles and cans, in haste before they be half drunk off, and never hear anybody call (if they should chance to mark you) till you ha' brought fresh, and be able to forswear 'em. (2.2.86–94)

Thus Knockem, like Overdo, voices a legitimate fear when he asks, shortly hereafter, "Thou'lt poison me with a newt in a bottle of ale, wilt thou? Or a spider in a tobacco pipe, Urs?" (2.3.18–19). Ursla outdoes her prototype, Elinour Rumming, by adulterating her ale *and* her tobacco.

That (male) identity and (female) adultery in *Bartholomew Fair* is represented metaphorically – via commodity adulteration – can be seen in its connection with tobacco and syphilis, in the polluted "progeny" of Joan Trash's gingerbread children, and particularly in the way the play links Ursla, the chief adulteress, with Original Sin. "I shall e'en melt away to the first woman, a rib again," she suggests (2.2.47–48), and Knockem feels that out of her another Bartholomew Fair – a Fair frequently described as a microcosm, a world in miniature (cf. 2.3.2–3; 3.6.30–33; 4.3.110) – might be created: "Art thou alive yet? With thy litter of pigs to grunt out another Bartholomew Fair, ha?" (2.3.1–3). When Overdo overhears Ursla's tutorial in mangonism he exclaims "this is the very womb and bed of enormity! Gross as herself!" (2.2.95–96). His use of "womb" is telling, for commercial transaction in the Fair metaphorically figures sexual transaction in the World. The fear of woman's innate corruption, something suspected by Overdo and Knockem, is emblematized in the gingerbread progeny, the ale, and tobacco sold in the Fair. This kind of adultery, as well as that feared in the cuckold's anxieties, posed an almost insurmountable difficulty in the construction of male identity: if man is dependent on woman in the same way that the spiritual depends on the corporeal, the subjective upon the objective, how can an autonomous integrity exist?

While references to tobacco saturate Jonson's *oeuvre*, Shakespeare, in all his works, never mentions the weed.[38] Several possible explanations for this disparity exist, among them the respective country/city origins of the playwrights (the taking of tobacco at this time seeming to be a predominantly urban phenomenon), and the fact that Shakespeare, nearly a decade older than his fellow dramatist, came from and looked to a different formative age – one characteristically emphasizing the abstract over the quotidian. Othello's "magic in the web" speech might appear in this light almost as a self-parody of Shakespeare's habit of romantically mystifying the ordinary. With the Jacobean drama, however, would come a greater degree of concreteness and specificity in metaphorical language and narrative symbolism. Adriana, for example, delivers her complaint in the quintessentially Tudor *The Comedy of Errors* in a straightforward equation:

> I am possess'd with an adulterate blot;
> My blood is mingled with the crime of lust:
> For if we two be one, and thou play false,

I do digest the poison of thy flesh,
Being strumpeted by thy contagion.

(2.2.140–44)

Here reciprocity forms the center of her argument: marriage partners are
equally responsible for and affected by the consequences of infidelity.
Correspondingly, the confusion over rings and chains in the play arises
from their location, not their composition: "where have you left the
money I gave you?" The drama of later Elizabethan and early Stuart
England, in contrast, emphasizes the interiority of the object: "nothing
but what's wholesome." Visible in a move from spiritual to satiric, from
abstract to particular, this shift bore signal – if counterintuitive – implications for the social practice of valuation: with worth and identity
assigned from without by subjects beginning to struggle with the complications of interiority and urban alienation, value itself began what can
only be described as a paradoxical movement away from the inherent
toward the ascribed, from Hector's "value dwells not in particular will" to
Troilus's "what's aught as 'tis valued?" As London placed increasing
emphasis on the objective's essence, ascription of value likewise became,
theatrically, the internalized property of the early modern subject.

And while it lies beyond the scope of this chapter to prove that the
drama of this period captured the extent or actuality of the social transformation evidenced more objectively in "historical" (i.e. extra-literary)
sources, it is clear that the playhouses clearly took their energy and their
direction from a city in the midst of sweeping economic changes. Using an
image uncannily descriptive of such alteration, Feste contrasts his youth
with his later life: "When that I was and a little tine boy ... A foolish thing
was but a toy" / "when I came to man's estate ... 'Gainst knaves and
thieves men shut their gate." Although it is extremely doubtful that the
Clown refers here to anything like English society's accommodation to
the market, his musical epigraph to *Twelfth Night* (1601) might nonetheless be seen as offering an abbreviated delineation of the effects of rapid
economic and cultural change on Shakespeare's London. Characterized
by a growing seriousness over ownership and commodity, the materialist
vision transformed the way dramatists of the English Renaissance con-
figured the connections between purse and person. The questions *Jack
Juggler* posed about the relationship between individual and object in a
religious context shortly after midcentury were rephrased, around 1600,
with pressing commercial implications. One could describe the plays of
1590–1620, in fact, as secularly recusant, in that, following the bulls of the
market, they reinscribed identity into a worldly commodity.

7 "The alteration of men": *Troilus and Cressida*, Troynovant, and trade

I have an excellent thought: if some fifty of the Grecians that were crammed in the horse belly had eaten garlic, do you not think the Trojans might have smelt out their knavery?

Sly, in Webster's Induction to *The Malcontent* (1604)

We are so asotted with these delights, so blinded with the love, and drunken with the sweetness of these vanities, that greedily we flock together, and with our brainsick assemblies not unlike to the Troyans hale in the horse, whose bowels have been many times gaged with the sword of his truth ...

Stephen Gosson on London's playhouses, in *Plays Confuted* (1582)

When, in *Twelfth Night* (1601), one coin already well in hand, Feste begs another of Viola, he applies a commercial gloss to the Troilus and Cressida legend:

> FESTE. Would not a pair of these have bred, sir?
> VIOLA. Yes, being kept together, and put to use.
> FESTE. I would play Lord Pandarus of Phrygia, sir, to bring a Cressida to this Troilus.
> VIOLA. I understand you, sir. 'Tis well begg'd.
> FESTE. The matter, I hope, is not great, sir – begging but a beggar: Cressida was a beggar.
>
> (3.1.49–55)

In personifying the two coins – the one as Troilus, the other Cressida – and endowing them with desires and traits of their own, Feste participates in what I have described in the preceding pages as the tendency of Elizabethan and Jacobean drama to objectify the personal. Significantly, the project he hints at here would be carried out extensively in a play written during the same period: Shakespeare's own *Troilus and Cressida* (1602).[1] In one of this play's more engaging scenes, Diomedes and Cressida enter the camp of the Greek leaders only to see Cressida "kiss'd in general" (4.5.21), passed about in a potentially disturbing sexual tableau. Agamemnon, Nestor, Achilles, Patroclus, and Menelaus all step forward to kiss her. By the time the fifth Greek has done so, Cressida –

97

whom we have just heard, in the preceding scene, ask Troilus if he will remain faithful to her (4.4.99) – appears to realize the nature of her predicament, and flirtatiously moves to assert control over her own value and use:

> I'll make my match to live,
> The kiss you take is better than you give:
> Therefore no kiss ...
> You are an odd man: give even or give none.

(4.5.37–41)

When she exits shortly after this, Nestor calls her "A woman of quick sense" (4.5.54), a description which might be paraphrased as "quick witted" (with a glance, perhaps, at something like "sensuous passion"). The reference to her quick wit undoubtedly refers to her skill at repartee in the exchange with the Greeks ("You are an odd man: give even or give none"), but it also explains, in a way that does not seem intended, Cressida's quick-witted realization of her circumstances, and her decision to make the best of them. Realizing that she is seen as a commodity, Cressida decides to take control of her commodity function.

In the previous scene, as part of their assurance to one another of their eternal fidelity, Cressida and Troilus had exchanged love tokens: she gave him a glove, and he, in return, entrusted her with a sleeve (4.4.60–70). It is this sleeve that Troilus, in the voyeuristic, multi-levelled observation scene around Diomedes' tent (5.2), sees Cressida give to Diomedes. All the characters in this scene seem to recognize the sexual implications of the gift: Diomedes pledges to wear it as a taunt to Troilus, and Troilus swears to "lose my arm, or win my sleeve" (5.3.96). When Thersites comes forward to describe the ensuing battle between the two warriors, he notes that: "That dissembling abominable varlet Diomed has got that same scurvy, doting, foolish knave's sleeve of Troy there in his helm. I would fain see them meet, that that same young Trojan ass, that loves the whore there, might send that Greekish whoremasterly villain with the sleeve back to the dissembling luxurious drab of a sleeveless errand" (5.4.2–9). His final phrase plays on "sleeveless errand" as meaning a fruitless trip or journey, as well as on the image of Cressida as "sleeveless," as lacking the symbol of sexual fidelity and union (an arm in a sleeve, a hand in a glove) which Troilus had given her. "Soft: here comes sleeve, and t'other," Thersites continues (18), now objectifying Diomedes as the "sleeve." When they begin their fight, Thersites encourages them with "Hold thy whore, Grecian! Now for thy whore, Trojan! Now the sleeve, now the sleeve!" By this point in the drama, Cressida has become the sleeve – or rather, the sleeve has become Cressida. Among the many epistemological conjunctions it works to straddle, then, Troilus' famous "This is, and is not, Cressid" (5.2.145) – coming in the context of her gift of the sleeve to Diomedes – might be seen as an attempt, by Troilus, to come to grips with the fluidity of commodity and the problems of controlling objects. The drama continually concerns itself with problems of the material, with exchange and its effects on actions, language, and thought. With its likely date of 1602 *Troilus and Cressida* can be said to straddle the division between what are usually seen as distinct periods in the history of English Renaissance drama: the Elizabethan period, up to the development of humours comedy and the satiric strain in the late 1590s, and the (extended) Jacobean period, encompassing the rise of satiric drama and the rebirth of revenge tragedy from the late 1590s on.

It was no accident that Shakespeare chose the Troy myth for his satirical "comedy." During the English Renaissance, London looked on Troy as its progenitor and its double, a historical center of nobility, luxury, and desire. Tudor historians, eager to champion the integrity of the ruling family's lineage, readily embraced Geoffrey of Monmouth's claim that Britain had been founded by Brutus, the grandson of Aeneas. As Robert Kimbrough points out, the years around the turn of the century witnessed a remarkable outpouring of literary works based on the events of the Trojan War.[2] In the period from 1596 to 1602, for instance, new editions were published of the medieval versions of the Troy story by Caxton, Chaucer, and Henryson; these joined new works by Chapman, Chettle and Dekker, and others in what may be described as a rising fin-de-siècle interest in the fall of Troynovant's eponymic city. Underscoring this interest was a considerable anxiety over the logical implications of the Troy/London parallel: if Troy fell, so must London. In *Troilus and Cressida* Shakespeare incorporates this anxiety in a portrayal of the Trojan War which draws its energy from the growing restlessness and uncertainty of the late Elizabethan era. Like other turn-of-the-century versions of the Troy myth, Shakespeare's play attempts to attribute blame for what appeared to be the imminent decline of London. London's penchant for stressing the role of appetite in the Troy story (evident in the Sly epigraph above) is most clearly revealed in *Troilus and Cressida* in the role played by commercial and domestic metaphors. Like *A Larum for London* (1599) – a play portraying the fall of Antwerp at the hands of the Spanish and, significantly, printed in 1602 – *Troilus and Cressida* echoes traditional reservations over mercantile exchange and merchant adventurism, locating the source of the city's ills in the uncontrolled dynamism of the market.

Viola's pun on "use" as usury underscores the basis of Feste's analogy: for him the myth of Troy survives only to draw coins from strangers.[3] Following Chaucer in representing Cressida as a beggar, Feste compares himself to the original broker, Pandarus, who dealt in a human commodity. That Pandarus' name had come to be a generic label for merchants of flesh in Elizabethan England points up the fact that, for many of Shakespeare's contemporaries, Troy symbolized the City of Commerce.[4] While Homer, for example, pictures an epic Odysseus, counselor and warrior, George Peele describes him "with his toys and trifles trim, / in pedlar's base array,"[5] ironically prefiguring Shakespeare's Autolycus – maternal grandfather of Ulysses – in *The Winter's Tale* (1610). Similarly Troy lived on for the Elizabethans in popular, domestic nicknames. "Merrygreek," as *Troilus and Cressida* seems to argue (1.2.110; 4.4.55), could refer to a person of loose behavior, perhaps a prostitute; "greek" in itself frequently described a wily person, particularly a card sharp. T. J. B. Spencer argues that the "during Shakespeare's lifetime, *Greek* was a household word for a voluptuary or a crook."[6] And while "true trojan" might mean honest character, alone, or with a modifier – as in Pistol's "base trojan" – "trojan" often meant something like "dissolute roisterer."[7] Steevens, for one, thought that Gadshill's "tut, there are other Trojans that thou dreamst not of" in 1597's *1 Henry IV* (2.1.66) was "perhaps only a more creditable term for a thief."[8] Individual names carried equal significance. Harington's *The Metamorphosis of Ajax* (1596) revolves around the popular pun of "Ajax" and "a jakes" – that is, a toilet. Nashe also reminds us of the pun's currency when in one place he reviles "the most contemptible Mounsier Ajaxes of excremental conceipts and stinking kennel-rakt up invention."[9] In two works at around 1600 one finds a pun on Cressida as "cresset light," or torch: in (?) John Marston's *Histriomastix* (1599) "Come Cressida, my Cresset light;" and in Samuel Rowlands' *The Letting of Humor's Blood* (1600) "Be thou the lady Cressit-light to me / Sir Trollelolle I will prove to thee." [10]

"Troy weight," of course, measured gold and other precious metals, as well as jewels and bread. In *The Old Law*, a collaborative play probably dating from around 1618, Gnotho the clown – a character much like Feste – connects this unit of weight with Cressida.[11] His fooling repartee with the Cook, the Tailor, and the Bailiff also includes Helen and Paris:

> COOK. That Nell was Helen of Greece too.
> GNOTHO. As long as she tarried with her husband, she was Ellen; but after she came to Troy, she was Nell of Troy, or Bonny Nell, whether you will or no.
> TAILOR. Why, did she grow shorter when she came to Troy?
> GNOTHO. She grew longer, if you mark the story. When she grew to be an ell, she was deeper than any yard of Troy could reach by a quarter; there was Cressid was Troy weight, and Nell was avoirdupois; she held more, by four ounces, than Cressida.
> BAILIFF. They say she caused many wounds to be given in Troy.

GNOTHO. True, she was wounded there herself, and cured again by
plaster of Paris, and ever since has been used to stop holes with.

Gnotho's bawdy etymologies for Troy weight and plaster of Paris, along
with the Helen/ell pun – ell being a unit of measure – continue the
domestic reduction of the Iliadic tradition. A similar Troy parody comes
from the Clown in Heywood's *Love's Mistress* (1634), a court masque:

But hear me, oh you miss of misunderstanding: this Troy was a village of some
twenty houses; and Priam, as silly a fellow as I am, only loving to play the good
fellow, he had a great many bowsing lads, whom he called sons. . . . By this Troy
ran a small brook, that one might stride over; on the other side dwelt Menelaus,
a farmer, who had a light wench to his wife called Helen, that kept his sheep,
whom Paris, one of Priam's mad lads seeing and liking, 'ticeth over the brook,
and lies with her despite of her husband's teeth; for which wrong, he sends for
one Agamemnon his brother, that was then High Constable of the hundred, and
complains to him; he sends to one Ulysses, a fair spoken fellow, and Town-Clerk
and to divers others, amongst whom was one stout fellow call'd Ajax, a butcher,
who upon a holy day, brings a pair of cudgels, and lays them down in the midst,
where the Two Hundreds were then met, which Hector, a baker, another bold
lad of the other side, seeing, steps forth and takes them up: these two had a bout
or two for a broken pate; and here was all the circumstance of the Trojan
Wars.[12]

Classical legends often became the targets of parody in Renaissance
drama. But for Heywood's clown, as well as for Shakespeare's Feste and
The Old Law's Gnotho, the myth of Troy appears to have served a special
purpose: the urban and commercial replace the heroic; burlesqued, the
mythic is reformed into readier, mercantile shapes. Shakespeare's *Troilus
and Cressida* continually wavers between these opposites: while at times
heroic diction and display dominate, the drama also unfolds on the level
of Feste's jest, indeed enlarging his revision.

Thus, in addition to the works of Homer, Caxton, and Chaucer, the
literature of the City – the pamphlets of the nineties and early 1600s – and
the materialist vision of Shakespeare and his contemporaries infuse the
drama's language and action. And while several recent studies have taken
up the role of desire and valuation in the drama, few have addressed the
relation of *Troilus and Cressida* to the social life of Renaissance London.[13] (A notable exception, Eric Mallin's *The End of Troy: Elizabethan
Dissolution in Shakespeare's "Troilus and Cressida"*, suggests that – in
relation to the future of criticism concerning the play – the tide may be
turning.[14]) Twentieth-century productions of the play (significantly it is
only in this century, and, as Jeanne Newlin points out, mainly after the
horrors of the First World War, that revivals of Shakespeare's original
play have taken place[15]) often use properties and costumes evocative of an

idle aristocracy. Critics and directors alike have overspecified the play's aristocratic reference.

Yet even while recognizing the dangers of such a narrow focus, one should not separate the court and monarch from commerce and the domestic; *Troilus and Cressida* insists on their linkage, portraying the Trojan War, in part, as an amplified struggle between merchant powers. In the following remarks, I explore the play's social reference, demonstrating how Shakespeare employed contemporary interest in London's Trojan heritage as the basis of an allegorical satire of the City's growing commercialism and channeled the energies of the materialist vision into a Trojan history of the present.

The language of commerce

Troilus and Cressida repeatedly refers to merchants and to trade, large-scale and small, and its characters often use the language of commerce. The heroic diction of the prologue and the coarse language of commodity in the epilogue set up two poles of dramatic language in the drama: even as Latinity, parallelism, illeisms, and formal rhetoric appear in the play, so does the slang of the streets, satirical abuse, and mercantile talk – something several critcs have noticed. T. J. Stafford has discussed the mercantile images and commercial figures in the drama: terms like "price," "worth," "value," and "estimation" come, in his words, not "from the exterior of the play," but "from its thematic center."[16] Douglas Wilson points out that in *Troilus and Cressida* "Shakespeare couches his philosophic theme of value in imagery of merchandising."[17] Sandra Fischer places *Troilus and Cressida* with *Othello* and *King Lear* in a group of three plays "using economics as a secondary or supporting matrix addressing the role of money in society and the proper 'valuing' of human relations."[18] And seeing "transaction" at "the very core of the problem of human relationships that concerns Shakespeare in *Troilus and Cressida*," C. C. Barfoot suggests that "this concern is signified by the prevalence of the mercantile metaphor that runs through the play."[19] Of course the language of Shakespeare's plays typically operates on many registers, as characters often use diction and images coextensive with their social station. Almost inevitably, commercial references spring up in the language of particular characters in each play. Thus although it comes as no surprise, for example, to hear Pandarus talking like a seedy businessman – by Shakespeare's time, as I mentioned above, his name had become a professional epithet, the etymology of which one actually hears constructed (3.2.195–202) – it seems strange to discover most of the other characters following his lead, the parlance of the market forming a readily recognizable dialect in *Troilus and Cressida*.

Early in the play Troilus speaks of Cressida, and with a striking image declares that

> Her bed is India; there she lies, a pearl.
> Between our Ilium and where she resides,
> Let it be call'd the wild and wand'ring flood,
> Ourself the merchant, and this sailing Pandar
> Our doubtful hope, our convoy and our bark.
>
>   (1.1.100–104)

Here Petrarchan imagery predicts an analogy repeated in the drama.[20] Troilus labels himself a merchant, Cressida the goal and reward of trade. This move reflects something occurring in the play generally: love and war become commercial endeavors, and relations – social, political, and personal – take place on the material plane. By "Petrarchan," of course, I mean the efforts of the school of Petrarch rather than the poet's own literary production. Significantly, only once during the repeated nautical images in the *Rime sparse* does Petrarch refer to Laura as a treasure ship:

> *Indi per alto mar vidi una nave*
> *con le sarte di seta et d'or la vela,*
> *tutta d'avorio e d'ebeno contesta;*
>   *e'l mar tranquillo et l'aura era soave*
> *e'l ciel qual è se nulla nube il vela,*
> *ella carca di ricca merce onesta.*

Then on the deep sea I saw a ship with ropes of silk and sails of gold, all fashioned of ivory and ebony; and the sea was calm and breeze gentle and the sky such as when no cloud veils it, and the ship was laden with rich, virtuous wares.[21]

Petrarch carefully stresses that while her *merce* – cargo – is *ricca*, "rich," no less is it *onesta*, "virtuous." Richness here intensifies virtue. Most often Petrarch's venturing bark represents the hopeful container of his heart, love, or soul.

Taking up this figure, many English sonneteers neglected the *onesta* while employing the *ricca* as sole modifier, conflating amatory and mercantile valuation without moral reference. The conceit was common. The opening of the first sonnet in Drayton's *Idea* – "Like an adventurous Sea-farer am I, / Who hath some long and dang'rous Voyage been / And call'd to tell of his Discovery" – is directly comparable to Donne's celebration of his love as America, his "new found land."[22] Spenser likewise praises his love "when her breast like a rich laden bark, / With precious merchandise she forth doth lay."[23] But joining their enthusiasm for their mistresses with the national fascination over treasure returning from abroad, the sonneteers strayed far from the spiritual basis of Petrarch's own poetry.

Romeo, Shakespeare's young lover of the nineties, anticipates Troilus' conceit when he declares: "I am no pilot; yet, wert thou as far / As that vast shore washed with the farthest sea, / I should adventure for such merchandise" (2.2.82–84). Here Juliet joins, if only metaphorically, Kate, Portia, and Anne Page, women whose lovers confess to initial motivations of a mercenary kind: Petruchio, Bassanio, and Fenton all admit that profit first prompted their wooing.[24] Troilus, forced to part from his mistress, describes their courtship in commercial terms:

> We two, that with so many thousand sighs
> Did buy each other, must poorly sell ourselves
> With the rude brevity and discharge of one.

(4.4.38–40)

"Discharge" here refers both to the breathing out of the last sigh and to the "discharging" of a debt or obligation. Rephrasing his early image of Cressida, Troilus once more returns to the metaphor of the pearl in praising Helen: "Why, she is a pearl / Whose price hath launch'd above a thousand ships, / And turn'd crown'd kings to merchants" (2.2.82–84). This passage, remarkably compact in allusion and import, requires some comment. The pearl image, from "price," recalls and parodies Matthew 13:46 – "Again, the kingdom of heaven is like to a merchant man, that seeketh good pearls, / Who, having found a pearl of great price, went and sold all that he had, and bought it." Storing up their treasures on earth, the Greeks and Trojans pursue an empty goal. Christ is sometimes shown, in Matthew, using economic metaphors to support his spiritual message; Shakespeare imitates the practice, but frequently gives us characters like Shylock who read the letter of the image but not the spirit, "bond" symbolizing to the moneylender the material rather than the spiritual. Many characters in *Troilus and Cressida* likewise read too literally, a kind of anti-spirituality surfacing in their idolatry of the material.[25] "Price" in Troilus' passage (line 83) also echoes Faustus' "Is this the face that launched a thousand ships?" Troilus, however, substitutes "price" for "face:" ascribed worth replaces essential value, a shift, again, mirrored in the action of the play generally. And Troilus sees the Grecian forces, even as he saw himself, as members of a merchant convoy.

The last line of Troilus' passage – "And turn'd crown'd kings to merchants" – recalls the Bastard's humour in *King John* (1591): commodity. Calling commodity "the bias of the world" (2.1.574), Philip Faulconbridge, in a soliloquy resembling Ulysses' oration on degree, describes a world unsettled by commodity; he sees

The world, who of itself is peized well,
Made to run even upon even ground,
Till this advantage, this vile-drawing bias,
This sway of motion, this commodity,
Makes it take head from all indifferency,
From all direction, purpose, course, intent ...

                                                            (2.1.575–580)

The word "commodity" is a kind of "keyword" for the Renaissance, with a shifting constellation of meanings speaking to a society changing along, and through, the axes which it could represent. It functioned, as we have seen, as a bawdy quibble for the pudendum, and in the Bastard's description of "this vile-drawing bias" one sees a prefigurement of the role which women play in *Troilus and Cressida*.

The Bastard concludes his speech with a cynical apostrophe: "Since kings break faith upon commodity, / Gain, be my lord, for I will worship thee!" (597–98). Even as Ulysses rigs the warriors' lottery after delivering a sermon on rightful order, Philip contradicts his moral and political criticism through a cynical pragmatism. Both men, lifted above the other characters by intelligence, share a strong affinity with the figure of the Morality Vice. Not coincidentally are several of Plautus' tricky slaves compared to Ulysses: Shakespeare's wily Greek orator and the Bastard trace their dramatic lineage to just such comedic characters.[26] Richard's famous soliloquy in *3 Henry VI* (1591), of course, draws the many faces of the Vice together into an Iliadic mask: "I'll play the orator as well as Nestor, / Deceive more slily than Ulysses could, / And like a Sinon, take another Troy" (3.2.188–90). The myth of Troy provides Richard with the disguises he needs to complete his black comedy. Like Richard, Philip, Iago, and Edmund, Ulysses uses his intelligence to further his vested interest in the drama's intrigue. Cicero perceptively pointed out that "it was not Ajax, or Achilles, whom Homer called 'City-Sacker,' but Ulysses."[27]

Troilus engages in a significant commercial analogy during his famous forensic speech. Debating Hector over the disposition of Helen he argues: "We turn not back the silks upon the merchant / When we have soil'd them, nor the remainder viands / We do not throw in unrespective sieve / Because we now are full" (2.2.70–73). Helen, as Paris later agrees, is soiled silk, left-over scraps of food. But the laws of the marketplace govern commodity, and so demand her retention. Other characters follow Troilus' metaphorical lead. Paris describes Diomedes' condemnation of Helen as akin to the methods of "chapmen" who "Dispraise the thing that they desire to buy." He includes himself in the analogy: "We'll not commend, that not intend to sell" (4.1.76–79). Ulysses, contriving to have

Ajax – instead of Achilles, their best warrior – meet Hector in combat, proposes that the Greeks: "like merchants / First show foul wares, and think perchance they'll sell: / If not, / The lustre of the better shall exceed / By showing the worse first" (1.3.359–62). The irony of this marketplace stratagem reverberates loudly: the Greeks attempt to convince Achilles he is worth nothing precisely when they need him most. Ulysses' plan paints the Greek generals as petty merchants engaged in a game of buying and selling. Shortly after this speech Ulysses describes his strategem as a "project" (384), revealing at least a nominal kinship with a host of projectors in comedies dealing with urban intrigue. Much in this vein, Thersites describes Ajax as a tavern hostess (3.3.251–253) and Cressida jestingly calls Troilus a "lifter" (1.2.119), calling up the vocabulary of Greene's cony-catching pamphlets and the Elizabethan underworld.

Wolfgang Clemen observed that Shakespeare often "smuggles in the images" in his tragedies, the image "only touched upon and hinted at."[28] The "smuggled" commercial metaphors of *Troilus and Cressida* are often recognizable to us as such only through scholarly apparatus. Pandarus describes the dents in Troilus' helmet – "there's laying on, take't off who will, as they say" (1.2.209) – in terms of a bond transaction, a reference more veiled than his vicarious enjoyment of the lovers' first meeting: "go to, a bargain made: seal it, seal it" (3.2.195). With this contractual imagery, Ulysses hails Troilus' efforts on the field of battle, the young Trojan "engaging and redeeming himself" like a bond (5.5.39). Cressida, calling herself the Greek generals' "debtor" (4.5.51), inquires of them whether, "in kissing, do you render or receive?" (4.5.36). Priam, quoting Nestor, relays it to the Trojans that if they "deliver Helen," "all damage else ... / Shall be struck off" (2.2.3–7), as though the conflict between the nations were one, instead, between Thersites' hostess and a penniless customer.

Pandarus' salacious remark to Troilus after the young prince and Cressida have consummated their affair – "How now, how now, how go maidenheads?" (4.2.23) – recalls Hal's predatory expectation of the booty which war may provide: "if there come a hot June, and this civil buffeting hold, we shall buy maidenheads as they buy hob-nails, by the hundreds" (*1H4*; 2.4.357–59). Value becomes especially relative during war, and in *1 Henry IV*, as in *Troilus and Cressida*, Shakespeare connects military conflict with the commodification of sex. The commercialism of the tavern world, lingering through the Battle of Shrewsbury in punning and direct allusions to coins, garments, and commodities, almost completely disappears with the political negotiations in the play's closing scene. But Shakespeare inverts this pattern in *Troilus and Cressida*: if the heroic, Latinate prologue says nothing of the lovers' plot, Pandarus' epilogue in turn mentions neither the war nor the general political situation. His remarks instead deal with dealing – what it means to procure and pass on merchandise – and in doing so he uses the vocabulary of the marketplace.

The tension between the heroic and the commercial appears frequently in Shakespeare's works: one could argue, even, that his historical vision saw them as the antithetical entities of past and present. Coriolanus, representative of a Roman *virtus* long forgotten, battles with the plebians of the marketplace in a struggle between the martial and the mercenary. Hotspur, catching Lady Percy swearing "like a comfit-maker's wife," rails against the language of the "velvet-guards and Sunday-citizens" (*1H4* 3.1.247–56). Yet Finsbury triumphs over Northumberland, and the heroic grudgingly gives way to the commercial. With the romantic ceding to the cynical, the Troy story begs this diphasic structure. The first Player's Speech in *Hamlet* (1601), for example, shows the Danish prince a world – and, not coincidentally, an Iliadic one – that he, "dull and muddy-mettled rascal," cannot recreate. The lofty language of the past can be recalled only in a play. As the final couplet of *King Lear* suggests, history exists to belittle the present, creating an invidious diptych. The world of Talbot, even in the nineties appearing to elude attainability, with *Troilus and Cressida* – and later *Coriolanus* (1608) – falls before the citizenry and the City's growing commercialism. *Troilus and Cressida* is about this fall.

Troynovant

"All large towns in the plays," Empson suggested, "are conceived as London."[29] While this might seem a sweeping generalization, certainly the portrait of Troy in Shakespeare's play begs comparison with Renaissance London. By 1602, the idea of Troy as London's seminal city – through Aeneas, Rome, and Brutus the founder of Britain – was deeply ingrained in the English consciousness: the Tudors, as mentioned above, sought ratification of their lineage in Geoffrey of Monmouth's *Historia Regum Britanniae*. Lluellen, in Peele's *Edward I* (1591), claims that he is "Descended from the loins of Trojan Brute, / And ... the traitorous Saxons, Normans, Danes, / Have pent the true remains of glorious Troy / Within the western mountains of this Ile" (2.[272–75]).[30] Likewise Thomas Hughes' misfortunate Arthur calls Britain "th' auncient type of Troy" (3.3.50).[31] The comparison of capital cities had long been favorably received. The author of 1501's *In Honour of the City of London*, for example, welcomed the analogy: "Gladdeth anon, thou lusty Troynovant, / City that some time cleped was New Troy; / In all the earth, imperial as thou stant, / Princess of towns ..."[32] Robert Fabyan, in his 1516 *Prologue to a Chronicle*, also saw the comparison as desirable: "This city I mean is

Troynovant, / Where honour and worship doth haunt, / With virtue and riches accordant, / No city to like."[33] Spenser followed this tradition in asserting the nobility of London's Greek lineage without seeming to recognize the inherent danger of such an analogy. Troy provided a magic mirror into which London looked and saw what it wanted to see.

Yet to others the fin-de-siècle pessimism increasing with Elizabeth's age and illness – she was childless and sixty-nine in 1602 – deepened the significance of the Troy/London parallel and prompted a more linear, historical interpretation of the link. Several of Shakespeare's contemporaries admitted to the logical conclusion of the pairing in showing the inevitable fall of the city. George Peele's "The Tale of Troy" (1589), I. O'.s *The Lamentation of Troy for the Death of Hector* (1594), and Thomas Heywood's *The Iron Age* (1612, *1* and *2*) are just a few of such works focusing on Troy's fall. John Speed came out vehemently against this mythological heritage, arguing in 1611 "neither is it any honour to derive these Britains from the scum of such conquered people as the Troians were," and going further

to conclude; (by what destiny I know not) nations desire their originals from the Troians, yet certain it is, that no honour from them can be brought, whose city and fame stood but for six descents ... during which time they were thrice vanquished.

The marginal gloss summarizes his argument: "To have a descent from Troy cannot be an honour to any Nation."[34] Thomas Dekker's macabre pamphlet, *The Wonderful Year*, describing the horrors of the great plague of 1603, sustains the Troy/London link even as it details Elizabeth's death and the ascension of James. From the eerie placement of this political narration, it becomes clear that Dekker's London is re-enacting Troy's final moments.

Dekker's pamphlet damns the Earthly City. The plague, in a "siege of the City," knocks down London's gates; Death marches with impunity "through Cheapside and the capital streets of Troynovant."[35] Commodity, the eighth Deadly Sin in the pamphlet's morality framework, incites the gluttony of Priam and the Trojans as they fiddle while Troy burns:

Whilst Troy was swilling sack and sugar and mousing fat venison the mad-Greeks made bonfires of their houses. Old Priam was drinking a health to the wooden horse and, before it could be pledged, had his throat cut.[36]

With its contempt for worldly goods and its view of the plague as an unpredictable leveler, *The Wonderful Year* exhibits the perverse democracy of the Dance of Death performed in New Troy. Dekker hints at a

more specific reason for Troynovant's fall. In a section on the events
following James' coronation, he cites the false security felt by "citizens"
who subsequently resolve "to worship no saint but money."[37] Tailors,
through an alchemical process, mortgage their shops into ships, and sail
"to the West Indies for no worse stuff to make hose and doublets of than
beaten gold."[38] It was in 1600 that the English East India Company began
issuing stock and setting up trading posts in India and Indonesia, but the
previous decade and a half had seen wealth pour into the country from
trade and privateering in the West Indies. Indeed, this transference of
name from east to west, old to new, only repeated the practice that
London followed in linking itself with Rome and Troy. Dekker's citizens
look as feverishly toward their West Indies as Troilus to Cressida and her
bed of India. Perhaps it is this commercialism Nashe had in mind when
he called London "this great Grandmother of Corporations, Madame
Troynovant."[39]

Dekker's condemnation of merchant adventurism as a socially dangerous enterprise has its correspondence in the classical connection between
Tiphys' sea travel in the *Argo* and the fallen, Iron Age. Things fell apart,
the story held, when sea travel began. Several of the women connected
with Jason understandably complain about Tiphys' daring.[40] In a section
of *The Republic*, Cicero typifies the conservative animus against sea trade
in ascribing the decay of maritime kingdoms to the change which
commercial exchange brings to a state:

> ... their inhabitants do not cling to their dwelling places, but are constantly being
> tempted far from home by soaring hopes and dreams; and even when their bodies
> stay at home, their thoughts nevertheless fare abroad and go wandering. In fact,
> no other influence did more to bring about the final overthrow of Carthage and
> Corinth ... than this scattering and dispersion of their citizens, due to the fact that
> the lust for trafficking and sailing the seas had caused them to abandon agri-
> culture and the pursuit of arms. Many things too that cause ruin to states as being
> incitements to luxury are supplied by the sea, entering either by capture or import;
> and even the mere delightfulness of such a site brings in its train many an
> allurement to pleasure through either extravagance or indolence.[41]

Similarly, Vergil's prophecy to the anonymous child of the fourth Eclogue
mentions Tiphys even as it expects another Trojan War:

> Yet shall some few traces of olden sin lurk behind, to call men to essay the sea in
> ships, to gird the towns with walls, and to cleave the earth with furrows. A second
> Tiphys shall then arise, and a second *Argo* to carry chosen heroes; a second
> warfare, too, shall there be, and again shall a great Achilles be sent to Troy.[42]

In connecting the nautical impulse with the idea of an older, communal
sin (*fraus prisca*), Vergil brings to mind the Athenian notion of *polu-*

pragmosune, which William Arrowsmith defined as "that quality of spectacular restless energy that made the Athenians both the glory and the bane of the Hellenic world."[43] Arrowsmith describes how,

in political terms, *polupragmosune* is the very spirit of Athenian imperialism, its remorseless need to expand, the *hybris* of power and energy in a spirited people; in moral terms, it is a divine discontent and an impatience with necessity, a disease whose symptoms are disorder, corruption, and the hunger for change.

The compression of time and event in Vergil's prophecy – the *Argo*'s voyage indistinct from the Achaean flotilla – underscores the *polupragmosune* of Roman ambition. Liddell and Scott gloss the term – verb, noun, and adjective – with "to be busy about many things," "to be curious after knowledge;" "officiousness, meddlesomeness;" "prying."[44] And while the lexicographers mention that it was an epithet "often given to "the ever restless Athenian," perhaps no term better describes Elizabethans like Drake, Raleigh, and Essex. Appian's history, published in London in 1578 as *An Auncient History and Exquisite Chronicle of the Romans' Wars, both Civil and Foreign*, ominously features on its title page a moral table of its contents, "in the which is declared:" "Their greedy desire to conquer others. / Their mortal malice to destroy themselves. / Their seeking of matters to make war abroad."[45]

The restlessness behind *polupragmosune* and Vergil's "olden sin," luring the men to sea for purposes military and mercantile, also describes the heady spirit of ambition in England in the decade following the Armada. *Troilus and Cressida* is linked with the disappointment following that enthusiasm. Indeed, the war between England and Spain, in 1602 being waged at sea as well as in Ireland and the Low Countries, may well have prompted the sense of disillusionment with war in *Troilus and Cressida*. Sapping the populace, wealth, and vitality of England, this conflict sprang essentially from a struggle between trading rivals. It requires no revisionist ideology to note that privateering incidents increased the tensions leading to war, and that much of England's finances as well as military strategy revolved around the predatory mariners. *Pecunia nervus belli*, after all, for good reason held proverbial currency throughout the Renaissance.

Thomas Heywood's *Troia Britanica, or Great Britaine's Troy* (1609), very clearly connects both Jason and the Trojan War with Elizabethan privateering. "As brave a General Martial'd our great Fleet," he argues,

> As that bold Greek that sought the fleece of Gold,
> Hoping by sea an enemy to meet,
> Fiercer than Jason's, and more warlike bold,
> Renowned Essex, at whose warlike feet

Spain's countless spoils and Trophies have been told,
Who from Hesperia brought to England's Greece,
More Gold than would have weigh'd down Jason's fleece.

$(7.51)^{46}$

"England's Greece:" it is interesting to observe how easily Heywood
transposes national identities, here going in the face of the Trojan analogies in both titles he gives his work. He elaborates on this inversion
shortly thereafter:

So by the English was great Calix surprised
And entered, with the Spaniards that retire,
They that at the first the generals name despisd,
Now at the last are forced his fame t'admire,
English and Dutch in Spanish wealth disguised,
Laden their fleet with pillage, whilst bright fire
    Consumes the Town, which twice the English take,
    As Greece did Troy, great Essex and bold Drake.

(7.87)

Elsewhere Heywood calls on Richard Grenville and the *Revenge* as
modern representations of these classical types.

The 1590s saw a spate of authors make such typological connections
between Greece and England. In Samuel Daniel's *The Civil Wars* (1595),
the ghost of Henry V appears to the author and asks why he seeks to
invent "feigned Paladins" to confer glory on the deeds of men like Talbot
and Willoughby, English warriors who have produced matter "whence
new immortal Iliads might proceed!"[47] In his dedication to the *Seven
Books of the Iliads* (1598), George Chapman refers to Essex as "The Most
Honored now living Instance of the Achillean virtues eternized by divine
Homer" and, more bluntly, addresses him as "Most true Achilles ...
whom by sacred prophecy Homer did but prefigure in his admirable
object."[48] For the Elizabethans to conflate history and myth, past and
present, James Bulman argues, was more the rule than the exception:
"Myth and history merged to make legend, and historical figures acquired
the patina of their bronze-age prototypes. In the Elizabethan imagination, Henry V *was* an Alexander; Talbot *was* a Hector; Essex, at least for
Chapman, *was* an Achilles."[49]

The connections between Chapman's Homer and Shakespeare's
Troilus and Cressida have been examined by many critics.[50] In an essay on
Chapman's *Seven Books of the Iliads* and its relationship to the Earl of
Essex, John Briggs argues persuasively for specific allusions to England's
contemporary political situation throughout Chapman's translation:

From late 1597 and throughout 1598 important trends in Elizabethan foreign
policy and politics were converging toward a crisis catalyzed by Essex. In fact,

history had conspired to make prominent certain analogies between Essex and Achilles; the opening books of the *Iliad* apparently struck Chapman in 1598 as preternatural reflections and foreshadowings of Essex's career.[51]

Chapman's "first translation of Homer," Briggs maintains, "is an attempt to absorb the career of Essex into the epic of Troy."[52]

To many of Essex's mind the war was not only noble, but in fact lucrative, for it produced an enormous amount of wealth through plunder. The capture in 1592 of the *Madre de Dios*, a Portuguese treasure ship, touched a popular vein, with many contemporary accounts enthusiastically detailing the carrack's rich cargo. In 1601 Thomas Wilson observed "it is incredible what treasure hath been brought into England by prize and from the Indies this 12 or 16 years."[53] The English reacted to such treasure with wide-eyed amazement, for wealth of this sort reinforced their convictions about England's providentially-assured place in the international community. Thus it came that financial considerations often preceded and sponsored military planning. To R. B. Wernham "indeed, it looks as if finance, almost by itself, can explain much, not only of the character but also of the course of the offensive war, the war at sea."[54] K. R. Andrews notes that "commerce and warfare were so intimately and variously connected as to make this struggle total, in the sense that every aspect affected every other."[55] Michael Howard echoes Andrews in calling it "a period when war, discovery, and trade were almost interchangeable terms," and relates that "for a time the distinction between warship and merchantman almost disappeared."[56] Like Andrews, Howard also sees the link between trade and war as inextricable:

The capacity to sustain war and so maintain political power in Europe became, during the seventeenth century, increasingly dependent on access to wealth either extracted from the extra-European world or created by the commerce ultimately derived from that wealth. There was in fact a continual interaction between the expansion of European enterprise overseas and the internecine conflicts between the Europeans themselves. Expansion provided further resources for those conflicts and was to a considerable extent generated by them.[57]

Drake, Hawkins, and Frobisher succeeded as the nation's triumphant warriors and as its merchants, attaining both titles simultaneously: nothing divided plunder and patriotism in Renaissance England save post hoc rulings on the legality of prize. Essex, less successful at privateering than some of his contemporaries, knew that the way to the King of Spain was through his purse: "The hurt that our State should seek to do him is to intercept his treasures, whereby we shall cut his sinews and make war on him with his money."[58] The years immediately surrounding the turn of the century were particularly imperialistic, at least with respect to theatrical productions: 1598 witnessed John Day and Henry Chettle's *1 The Conquest of Brute, with the First Finding of the Bath*, and Chettle's continuation, *2 The Conquest of Brute*; in 1601 Henslowe backed Day, Hougton, and Smith's *The Conquest of the West Indies* as well as the unfinished *The Conquest of Spain by John of Gaunt*, by Hathway and Rankins.[59]

As the war continued, London itself came more and more to dominate the business of privateering, and piracy became, increasingly, a joint-stock endeavor centered in that city. "The superior financial resources of the London merchants," Andrews notes, "gave them advantages over most of the outport men."[60] Shakespeare's London formed the nucleus of the nation's maritime predation. In fact, if Shakespeare had failed at the Globe, he might have sought his fortunes at sea: Lording Barry's debut as amateur, illegal, pirate in 1607 offers one view of the avenues open to unsuccessful playwrights and theater owners even as it suggests the proximity of illegal and legal commercial activity. After an aborted attempt with Drayton to manage Whitefriars, Barry helped commandeer a waterman's boat before raiding a Flemish vessel near Tilbury. And although this escapade led most of his accomplices to the gallows, it eventually carried Barry to the status of ship Captain, a brief association with Raleigh, and part-ownership in a trading vessel before his peaceful death in London.[61] Significantly, Barry's sole surviving play is a "city comedy," *Ram Alley* (1608). As is true for the generals of *Troilus and Cressida*, the energy of the marketplace was, in Barry's career, successfully channeled into piracy.

Commerce and society

If commercial struggle leads to political rivalry, it also fundamentally alters personal relations. Troilus himself complains of the prophylactic role played by commerce in his quest for Cressida: "I cannot come to Cressid but by Pandar; / And he's as tetchy to be woo'd to woo / As she is stubborn-chaste against all suit" (1.1.95–97). The lengthening line of dependencies established by commerce and its needs separates Troilus and his love. Pandarus is at once a bridge and a barricade; depending on him necessitates a second wooing, one as difficult as engaging Cressida. The complexities of commercial dealing drain Troilus' patience and faculties.

Trade and war themselves received fair amounts of criticism for draining away the resources of England. One of the surviving state papers from the beginning of Elizabeth's reign, "The Distresses of the Commonwealth, with the Means to Remedy Them," lists seven causes for the present diseases of the nation. War, the author argues, has consumed England's "captains, men, money, victuals, and lost Calais."[62] Ironically, the author of 1621's *A Discourse of Trade, From England unto the East Indies*, through what he means to be straw-man arguments easily overcome by his pro-trade logic, reveals contemporary resistance toward trade in several of his stock objections:

It were a happy thing for Christendom (say many men) that the Navigation to the East-Indies, by way of the Cape of Good Hope, had never been found out; for in the fleets of ships which are sent thither yearly out of *England, Portingall*, and the *Lowcountries*; The gold, silver, and coin of Christendom, and particularly of this kingdom, is exhausted, to buy unnecessary wares.[63]

This repeats a mercantilist version, slightly modified, of the classical lament over Tiphys' nautical hubris: trade weakens because it overextends and, as in *A Discourse of Trade*, exhausts through imbalance of specie. Thus the Iron Age replaces the Bronze. The second objection the author puts into the mouths of his opponents centers on England's resources:

The timber, plank, and other materials, for making of shipping, is exceedingly wasted, and made dearer, by the building of so many great ships, as are yearly sent to Trade in the *East-Indies*; and yet the State hath no use of any of them upon occasion. For either they are not here, or else they come home very weak, and unserviceable.[64]

When Lady Lucre in Robert Wilson's morality, *The Three Ladies of London* (1581), asks Mercator, an Italian merchant, "dare you not to undertake / Secretly to convey good commodities out of this country for my sake?" she delineates the malign disparity of the exchange: "leather, tallow, beef, bacon, bell-metal and everything, / And for these good commodities trifles into England thou must bring; / As bugles to make bable, coloured bones, glass beads to make bracelets withal".[65] The psychological subtext of the anxiety behind Lady Lucre's speech is predicated on transaction. "We're tapers too, and at our own cost die," as Donne rephrases the contemporary superstition concering intercourse's detrimental effect on longevity in "The Canonization." Transaction, whether interpersonal or international, always involves risk. Who gets the best of the trade?

For this reason, desire's effect on social stasis figures importantly in *Troilus and Cressida*. In an essay entitled "The Politics of Desire in *Troilus and Cressida*," René Girard points out the drama's habit of collapsing what might seem separate entities: eroticism and power, lechery and war.[66] The problem of location underlies what is to Girard (as well as to the characters of the play) a central question: "Can the erotic prestige of one woman really be transferred to someone else, or something else?"[67] This query emphasizes the slipperiness of categorical boundaries in the play. The object of male desire, for instance, wavers in *Troilus and Cressida*. Significantly, much of the play's homosocial attraction surfaces both in the urge to combat and in a form of commercial desire. Male and female – like struggle and purchase, and man and material – are conflated. Patroclus, of course, forms homosexuality's *locus classicus* in Western literature; accordingly, this play draws the only outright reference to homosexuality in Shakespeare's plays. Troilus establishes this theme early when he states, three times, that he feels like a woman (1.1.9; 1.1.11; 1.1.106–07). Patroclus warns Achilles that "A woman impudent and mannish grown / Is not more loath'd than an effeminate man / In time of action" (3.3.216–18), yet not twenty lines later Achilles claims "I have a woman's longing, / An appetite that I am sick withal, / To see great Hector in his weeds of peace" (236–38). One might remember that Ovid portrayed Achilles in cross dress, that Aeschylus hinted at the amatory relationship between Achilles and Patroclus, and that Servius, glossing a line in the *Aeneid*, related "that Achilles, drawn to Troilus out of love, placed doves in his way, in which Troilus delighted: when he wished to take them up, caught by Achilles he died in his embrace. But the poet changes this, unworthy, as it were, of a heroic poem."[68]

Classical myth, with its homocentric argument, connected Troy's fall with the fate of certain individuals. Several legends existed positing the *sine qua non* conditions for the fall of Troy. Perhaps the most widely known held that the city would stand while the Palladium – the statue of Pallas Athena – remained in the citadel of Troy. In the *Aeneid*, the Greeks' fulfillment of this requirement contains highly sexual connotations:

Sacrilegious Diomede and Ulysses, always quick to invent new crimes, crept up to wrest Troy's talisman, the image of Minerva, from your hallowed temple, cut down the sentries guarding the upper citadel, seized the holy figure, and actually touched the virgin headband of our goddess with blood still on their hands.[69]

Roman women often wore a *vitta* – translated as "headband" above – as an indicator of virginity or chastity. For Ulysses and Diomedes to touch the chastity emblem of the chastity symbol itself was a flagrant act of sacrilege. Thus Troy falls sexually, the city assaulted physically.[70] The Ulysses of Heywood's *The Iron Age* puts it more bluntly: "I ventur'd through *Troy's* gates, and from the Temple / Rap't the *Palladium*, then I conquered *Troy*."[71] Lust, in the *de casibus* tradition, leads to a fall. Golding's Ovid tells how King Laomedon cheated Phoebus and Neptune out of their due wages for their help in building Troy, and how an angry Neptune "caused all the surges of the sea to rush upon / The shore of covetous Troy."[72]

Commodity brings change to society even as the lust for Helen-as-chattel changes Troy. Language is particularly revealing of this in *Troilus and Cressida*, as words and concepts undergo peculiar metamorphosis. In the same way that the metaphor for war changes, over the course of the play, from war as domestic economic endeavor – "And like as there were husbandry in war, / Before the sun rose he was harness'd" (1.2.7–8) – to war as sport – "Though't be a sportful combat / Yet in the trial much opinion dwells" (1.3.335–36) – to war as hunting – "By Jove, I'll play the hunter for thy life / With all my force, pursuit and policy" (4.1.18–19); "Why then, fly on; I'll hunt thee for thy hide" (5.6.31), so Calchas' term for the business deal whereby Antenor is traded for Cressida moves from "exchange" (3.3.21) to "change" (27) to "interchange" (33) in the space of twelve lines. Significantly, such variation forms the stylistic basis of the prefatory epistle, paronomasia an important component of the author's discourse:

And were but the vain names of comedies changed for the titles of Commodities, or of Plays for Pleas; you should see all those grand censors, that now style them such vanities, flock to them for the main grace of their gravities: especially this author's Comedies, that are so framed to the life, that they serve for the most common Commentaries . . .

Here wit beats the raw material of words into new forms. Beneath the surface appearance, however, they retain a semblance of their former shapes. Gradually, such puns form an associative whole. The author describes a hypothetical day when comedies might be "changed" for commodities, later pointing out "when he is gone, and his Comedies out of sale, you will scramble for them." The letter stands before the play as a barker outside a circus tent, one who uses humorous and contorted phrasing to catch the ear and the coin. Commerce, a worldly figure of *variatio*, alters language as well as material.

That Shakespeare, in *Troilus and Cressida*, would be anxious over the fate of his nation and its parallels to Troy places him in a situation roughly analogous to that of the Roman general Scipio, who, when surveying the ruins of Carthage in one of Polybius' firsthand accounts, made the connection with his own city. The quotation is from the 1578 edition of Appian referred to above:

Scipio seeing the City that had continued seven hundreth years, ruling over so many nations about them, of such power on the land, and also of ships by sea, and Islands in the same, full of armor, navy, Elephants and money, equal with the greatest kingdoms, and in boldness and courage surpassing: the which, when they were spoiled of their ships, and all their armor, yet abode the war three whole years,with so great famine. Then seeing it utterly destroyed by extreme siege, they say he wept, and openly pitied them that were overcome, calling to his remembrance, and perceiving, that all cities, nations and kingdoms, were subject to mutation, as the destinies of men. So suffered Troy, a noble city. So suffered the Assyrians, the Medians, and Persians, which were the great monarchs of the world, and lastly, the most glorious state of Macedonia, so that either of purpose, or by chance, this word fell from him.

The day shall come when mighty Troy must fall,

And Priamus and his warlike nation all.

Polybius that was his schoolmaster, did ask him freely, what he meant by that speech, and that he said, not forbearing to name his own country plainly, of the which he was afraid for the alteration of men.[73]

In *Troilus and Cressida* Shakespeare answers, as Milton and so many others have answered, Marx's question – "is Achilles possible when powder and shot have been invented? And is the Iliad possible at all when the printing press and even printing machines exist?"[74] – by showing us that Achilles and the *Iliad* are all *about* just such inventions, *about* the passing of the old and the coming of the new, that Troy's fall is *about* change.

Left to be answered is the question whether Shakespeare, with *Troilus and Cressida*, was criticizing lapsed morality or whether he was commenting on an entire system of commerce. G. Wilson Knight's reading of *Timon of Athens* endorses the former argument: "it condemns no system, but rather men as individuals, found incapable of handling private wealth which is, finally, equivalent to personal responsibility and personal power."[75] It is tempting to adopt such a view, reading the world of *Troilus and Cressida* as Thersites reads it, as a world thrown into war by lechery. Shakespeare would find in contemporary satire the tools and pattern for such a dramatic morality. But there is some evidence that Shakespeare's complaint, in this play, goes beyond the moral to the systemic. The play admits and condemns the fallibility of *humanum genus*, yet refers again and again to an economic system that apparently distorts human relationships and actively encourages the lapses in morality once ascribed to the machinations of abstract sins and commodities. Although the long war with Spain was to end shortly after James' ascension to the throne, the flood of merchant adventurers who, like Troilus, were seeking their own pearls in India and the Americas rose throughout the decade. Not until 1611 and *The Tempest*, however, would Shakespeare direct his attention to the other end of the voyage.

Notes

PREFACE

1 Thomas Lodge and Robert Greene, *A Looking Glass for London and England*, in Russell A. Fraser and Norman Rabkin, eds., *Drama of the English Renaissance*, vol. 1: *The Tudor Period* (New York: Macmillan, 1976).
2 On the "near and the far" in Renaissance drama, see Richard Marienstras, *New Perspectives on the Shakespearean World*, trans. Janet Lloyd (Cambridge: Cambridge University Press, 1985).

1 TOWARD A MATERIAL THEATER

1 For information pertaining to the construction of the Red Lion Theater in 1567, see Janet Loengard, "An Elizabethan Lawsuit: John Brayne, His Carpenter, and the Building of the Red Lion Theatre," *Shakespeare Quarterly* 34 (1983): 298–310. As Herbert Berry makes clear, the Red Lion was by no means as physically sound as the Theater and later playhouses. It would, in Berry's words, have had "no walls or roofs, and the turret was to rest on plates on the ground rather than on secure footings, along with, one might guess, the stage and galleries." Berry, "The First Public Playhouses, Especially the Red Lion," *Shakespeare Quarterly* 40 (1989): 133–48. See also John H. Astington, "The Red Lion Playhouse: Two Notes," *Shakespeare Quarterly* 36 (1985): 456–57. On the rise of the public theater – both in England and on the continent – see Walter Cohen, *Drama of a Nation: Public Theater in Renaissance England and Spain* (Ithaca: Cornell University Press, 1985).
2 Quoted in Chambers, vol. 4, p. 269.
3 John Northbrooke, *A Treatise Against Dicing, Dancing, Plays, and Interludes*, ed. J. P. Collier (London: Shakespeare Society, 1843), pp. 102, 85.
4 Chambers, vol. 4, p. 197.
5 Andrew Gurr, *Playgoing in Shakespeare's London* (Cambridge: Cambridge University Press, 1987), p. 4.
6 For a dissenting view of the "mixed-audience" tradition, however, see Ann Jennalie Cook, *The Privileged Playgoers of Shakespeare's London, 1576–1642* (Princeton: Princeton University Press, 1981). Martin Butler responds to Cook's argument in Appendix II, "Shakespeare's Unprivileged Playgoers 1576–1642," in his *Theatre and Crisis 1632–1642* (Cambridge: Cambridge University Press, 1984), pp. 293–306.

7 See Norman Rabkin, *Shakespeare and the Common Understanding* (New York: Free Press, 1967).

8 Bertolt Brecht, "Radio as a Means of Communication: A Talk of the Function of Radio" (1930), in Armand Mattelart and Seth Siegelaub, eds., *Communication and Class Struggle*, vol. 2, "Liberation, Socialism" (New York: International General, 1983), pp. 169–71, p. 169.

9 John Stowe, *A Survey of London* (1603), 2 vols., ed. Charles Lethbridge Kingsford (Oxford: Clarendon Press, 1908), vol. 1, p. 193.

10 Frederick, Duke of Wirtemberg, in William Brenchley Rye, ed., *England as Seen by Foreigners in the Days of Elizabeth and James the First* (London: John Russell Smith, 1865), p. 8.

11 Lawrence Stone, "Inigo Jones and the New Exchange," *Archaeological Journal* 114 (1957): 106–07.

12 Stone, "Inigo Jones," p. 115.

13 Thomas Heywood, *If You Know Not Me, You Know Nobody*, Part Two, in *The Dramatic Works*, vol. 1, p. 291.

14 Webster in Lucas, vol. 4, p. 42. Whether the theaters were actually round, the conceit seems to have been a commonplace: in Middleton's *Hengist, King of Kent, or The Mayor of Queenborough* (1618), for instance, we encounter the theater described as "this fair round ring"; and in E. V.'s poem on *Sejanus* (1603), "When in the Globe's fair ring, our world's best stage." Cited by Joseph Quincy Adams in his edition of Middleton's *The Ghost of Lucrece* (New York: Charles Scribner's Sons, 1937), p. 5, n. 4.

15 See, for example, Thomas Middleton's *Michaelmas Term* (1606), ed. Richard Levin (Lincoln: University of Nebraska Press, 1966), *Dramatis Personae* lines 7–8, note; 1.1.81–83, notes.

16 An aural dimension may also have obtained; compare, for instance, the (unwanted) level of theatricality in Thomas Nashe's *The Return of Pasquill* (1589), where – deep in conversation with Pasquill at the Royal Exchange – Marforius tells his companion to lower his voice:

> Speak softly, *Cavaliero*, I perceive two or three lay their heads at one side like a ship under sail, and begin to cast about you: I doubt they have over-heard you. This Exchange is vauted [i.e. "vaulted"] and hollow, and hath such an Echo, as multiplies every word that is spoken, by Arithmetic; it makes a thousand of one, and so imps so many feathers into every tale, that it flys with all speed into every corner of the Realm.

In Thomas Nashe, *The Works of Thomas Nashe*, 5 vols., ed. R. B. McKerrow (London: A. H. Bullen, 1904–1910), vol. 1, p. 82.

17 Stephen Gosson, *Plays Confuted in Five Actions*, in W. C. Hazlitt, ed., *The English Drama and Stage under the Tudor and Stuart Princes, 1543–1664* (London: 1869), pp. 157–218; pp. 214–15.

18 Thomas Middleton, *A Chaste Maid in Cheapside*, ed. R. B. Parker (London: Methuen, 1969).

19 Arthur Gorges, *A True Transcript and Publication of His Majesties Letters Patent. For an Office to be Erected and called the Public Register for General Commerce. Whereunto is Annexed an Overture and Explanation of the Nature and Purport of the Said Office, for their Better Understanding and Direction that Shall Have Occasion to Use It.* (London: 1611), D2^r–D3^v. Significantly, the pamphlet was printed at "Britain Burse" – that is, at the Royal Exchange.

20 John Hall, *The Advancement of Learning*, ed. A. K. Croston (Liverpool: Liverpool University Press, 1953), p. 37.

21 Thomas Dekker, *The Gull's Horn Book* (1609), from *Thomas Dekker*, ed. E. D. Pendry, in The Stratford-upon-Avon Library, vol. 4 (Cambridge, Mass.: Harvard University Press, 1968), p. 98.

22 Sandra Clark, *The Elizabethan Pamphleteers: Popular Moralistic Pamphlets 1580–1640* (London: Athlone Press, 1983), p. 27.

23 Thomas Middleton and Thomas Dekker, *The Roaring Girl*, ed. Andor Gomme (London: Ernest Benn, 1976). "To the Comic Play-Readers, Venery and Laughter," p. 3, lines 1ff. Middleton's name appears alone at the end of this epistle.

24 "The Induction on the *Stage*," lines 57ff. On the play-as-commodity conceit, see Joseph Loewenstein, "The Script in the Marketplace," in Stephen Greenblatt, ed. *Representing the English Renaissance* (Berkeley: University of California Press, 1988), pp. 265–78; and Robert Ashton, "Popular Entertainment and Social Control in Later Elizabethan and Early Stuart London," *London Journal* 9 (1983): 3–19.

25 Stephen Gosson, *Plays Confuted*, in Hazlitt, ed., *English Drama*, p. 166.

26 Jean-Christophe Agnew, *Worlds Apart: The Market and the Theater in Anglo-American Thought, 1550–1750* (New York: Cambridge University Press, 1986), pp. xi, x.

27 Agnew, *Worlds Apart*, p. xi. Agnew repeats the "laboratory" metaphor on p. 54.

28 Agnew, *Worlds Apart*, p. 11.

29 Agnew, *Worlds Apart*, p. 118. Jonson's play has a way of collapsing arguments which insist upon (or imply) categories of separation. As Don Wayne has shown, *Bartholomew Fair* constituted a signal omission from L. C. Knights' influential *Drama and Society in the Age of Jonson*, left out, most probably, because it did not feature the kind of moral criticism of the social order that Knights saw in Jonson's earlier plays. Don E. Wayne, "Drama and Society in the Age of Jonson: Shifting Grounds of Authority and Judgment in Three Major Comedies," in Mary Beth Rose, ed., *Renaissance Drama as Cultural History: Essays from "Renaissance Drama" 1977–1987* (Evanston: Northwestern University Press, 1990), pp. 3–29.

30 Agnew, *Worlds Apart*, p. 103.

31 Steven Mullaney, *The Place of the Stage: License, Play, and Power in Renaissance England* (Chicago: University of Chicago Press, 1988), p. 136. I should make it clear that my argument here with Mullaney's book is intended to reflect the real debt I owe him for making possible the kind of thesis I am advancing.

32 Mullaney, *Place of the Stage*, pp. ix–x.

33 Mullaney, *Place of the Stage*, p. 9.

34 When Mullaney takes up the conjunction of market and theater in the brothel scene of *Pericles*, he addresses the question of the relationship between the two by marginalizing merchants, thus connecting market and playhouse in terms of their ambivalent status and the discomfiture and anxiety he sees them causing their cultures (pp. 141–43). My argument is that the two are related not by marginality, but by institutionalization and centrality.

35 Kathleen McLuskie, "The Patriarchal Bard: Feminist Criticism and Shakespeare: *King Lear* and *Measure for Measure*," in Jonathan Dollimore and Alan Sinfield, eds., *Political Shakespeare: New Essays in Cultural Materialism*, (Ithaca: Cornell University Press, 1985), pp. 88–108; p. 92.

36 Joan Thirsk, *Economic Policy and Projects: The Development of a Consumer Society in Early Modern England* (Oxford: Clarendon Press, 1978), pp. 11, 51–105.

2   DRAMA AND THE AGE

1 Fernand Braudel, *The Wheels of Commerce: Civilization and Capitalism, 15th–18th Century* (New York: Harper & Row, 1982), p. 448.

2 Margot Heinemann, *Puritanism and Theatre: Thomas Middleton and Opposition Drama under the Early Stuarts* (Cambridge: Cambridge University Press, 1980), p. 3.

3 Agnes Heller, *Renaissance Man*, trans. Richard E. Allen (New York: Schocken Books, 1981), p. 2.

4 See for example David Aers, "Rewriting the Middle Ages: Some Suggestions," *The Journal of Medieval and Renaissance Studies* 18 (2) (1988): 221–40. Aers expanded this essay in *Community, Gender, and Individual Identity: English Writing 1360–1430* (London: Routledge, 1988); see also his *Chaucer, Langland and the Creative Imagination* (London: Routledge & Kegan Paul, 1980). Christopher Dyer's *Standards of Living in the Later Middle Ages: Social Change in England c. 1200–1500* (Cambridge: Cambridge University Press, 1989) also creates a persuasive picture of an era in flux. In "Discourse, Ideology and the Crisis of Authority in post-Reformation England," Robert Weimann delineates the influence of the Reformation on ideological stability in early and mid sixteenth-century England. *REAL: The Yearbook of Research in English and American Literature* 5 (1987): 109–40. A recent study of cultural poetics which traces the influence of market forces in the sixteenth and early seventeenth centuries is Richard Halpern's *The Poetics of Primitive Accumulation: English Renaissance Culture and the Genealogy of Capital* (Ithaca: Cornell University Press, 1991).

5 Lawrence Stone, *The Crisis of the Aristocracy 1558–1641* (London: Oxford University Press, 1965), p. 15. On the nature and extent of social transformation in the English Renaissance, see Raymond Williams, *Culture* (London: Fontana, 1981), pp. 158–59; Conrad Russell, *The Crisis of Parliaments* (London: Oxford University Press, 1971), pp. 195–217; and David Morse, *England's Time of Crisis* (Basingstoke: Macmillan, 1989).

6 Harry Levin, "English Literature of the Renaissance," in *The Renaissance: A Reconsideration of the Theories and Interpretations of the Age*, ed. Tinsley Helton (Madison: University of Wisconsin Press, 1961), p. 129. Levin is responding to J. M. Keynes, who attributed the literary achievements of the English Renaissance to the profit inflations sparked by the New World gold, holding that "by far the larger proportion of the world's greatest writers and artists have flourished in the atmosphere of buoyancy, exhilaration and the freedom from economic cares felt by the governing class, which is engendered

by profit inflations." J. M. Keynes, *A Treatise on Money*, 2 vols. (1930; London: Macmillan, 1965), vol. 2, p. 154, n. 3.

7 See, for example, Alfred Harbage, "Copper Into Gold," in Standish Henning et al., eds., *English Renaissance Drama: Essays in Honor of Madeleine Doran and Mark Eccles* (Carbondale: Southern Illinois University Press, 1976): 1–14; Lauro Martines, *Society and History in English Renaissance Verse* (New York: Basil Blackwell, 1987); Marc Shell, *Money, Language, and Thought: Literary and Philosophical Economies from the Medieval to the Modern Era* (Berkeley: University of California Press, 1982); and Sandra K. Fischer, *Econolingua: A Glossary of Coins and Economic Language in Renaissance Drama* (Newark: University of Delaware Press, 1985).

8 L. C. Knights, *Drama and Society in the Age of Jonson* (London: Chatto and Windus, 1937).

9 Nicholas Breton, *Pasquil's Madcap*, in *The Works in Verse and Prose of Nicholas Breton*, ed. Alexander B. Grosart, 2 vols. (Edinburgh: Edinburgh University Press: 1875–1879), vol. 1, e, p. 6, B.

10 Karl Marx, *Capital*, 3 vols. (New York: International Publishers, 1987), vol. 1, p. 132, n. 1.

11 Paul Brown, "'This thing of darkness I acknowledge mine': *The Tempest* and the Discourse of Colonialism," in Jonathan Dollimore and Alan Sinfield, eds., *Political Shakespeare* (Ithaca: Cornell University Press, 1985), p. 68.

12 Roger B. Manning, *Village Revolts: Social Protest and Popular Disturbances in England, 1509–1640* (Oxford: Clarendon Press, 1988), p. 187.

13 Manning, *Village Revolts*, p. 187.

14 Andrew Gurr, *Playgoing in Shakespeare's London* (Cambridge: Cambridge University Press, 1987), p. 141.

15 E. H. Phelps Brown and Sheila V. Hopkins, "Seven Centuries of the Prices of Consumables, Compared with Builders' Wage Rates," in Peter H. Ramsey, ed., *The Price Revolution in Sixteenth-Century England* (London: Methuen, 1971), p. 30. The findings of Brown and Hopkins have been challenged and modified by other historians. See, for example, Donald Woodward, "Wage Rates and Living Standards in Pre-Industrial England," *Past and Present* 91 (1981): 28–46; E. A. Wrigley and R. S. Schofield, *The Population History of England, 1541–1871: A Reconstruction* (New York: Cambridge University Press, 1989), pp. 401ff.; Steve Rappaport, *Worlds Within Worlds: Structures of Life in Sixteenth-Century London* (Cambridge: Cambridge University Press, 1989), pp. 123–61; and John Walter and Keith Wrightson, "Dearth and the Social Order in Early Modern England," *Past and Present* 71 (1976): 22–42, especially n. 2.

16 Ramsey, ed., *Price Revolution*, p. 14.

17 Ramsey, ed., *Price Revolution*, pp. 14–15.

18 Ramsey, ed., *Price Revolution*, pp. 14–15. On social problems associated with poverty during this period, see Paul Slack, *Poverty and Policy in Tudor and Stuart England* (New York: Longman, 1988); and A. L. Beier, "Poverty and Progress in Early Modern England," in Beier et al., eds. *The First Modern Society: Essays in English History in Honour of Lawrence Stone* (New York: Cambridge University Press, 1989), pp. 201–39.

19 This table is a combination of figures provided by Wrigley and Schofield, *The*

Population History of England, pp. 531–32 (England), and Ann Jennalie Cook, *The Privileged Playgoers of Shakespeare's London, 1576–1642* (Princeton: Princeton University Press, 1981), p. 94. Other scholars have offered different figures. Roger Finlay, for instance, suggests that "at present, the best estimates suggest that the population increased from just over 100,000 in 1580 to about 200,000 in 1600 and 400,000 by 1650." Roger Finlay, *Population and Metropolis: The Demography of London 1580–1650* (Cambridge: University Press, 1981), p. 6. Arguing that estimates of this kind are most probably exaggerated, Valerie Pearl none the less admits that "the predominance of the metropolis and its phenomenal growth are not in doubt." Valerie Pearl, *London and the Outbreak of the Puritan Revolution* (Oxford: Oxford University Press, 1961), p. 14. Whatever set of figures one chooses to accept, it is clear that both England and London grew tremendously during this time, with the rate of London's growth by far exceeding that of England.

20 A. L. Beier and Roger Finlay, eds., *London 1500–1700: The Making of the Metropolis* (London: Longman, 1986), "Introduction: The Significance of the Metropolis," p. 11.

21 Quoted (in slightly altered form) by Braudel in *The Wheels of Commerce*, p. 41. Braudel goes on to observe: "what London was really 'eating up' was not merely the English interior, but also so to speak its exterior – at least two-thirds, possibly three-quarters or four-fifths of its foreign trade." On London's economic relations with the nation as a whole, see J. A. Chartres, *Internal Trade in England, 1500–1700* (London: Macmillan Press, 1977); and the essays collected in F. J. Fisher, *London and the English Economy, 1500–1700*, ed. P. J. Cornfield and N. B. Harte (London: Hambledon Press, 1990). For economic history generally, I have found useful Braudel's three-volume work, *Civilization and Capitalism, 15th–18th Century* (English translation, New York: Harper & Row, 1981–1985), the individual volumes of which are entitled, respectively, *The Structures of Everyday Life, The Wheels of Commerce*, and *The Perspective of the World*. Also informative are volumes 4, *The Economy of Expanding Europe in the Sixteenth and Seventeenth Centuries*, and 5, *The Economic Organization of Early Modern Europe*, in *The Cambridge Economic History of Europe*, both edited by E. E. Rich and C. H. Wilson (Cambridge: Cambridge University Press, 1967; 1977); the older but still useful *Religion and the Rise of Capitalism* by R. H. Tawney (1926; Gloucester, Mass.: Peter Smith, 1962); and Max Weber's much-debated *The Protestant Ethic and the Spirit of Capitalism*, translated by Talcott Parsons (1904–1905; London: Counterpoint, 1985). Two articles by Robert Brenner have also helped me in formulating the present argument: "Agrarian Class Structure and Economic Development in Pre-Industrial Europe," *Past and Present* 70 (1976): 30–75; and "The Agrarian Roots of European Capitalism," *Past and Present* 97 (1982): 16–113.

22 Robert Gray, *A Good Speed to Virginia* (London: 1609), B4r.

23 "Prohibiting Further Building or Subdividing of Houses in London," June 22, 1602, 44 Elizabeth 1, reprinted in Paul L. Hughes and James F. Larkin, eds., *Tudor Royal Proclamations*, 3 vols. (New Haven: Yale University Press, 1964–69), vol. 3, pp. 245–48; pp. 245–46.

24 Paul Slack, *The Impact of Plague in Tudor and Stuart England* (London: Routledge & Kegan Paul, 1985), p. 152.

25 Lawrence Manley, "From Matron to Monster: Tudor-Stuart London and the Languages of Urban Description," in Heather Dubrow and Richard Strier, eds. *The Historical Renaissance: New Essays on Tudor and Stuart Literature and Culture* (Chicago: University of Chicago Press, 1988), p. 350.
26 J. M. Keynes, *A Treatise on Money*, 2 vols. (New York: Macmillan, 1930), vol. 2, p. 154.
27 William Empson, *Some Versions of Pastoral* (Edinburgh: Edinburgh University Press, 1938), p. 14.
28 Significantly, most dramatists came to London from other areas of England. Of sixty-two London playwrights listed in a recent biographical dictionary of Renaissance authors, scholars and historians know with some degree of certainty the birthplace of thirty-eight (J. W. Saunders, *A Biographical Dictionary of Renaissance Poets and Dramatists, 1520–1650* (New Jersey: Barnes & Noble, 1983), pp. xxii–xxiv). Eleven of these, or roughly 29 percent, are Londoners by birth, including Chettle, Dekker, John Heywood, Jonson, Kyd, Middleton, Peele, Shirley, and Webster. The other 71 percent – dramatists such as Beaumont, Fletcher, Chapman, Day, Ford, Thomas Heywood, Lyly, Marston, Marlowe, Massinger, and Shakespeare – were born outside London, eventually making their way to this magnet of trade and traffic. For them England's major city seems likely to have been a foreign center of opportunity. What many of them would see in the city in all probability differed in scope, if not in nature, from the life they knew outside of London. The qualitative difference between rural and urban, in turn, appears to have influenced their literary production, sometimes inflating the pressures of the city even as it could exaggerate the patent novelty of the urban market.
29 Jonas Barish, *The Antitheatrical Prejudice* (Berkeley: University of California Press, 1981), p. 96.
30 Niccolo Machiavelli, *The Prince*, trans. Harvey C. Mansfield, Jr. (Chicago: University of Chicago Press, 1985), p. 88.
31 Cf. "politic" (*OED* 2.d), "political" (*OED* 5), "policy" (*OED* 3; 4; 4.b), and "politician" (*OED* 1).
32 See Gurr, *Playgoing*, pp. 13–22.
33 See John Gordon Sweeney, *Jonson and the Psychology of Public Theater* (Princeton: Princeton University Press, 1985), p. 229, n. 3.
34 See *2H4* Induction, 19; *2H6* 2.4.21, 3.2.135, 4.4.32, 4.8.56; *Cor.* 2.3.17; *Ham.* 4.3.4; *MV* 2.9.33; *Cym.* 3.6.85.
35 Barry Russell, "Launching the Swan," *Drama* 3 (1986): 11–12; p. 11.
36 For one reading of the thematic working-through of the acting experience, see Marjorie Garber, "'Infinite Riches in a Little Room': Closure and Enclosure in Marlowe," in Alvin Kernan, ed., *Two Renaissance Mythmakers: Christopher Marlowe and Ben Jonson* (Baltimore: Johns Hopkins University Press, 1977), pp. 3–21.
37 Quoted in Gurr, *Playgoing*, pp. 24, 210.
38 On the health issues and politics surrounding London's overcrowding in the early modern period, see Thomas G. Barnes, "The Prerogative and Environmental Control of London Building in the Early Seventeenth Century: The Lost Opportunity," *Ecology Law Quarterly* 1 (1971): 62–93; and Malcolm R Smuts, "The Court and Its Neighbourhood: Royal Policy and Urban Growth in the Early Stuart West End," *Journal of British Studies*, 30 (1991): 117–49.

Lawrence Stone charts the social impact of London's westward growth in "The Residential Development of the West End of London in the Seventeenth Century," in Barbara Malament, ed., *After the Reformation: Essays in Honor of J. H. Hexter* (Philadelphia: University of Pennsylvania Press, 1980), pp. 167–214. On social problems in London generally, see A. L. Beir, "Social Problems in Elizabethan London," *Journal of Interdisciplinary History* 9 (1978): 203–21.

39 Michael D. Bristol, *Carnival and Theater: Plebeian Culture and the Structure of Authority in Renaissance England* (New York: Methuen, 1985), p. 112.

40 Quoted in Chambers, vol. 2, p. 205.

41 Peter Thomson, *Shakespeare's Theatre* (London: Routledge & Kegan Paul), p. 27. Thomson's second chapter, "Balancing the Books," is a concise introduction to the economics of the Renaissance playhouse. See also Neil Carson's valuable study, *A Companion to Henslowe's Diary* (Cambridge: Cambridge University Press, 1988); Chambers, "The Actor's Economics," vol. 1, pp. 348–88; and Gerald Eades Bentley, *The Profession of Dramatist in Shakespeare's Time, 1590–1642* (Princeton: Princeton University Press, 1971), and *The Profession of Player in Shakespeare's Time, 1590–1642* (Princeton: Princeton University Press, 1984).

42 Thomson, *Shakespeare's Theatre*, p. 28.

43 R. A. Foakes and R. T. Rickert, eds., *Henslowe's Diary* (Cambridge: Cambridge University Press, 1961), p. 240.

44 Chambers, for instance, tells us that the ground-rent for the area the Globe was built on was around £15, while the rent that Richard Burbage received from Henry Evans – who would manage a company of child actors – for "the great hall or room, with the rooms over the same, situate within the precinct of the Black Friars" was £40 (Chambers, vol. 2, pp. 417, 508–09). One could draw a loose analogy with the drive-in movie theater in the United States in the middle and later twentieth century, places of entertainment almost invariably situated in the then open areas outside towns and cities. Like them, the Renaissance stage provided entertainment for profit, and may have looked to rental and mortgage exigencies before the political. Recently, of course, small movie theaters in shopping malls (most often outside urban centers) have duplicated this topographical arrangement.

45 Quoted in Chambers, vol. 2., pp. 374–75.

3   "CITY COMEDY" AND THE MATERIALIST VISION

1 Emrys Jones, "London in the Early Seventeenth Century: An Ecological Approach," *The London Journal* 6 (1980): 126.

2 Jeremy Boulton, *Neighbourhood and Society: A London Suburb in the Seventeenth Century* (Cambridge: Cambridge University Press, 1987), pp. 289, 293.

3 "Subgenre" as used here is adapted from its employment in the genre study of Alastair Fowler, *Kinds of Literature: An Introduction to the Theory of Genres and Modes* (Cambridge, Mass.: Harvard University Press, 1982).

4 R. C. Bald, "The Sources of Middleton's City Comedies," *Journal of English and Germanic Philology* 33 (1934): 373–87.

5 Felix Schelling, *Elizabethan Drama, 1558–1642*, 2 vols. (Boston: Houghton Mifflin, 1908), vol. 1, pp. 492–93.

6 Wilbur Dwight Dunkel, *The Dramatic Technique of Thomas Middleton in His Comedies of London Life* (Chicago: University of Chicago Libraries, 1925), p. 12.
7 Wilhelm Creizenach, *The English Drama in the Age of Shakespeare* (translated 1916; reprinted, New York: Russell & Russell, 1967), p. 138.
8 Brian Gibbons, *Jacobean City Comedy* (Cambridge, Mass.: Harvard University Press, 1968), p. 15. Gibbons has published a slightly revised edition of this work: (New York: Methuen, 1980).
9 Gibbons, *Jacobean City Comedy*, p. 24.
10 Gibbons, *Jacobean City Comedy*, p. 17.
11 Susan Wells, *The Dialectics of Representation* (Baltimore: Johns Hopkins, 1989), p. 103. See also Theodore B. Leinwand, *The City Staged: Jacobean Comedy, 1603–1613* (Madison: University of Wisconsin Press, 1986); and Lawrence Venuti, *Our Halcyon Dayes: English Prerevolutionary Texts and Postmodern Culture* (Madison: University of Wisconsin Press, 1989), especially ch. 3, "Transformations of City Comedy," pp. 99–164.
12 Gamini Salgado, ed., *Four Jacobean City Comedies* (New York: Penguin, 1975), p. 9.
13 Wendy Griswold, *Renaissance Revivals: City Comedy and Revenge Tragedy in the London Theatre, 1576–1980* (Chicago: University of Chicago Press, 1986), pp. 15–25.
14 Lee Bliss, *The World's Perspective: John Webster and the Jacobean Drama* (New Brunswick: Rutgers University Press, 1983), pp. 7–8.
15 Alexander Leggatt, *Citizen Comedy in the Age of Shakespeare* (Toronto: University of Toronto Press, 1973), p. 4.
16 Wilhelm Creizenach noted long ago that Renaissance playwrights "generally forget all about their Italian background and write exactly as if the action were taking place in England." Creizenach, *English Drama*, pp. 159–60.
17 *The Oxford English Dictionary* (hereafter merely *OED*), *q.v.*.
18 Philip Sidney, *An Apology for Poetry*, ed. Forrest G. Robinson (Indianapolis: Bobbs-Merrill, 1970), p. 75.
19 Ben Jonson, *Every Man in His Humour: A Parallel-Text Edition of the 1601 Quarto and the 1616 Folio*, ed. J. W. Lever (Lincoln: University of Nebraska Press, 1971), p. xxi.
20 Harry Levin, *Playboys and Killjoys* (New York: Oxford University Press, 1987), p. 155. Levin fails to note, however, that one school of Renaissance genre theory habitually ascribed country settings and characters to comedy. See, for example, Thomas Randolph's *The Muses' Looking-Glass* (1630), 1.3: "The comic glass is full of merry strife, / The low reflection of a country life."
21 Levin, *Playboys and Killjoys*, p. 174.
22 Leah S. Marcus, *Puzzling Shakespeare: Local Reading and Its Discontents* (Berkeley: University of California Press, 1988).
23 Thomas Lodge, *The Wounds of Civil War*, ed. Joseph W. Houppert (Lincoln: University of Nebraska Press, 1969), 5.5.224–26.
24 David Wiles discusses a version of this phenomenon in relation to the names given to (or assumed by) clowns on the Renaissance stage. Wiles points out that "[Will] Kemp's clowns consistently have English names," even in plays where all other characters have names consonant with the foreign setting of the dramatic action, and that this homeliness may have been related to a primarily

Elizabethan project that, with Tarlton (and later, Kemp), "helped to foster in Londoners a new sense of community, shared values and active participation in the making of a culture" in a rapidly growing London which lacked the social rituals of smaller communities. David Wiles, *Shakespeare's Clown: Actor and Text in the Elizabethan Playhouse* (Cambridge: Cambridge University Press, 1987), pp. 146, 23.

25 Quoted in the New Variorum *Julius Caesar* (at 2.1.213), ed. H. H. Furness, Jr. (Philadelphia: J. B. Lippincott, 1913).

26 Gail Kern Paster, *The Idea of the City in the Age of Shakespeare* (Athens: University of Georgia Press, 1985), pp. 6–7.

27 Both William Harrison and Sir Thomas Smith divided English society into six categories: royalty, nobility, gentry, citizens, yeomen, and artificers/laborers. And certain legal codes, such as the 1574 Statute Against the Excess of Apparel (16 Elizabeth 1), commonly assumed there were or should be clear divisions along lines of income. But see J. H. Hexter, "The Myth of the Middle Class in Tudor England," published in *Reappraisals in History: New Views on History and Society in Early Modern Europe* (Chicago: University of Chicago Press, 1979), pp. 71–116. On class generally, see also David Cressy, "Describing the Social Order of Elizabethan and Stuart England," *Literature and History* 3 (1976): 29–44; and Keith Wrightson, ch. 1, "Degrees of People," in Wrightson, *English Society 1580–1680* (New Brunswick: Rutgers University Press, 1982), pp. 17–38. D. M. Palliser also argues that the idea might "mislead a reader attuned to modern concepts of social class, by implying that society was an agglomeration of individuals." D. M. Palliser, *The Age of Elizabeth* (New York: Longman, 1983), p. 60.

28 Leggatt, *Citizen Comedy*, p. 3.

29 Edward Sharpham, *Cupid's Whirligig*, ed. Allardyce Nicoll (London: Golden Cockerel Press, 1926), p. 41.

30 Sharpham, *Cupid's Whirligig*, p. 9.

31 I should state here that Margot Heinemann said of Middleton's *The Changeling* (1622) and *Women Beware Women* (1621) that one might "see in these last great plays – immeasurably his finest – something which we can fairly describe as 'city tragedy'." Heinemann, *Puritanism and Theatre: Thomas Middleton and Opposition Drama under the Early Stuarts* (Cambridge: Cambridge University Press, 1980), p. 172.

32 Fredric Jameson, *The Political Unconscious: Narrative as a Socially Symbolic Act* (Ithaca: Cornell University Press, 1981), p. 17.

33 Eric Auerbach, *Mimesis: The Representation of Reality in Western Literature*, trans. Willard Trask (Princeton: Princeton University Press, 1974), p. 313; on *sermo humilis*, see also the chapter of that name in Auerbach's *Literary Language and Its Public in Late Latin Antiquity and in the Middle Ages*, trans. Ralph Manheim (London: Routledge & Kegan Paul, 1965), pp. 27–66.

34 Michael D. Bristol, *Carnival and Theater: Plebeian Culture and the Structure of Authority in Renaissance England* (New York: Methuen, 1985), pp. 22–23, 190, 191, 207.

35 Wells, *Dialectics of Representation*, pp. 17, 19; see also Wells' concentrated examination of the "typical" in its various permutations in the works of Lukács, n. 35, pp. 179–81.

36 See, for example, Oscar James Campbell, *Comicall Satyre and Shakespeare's "Troilus and Cressida"* (Los Angeles: Adcraft Press, 1938).
37 Madeleine Doran, *Endeavors of Art: A Study of Form in Elizabethan Drama* (Madison: University of Wisconsin Press, 1954), p. 230.
38 *Discoveries*, in C. H. Herford, Percy Simpson, and Evelyn Simpson, eds., *Ben Jonson*, 11 vols. (Oxford: Clarendon Press, 1925–1952), vol. 8, lines 1437–43.
39 John Wheeler, *A Treatise of Commerce* (1601) (Facsimile; New York: Columbia University Press, 1931), pp. 6–7.
40 Joan Thirsk, *Economic Policy and Projects: The Development of a Consumer Society in Early Modern England* (Oxford: Clarendon Press, 1978), p. 2.
41 A. D. Nuttall, *A New Mimesis: Shakespeare and the Representation of Reality* (New York: Methuen, 1983), p. 1.
42 On science and the impact of the "New Philosophy" on poetry in the early seventeenth century, see Marjorie Hope Nicolson, *The Breaking of the Circle* (New York: Columbia University Press, 1960; revised).
43 On the historical background of London's role as a center for the distribution, display, and consumption of commodity, see F. J. Fisher's classic essay, "The Development of London as a Centre of Conspicuous Consumption in the Sixteenth and Seventeenth Centuries," in Fisher, *London and the English Economy, 1500–1700*, ed. P. J. Corfield and N. B. Harte (London: Hambledon Press, 1990), pp. 105–18.
44 Richard Horwich, "Wives, Courtesans, and the Economics of Love in Jacobean City Comedy," in *Drama in the Renaissance: Comparative and Critical Essays*, ed. Clifford Davidson et al. (New York: AMS Press, 1986), p. 270.
45 Coppélia Kahn, "The Rape in Shakespeare's *Lucrece*," *Shakespeare Studies* 9 (1976): 45–72; p. 61.
46 Lawrence Stone, *The Family, Sex and Marriage in England 1500–1800* (New York: Harper & Row, 1977), p. 216. Although Stone's thesis has drawn its share of criticism, compare Alice Clark on the detrimental effects of the developing market on the status of women in Clark, *Working Life of Women in the Seventeenth Century* (1919; London: Routledge, 1982).
47 See James T. Henke, *Courtesans and Cuckolds: A Glossary of Renaissance Dramatic Bawdy* (New York: Garland, 1979), "commodity," p. 47; and Eric Partridge, *Shakespeare's Bawdy* (New York: E.P. Dutton, 1948), pp. 90–91. *The Wandering Whore*, a "bawdy" work of the early Restoration, tells of a drunken prostitute who "laid belly naked on a table with a candle stuck in her commodity." Quoted in Roger Thompson, *Unfit for Modest Ears: A Study of Pornographic, Obscene and Bawdy Works Written or Published in England in the Second Half of the Seventeenth Century* (London: Macmillan, 1979), p. 66.
48 W. H. Auden, *The Dyer's Hand, and Other Essays* (London: Faber and Faber, 1963), p. 173.
49 Gibbons, *Jacobean City Comedy*, p. 30.
50 Lauro Martines, *Society and History in English Renaissance Verse* (New York: Basil Blackwell, 1987), p. 104.
51 Thomas Middleton and Thomas Dekker, *The Roaring Girl*, ed. Andor Gomme (New York: W. W. Norton, 1976). The idea became commonplace. The fishermen of Shakespeare's *Pericles* (1611) repeat this proverbial notion when one inquires "how the fishes live in the sea" only to be answered: "why, as men

do a-land: the great ones eat up the little ones" (2.1.27–29). F. D. Hoeniger, editor of the New Arden *Pericles*, points out parallels to this sentiment throughout Shakespeare, including both Albany's "Humanity must perforce prey on itself, / Like monsters of the deep" (*Lear*, 4.2.49–50) and what appears to be Shakespeare's hand in *Sir Thomas More* (1595): "men like ravenous fishes / Would feed on one another" (86–87). (Cited here from the Riverside "Additions Ascribed to Shakespeare.")

52 John Day, *The Isle of Gulls*, in *The Works of John Day* (reprinted from A. H. Bullen, ed.; London: Holland Press, 1963), p. 241.

53 Quoted and translated by Chambers, vol. 2, pp. 364–66.

4 HORNS OF PLENTY: CUCKOLDRY AND CAPITAL

1 "The same day [15 May 1562] was set up at the cuckold haven a great May-pole by butchers and fisher-men, full of horns; and they made great cheer." *The Diary of Henry Machyn, Citizen and Merchant-Taylor of London*, ed. John G. Nichols (London: Camden Society, 1848; rpt. New York: Johnson Reprint Corporation, 1968), 48: 283.

2 Edward H. Sugden, *A Topographical Dictionary to the Works of Shakespeare and His Fellow Dramatists* (Manchester: Manchester University Press, 1925), p. 140.

3 Thomas Dekker, *The Witch of Edmonton*, in Fredson Bowers, ed., *The Dramatic Works of Thomas Dekker*, 4 vols. (Cambridge: Cambridge University Press, 1953–61), vol. 3.

4 John Taylor, "A [New] Discovery by Sea, [with a Wherry] from London to Salisbury," in *All the Works of John Taylor, the Water Poet* (1630, facsimile; London: Scolar Press, 1977), p. 21.

5 Sugden, *Topographical Dictionary*, p. 140.

6 Nicholas Breton, *Cornu-copiae. Pasquil's Night-cap: or, Antidote for the Headache* (London: 1612), p. 53.

7 Pierre Bourdieu, *Outline of a Theory of Practice*, trans. Richard Nice (Cambridge: Cambridge University Press, 1977), p. 183.

8 See the punning on "tail" and "tally" in Chaucer's *Shipman's Tale*, and related critical discussion in Albert H. Silverman, "Sex and Money in Chaucer's *Shipman's Tale*," *Philological Quarterly* 32 (1953): 329–36; Paul S. Schneider, "'Taillynge Ynough': The Function of Money in the *Shipman's Tale*," *Chaucer Review* 11 (1976–77): 201–09; and Robert Adams, "The Concept of Debt in *The Shipman's Tale*," *Studies in the Age of Chaucer* 6 (1984): 85–102.

9 Breton, *Cornu-copiae. Pasquil's Night-cap*, pp. 43, 49.

10 Katharine Eisaman Maus, "Horns of Dilemma: Jealousy, Gender, and Spectatorship in English Renaissance Drama," *ELH* 54 (1987): 561.

11 C. L. Barber, *Shakespeare's Festive Comedy* (Princeton: Princeton University Press, 1959), p. 16. On the unique appropriation of rural festivity by urban theatrical centers, see Robert Weimann, *Shakespeare and the Popular Tradition in the Theater: Studies in the Social Dimension of Dramatic Form and Function* (Baltimore: Johns Hopkins University Press, 1978).

12 Text from E. C. Wickham, ed., *Horace*, 2 vols. (Oxford: Clarendon Press, 1903–12), 2, I.vii.28–31. Trans. by author.

13 Pliny, *Natural History*. Loeb Classical Library, trans. H. Rackham, 10 vols. (Cambridge, Mass.: Harvard University Press, 1950), vol. 8: 18.66.

14 In *The Comedy of Errors* (1592) (5.1.400), *Much Ado About Nothing* (1598) (4.1.215), *Pericles* (1608) (3. Prologue, line 52; 3.1.114) and *Henry VIII* (1613) (5.1.71), Shakespeare uses "travail" to describe the work of childbirth. "Labor," though appearing in his work to describe the *concept* of female labor – such as "great things laboring perish in their birth" (*Love's Labour's Lost* (1595) 5.2.520), "the birth of our own laboring breath" (*Troilus and Cressida* (1602) 4.4.38), "my Muse labors, / And thus she is deliver'd" (*Othello* (1604) 2.1.127–28), "[the hour is] Laboring for nine" (*Timon of Athens* (1607) 3.4.8), and "With news the time's with labor, and throes forth / Each minute some" (*Antony and Cleopatra* (1607) 3.7.80–81) – is never used to describe an actual woman in labor until Sir Thomas Lovell in *Henry VIII* announces: "The Queen's in labor, / They say in great extremity, and fear'd / She'll with the labor end" (5.1.18–20).

15 "Rachel shulde bere childe, for the hardness of birth she beganne to perish" (Wycliffe); "Rachel began to travail. And in travailling she was in peril" (Tyndale, 1530); "Rachel travailed, and the birth came hard upon her" (Coverdale, 1535); "Rachel travailed, and in travailing she was in peril" (Geneva, 1560); "Wherein Rachel was in travail, By reason of her hard labour" (Douai, 1609); "And Rachel travailed, and she had hard labour" (King James, 1611). Although in Middle English, "Labour" and "Labouren" were sometimes used to describe women in childbirth – see the *Middle English Dictionary*; L.1, *labour* 4.b, and *labouren* 3.a – not until the second decade of the seventeenth century would it become a commonplace.

16 Thomas Tusser, *Five Hundred Points of Good Husbandry* (1573), ed. E. V. Lucas (London: James Tregaskis, 1931), p. 12. Lucas' text is based on the edition of 1590.

17 Alexander Schmidt, *Shakespeare Lexicon and Quotation Dictionary*, 2 vols. (Berlin: Georg Reimer, 1902; rpt. New York: Dover, 1971).

18 I take these definitions from Schmidt's *Lexicon*.

19 St. Luke, of course, was the gospel writer associated with the ox, "presumably," George W. Ferguson suggests, because "the ox is a symbol of sacrifice." George Ferguson, *Signs and Symbols in Christian Art*, 2nd edn (New York: Oxford University Press, 1954), p. 131. See plate no. 91 in Ferguson's work, "St. Luke the Evangelist" by Giovanni di Paolo. Cuckold's Haven appears to have taken on a kind of festive association in its connection with St. Luke's day, much like the May pole and its holiday. Compare the "May-pole" of Machyn's description, note 1.

20 See Morris Palmer Tilley, *A Dictionary of the Proverbs in England in the Sixteenth and Seventeenth Centuries* (Ann Arbor: University of Michigan Press, 1950), S580.

21 Archie Mervin Tyson, ed., *Every Woman in Her Humour: A Critical Edition* (New York: Garland, 1980).

22 Eric Partridge, *Shakespeare's Bawdy* (New York: E. P. Dutton, 1948), p. 160, cites *Measure for Measure* (1604) 4.2.33–39, where Pompey and Abhorson play on the word, and suggests that "perhaps, too, there is a prophetic relevancy" in Othello's speech.

23 Doll Tearsheet in *2 Henry IV* (1597) somewhat unconvincingly laments that "these villains will make the word as odious as the word 'occupy', which was an excellent good word before it was ill sorted" (2.4.147–50). See also *Romeo and Juliet* (1596), 2.4.96–100.

24 On cuckoldry as a manifestation of homosocial bonding, see Eve Kosofsky Sedgwick, *Between Men: English Literature and Male Homosocial Desire* (New York: Columbia University Press, 1985), ch. 3, "*The Country Wife*: Anatomies of Male Homosocial Desire," pp. 49–66. Also significant here is Joel Fineman's "Fratricide and Cuckoldry: Shakespeare's Doubles" in *Representing Shakespeare*, ed. Murray M. Schwartz and Coppélia Kahn (Baltimore: Johns Hopkins University Press, 1980), pp. 70–109.

25 Linda Woodbridge, *Women and the English Renaissance: Literature and the Nature of Womankind, 1540–1620* (Urbana: University of Illinois Press, 1984), p. 174.

26 See Freud on money and anality, *Collected Papers*, 5 vols. ed. James Strachey (London: Hogarth Press, 1950), vol. 2, pp. 49–50; 168–71. Particularly apt are his remarks on gambling and sexuality in "Dostoevsky and Parricide" (1928), vol. 5, pp. 222–42.

27 Stephen Hannaford, "'My Money is my Daughter': Sexual and Financial Possession in English Renaissance Comedy," *Shakespeare Jahrbuch* (West) (1984): 102. See also G. R. Hibbard, "Love, Marriage, and Money in Shakespeare's Theatre and Shakespeare's England," in Hibbard, ed., *The Elizabethan Theatre VI* (Toronto: The Macmillan Company, 1978), pp. 134–55.

28 John Webster, *The White Devil*, ed. J. R. Mulryne (Lincoln: University of Nebraska Press, 1969).

29 Quoting a similar passage from the beginning of this play, Raymond Southall speaks of a new, "common bourgeois concern" that during this period begins to "mediate" relationships, public and private. "*Troilus and Cressida* and the Spirit of Capitalism" in Arnold Kettle, ed., *Shakespeare in a Changing World* (New York: International, 1964), pp. 218–19.

30 *The Honest Whore*, Part One, in Bowers, ed., vol. 2.

31 On the Christian as cuckold, see George Chapman's *All Fools* (1601), 3.1.50–51, and *passim* in the edition of Frank Manley in the Regents Renaissance Drama Series (Lincoln: University of Nebraska Press, 1968); John Florio's *Second Frutes* (1591) (rpt. Gainesville: Scholars' Facsimiles, 1953), p. 143; and Rabelais' *Gargantua and Pantagruel*, trans. Sir Thomas Urquhart and Peter Le Motteux (1653–94) Tudor Translations (London: David Nutt, 1900), 3 vols.; vol. 2, Book 3, ch. 28, pp. 146–47.

32 See James T. Henke, *Courtesans and Cuckolds: A Glossary of Renaissance Dramatic Bawdy* (New York: Garland, 1979), p. 62.

33 Ben Jonson, *Volpone*, in Wilkes, ed., *The Complete Plays*, vol. 3.

34 Thomas Middleton, *Michaelmas Term*, ed. Richard Levin (Lincoln: University of Nebraska Press, 1966).

35 Thomas Middleton, *The Family of Love*, in A. H. Bullen, ed., *The Works of Thomas Middleton*, 8 vols. (Boston: Houghton, Mifflin, 1885–86), vol. 3.

36 *Sir Thomas More*, in C. F. Tucker Brooke, ed., *The Shakespeare Apocrypha* (Oxford: Clarendon Press, 1918).

37 Jonson, Chapman, and Marston, *Eastward Ho!*, ed. C. G. Petter (London: Ernest Benn, 1973).
38 Ben Jonson, *Epigrams and The Forest*, ed. Richard Dutton (Manchester: Carcanet, 1984), p. 46.
39 William Fennor, *The Counter's Commonwealth*, in A. V. Judges, ed., *The Elizabethan Underworld* (New York: E. P. Dutton, 1930), p. 446.
40 Thomas Heywood, *The Brazen Age*, in *The Dramatic Works*, vol. 3, p. 266.
41 Edward Sharpham, *Cupid's Whirligig*, ed. Allardyce Nicoll (Waltham Saint Lawrence: Golden Cockerel Press, 1926), p. 41.
42 I am not familiar with any substantial discussion of the wittol phenomenon in Renaissance Drama. Alan H. Gilbert ("The Prosperous Wittol in Giovanni Battista Modio and Thomas Middleton," *Studies in Philology* 41 (1944): 235–37) gives a brief extract from Modio's *Il convito*, where wittolry is praised as the basis of a fruitful marriage: "*Si vede che i cornuti quasi per tutto vivono abbondantemente*" ("It shows that cuckolds – almost all of them – live in abundance") (p. 235).
43 John Marston, *The Dutch Courtesan*, ed. M. L. Wine (Lincoln: University of Nebraska Press, 1965).
44 Thomas Middleton, *A Chaste Maid in Cheapside*, ed. R. B. Parker (London: Methuen, 1969).
45 See the line note in the Revels edition.
46 See Max Weber, *The Protestant Ethic and the Spirit of Capitalism* (1904–1905; rpt., London: Unwin, 1987); R. H. Tawney, *Religion and the Rise of Capitalism* (1926; rpt. Gloucester, MA: Peter Smith, 1962). The critical debate over Weber's thesis has been intense. For a brief account of the controversy, see Anthony Giddens' introduction to the above edition, pp. xix–xxvi.
47 Coppélia Kahn, *Man's Estate: Masculine Identity in Shakespeare* (Berkeley: University of California Press, 1981), p. 172.
48 According to *The London Stage, 1660–1800*, ed. William Van Lennep et al., 5 parts (Carbondale: Southern Illinois University Press, 1965–1968), between 1700 and 1758 *The London Cuckolds* was performed on Lord Mayor's day (October 29 Old Style; November 9 New Style) a total of 37 times at Drury Lane, Lincoln's Inn Fields, and Covent Garden. During the 1748, 1749, and 1750 seasons, it was performed simultaneously at Drury Lane and Covent Garden, Drury Lane finally breaking the tradition in 1751 to put on *Eastward Hoe*. I am indebted to Howard Weinbrot for bringing Ravenscroft's play to my attention.
49 See Henry A. Harben, *A Dictionary of London* (London: Herbert Jenkins, 1918), pp. 189, 561.

5   THE OBJECTS OF FARCE

1 Georg Simmel, *The Philosophy of Money*, trans. Tom Bottomore and David Frisby (Boston: Routledge & Kegan Paul, 1978), p. 331.
2 Stanley Cavell, *Pursuits of Happiness: The Hollywood Comedy of Remarriage* (Cambridge, Mass.: Harvard University Press, 1981), p. 118.
3 Jiří Veltruský, "Man and Object in the Theater," pp. 83–91 in *A Prague School*

Reader on Esthetics, Literary Structure, and Style, trans. and ed. Paul L. Garvin (Washington: Georgetown University Press, 1964), p. 90.

4 C. B. Macpherson, "Capitalism and the Changing Concept of Property," in *Feudalism, Capitalism and Beyond*, ed. Eugene Kamenka and R. S. Neale (London: Edward Arnold, 1975): 105–06. See also Macpherson's highly influential study, *The Political Theory of Possessive Individualism: Hobbes to Locke* (Oxford: Oxford University Press, 1962).

5 Jean Baudrillard's suggestion that "Tous les objects ... se font femme pour etre achetes" ("All objects are made women in order to be bought") might be employed here as a starting position from which to understand the gender politics of objectification in nascent capitalism. *Le Système Des Objets* (Paris: Gallimard, 1968), p. 98. (For this reference, and other extremely useful observations, I am indebted to Karen Newman's insightful treatment of commodification in early modern London, "City Talk: Women and Commodification in Jonson's *Epicoene*," *ELH* 56 (1989): 503–18.) Indeed, I hope it will become apparent from the following remarks that the commercial inscription of subjectivity in the early modern theater – a process that tended to foreground the divisions of the gender system even as it worked to dissolve the fabricated boundaries between subject and object – anticipated in many ways what we consider to be quintessentially modern phenomena, activities associated with Baudrillard's "publicité" – that is, advertising.

6 Barbara Freedman, "Errors in Comedy: A Psychoanalytic Theory of Farce," in *Shakespearean Comedy*, ed. Maurice Charney (New York: New York Literary Forum, 1980), p. 235. Freedman has revised and extended some of the ideas advanced in this essay in "Reading Errantly: Misrecognition and the Uncanny in *The Comedy of Errors*," a provocative chapter of her study, *Staging the Gaze: Postmodernism, Psychoanalysis, and Shakespearean Comedy* (Ithaca: Cornell University Press, 1991): 78–113.

7 Albert Bermel, *Farce: A History from Aristophanes to Woody Allen* (New York: Simon and Schuster, 1982), pp. 14, 22.

8 Bermel, *Farce*, p. 25.

9 Bermel, *Farce*, pp. 27, 28.

10 Bermel, *Farce*, p. 29.

11 Henri Bergson, "Laughter" in *Comedy*, ed. Wylie Sypher (Garden City, New York: Doubleday, 1956), p. 84.

12 Bergson, "Laughter," p. 79.

13 Stanley Cavell, *In Quest of the Ordinary: Lines of Skepticism and Romanticism* (Chicago: University of Chicago Press, 1988), p. 155. See also Marjorie Garber's observation on Freud's denial of the uncanniness of Shakespeare's ghosts: "The essay on 'The Uncanny' plays a major part in my approaches to these plays, and it is an uncanny fact that the Shakespeare plays Freud singles out – precisely to demonstrate that their ghosts are *not* uncanny – are the plays that appear in my text: *Hamlet, Macbeth, Julius Caesar*." *Shakespeare's Ghost Writers: Literature as Uncanny Causality* (New York: Methuen, 1987), p. xiv.

14 Stephen Greenblatt, "Psychoanalysis and Renaissance," in *Literary Theory/ Renaissance Texts*, ed. Patricia Parker and David Quint (Baltimore: Johns Hopkins University Press, 1986), p. 220.

15 Simmel, *The Philosophy of Money*, p. 321.

16 Sigmund Freud, *Beyond the Pleasure Principle*, trans. James Strachey (New York: Norton, 1961), p. 8.
17 Freud, "Pleasure Principle," p. 9.
18 Freud, "Pleasure Principle," p. 10.
19 "In order to gain and to hold the esteem of men it is not sufficient merely to possess wealth or power. The wealth or power must be put in evidence, for esteem is awarded only on evidence." Thorstein Veblen, *The Theory of the Leisure Class* (1899; New York: Mentor, 1953), p. 42.
20 Guy Debord, *Society of the Spectacle* (Detroit: Black & Red, 1983), no. 17.
21 D. W. Winnicott, "The Use of an Object and Relating through Identifications," pp. 86–94 in *Playing and Reality* (New York: Basic Books, 1971), p. 91. See also "Transitional Objects and Transitional Phenomena," pp. 1–25 in the same volume.
22 Winnicott, "The Use of an Object," pp. 89–90.
23 Joel Fineman, *Shakespeare's Perjured Eye: The Invention of Poetic Subjectivity in the Sonnets* (Berkeley: University of California Press, 1986); Anne Ferry, *The "Inward" Language: Sonnets of Wyatt, Sidney, Shakespeare, Donne* (Chicago: University of Chicago Press, 1983); Jonathan Dollimore, *Radical Tragedy* (Chicago: University of Chicago Press, 1984); Stephen Greenblatt, *Renaissance Self-Fashioning* (Chicago: University of Chicago Press, 1980); Catherine Belsey, *The Subject of Tragedy: Identity and Difference in Renaissance Drama* (New York: Methuen, 1985). The *locus classicus* for discussion of the self's 'origination' in the Renaissance is, of course, Jacob Burckhardt's *The Civilization of the Renaissance in Italy* (originally published, 1860) (New York: Harper & Row, 1958) 2 vols. See, especially, vol. 1, "The Development of the Individual" and "The Perfecting of the Individual," pp. 143–50; and vol. 2, "The Discovery of Man – Spiritual Description in Poetry" and "Biography," pp. 303–33. Useful studies of subjectivity, identity, and the self in the Renaissance include Francis Barker, *The Tremulous Private Body: Essays on Subjection* (London: Methuen, 1984); the discussion of disguise and identity in Natalie Zemon Davis, *The Return of Martin Guerre* (Cambridge, Mass.: Harvard University Press, 1983), and her essay "Boundaries and the Sense of Self in Sixteenth-Century France," pp. 53–63 in *Reconstructing Individualism: Autonomy, Individuality, and the Self in Western Thought*, ed. Thomas C. Heller et al. (Stanford: Stanford University Press, 1986). Also contained in this volume is Stephen Greenblatt's "Fiction and Friction," pp. 30–52. A foundational essay (one important to Greenblatt's theory of "self-fashioning") is Thomas Greene's "The Flexibility of the Self in Renaissance Literature," pp. 241–64 in *The Disciplines of Criticism: Essays in Literary Theory, Interpretation, and History*, ed. Peter Demetz et al. (New Haven: Yale University Press, 1968). A. Bartlett Giamatti's "Proteus Unbound: Some Versions of the Sea God in the Renaissance," also in this volume (pp. 437–76), addresses the anxieties connected with self-mutability in Renaissance Humanism. See also William Kerrigan, "The Articulation of the Ego in the English Renaissance," pp. 261–308 in *The Literary Freud: Mechanisms of Defense and the Poetic Will*, ed. Joseph H. Smith (New Haven: Yale University Press, 1980); Linda Charnes, " 'So Unsecret to Ourselves': Notorious Identity and the Material Subject in Shakespeare's *Troilus and Cressida*", *Shakespeare*

Quarterly 40 (1989): 413–40; and Katharine Eisaman Maus, "Proof and Consequences: Inwardness and Its Exposure in the English Renaissance," *Representations* 34 (1991), pp. 29–52.

24 Werner Jaeger, *Paideia: The Ideas of Greek Culture*, 3 vols., trans. Gilbert Highet (Oxford: Basil Blackwell, 1939–1945), vol. 1, p. 350.

25 A cautionary note relating to current critical discourse of subjectivity in the Renaissance has been sounded by Lee Patterson, who, in an article entitled "On the Margin: Postmodernism, Ironic History, and Medieval Studies," argues against the way "the program of Renaissance humanism continues to control the writing of the cultural past." *Speculum* 65 (1990): 87–108. Ironically, Patterson's claim here begs the very question he would avoid.

26 On the importance of the individual to the Protestant project, see Barbara K. Lewalski, *Protestant Poetics and the Seventeenth-Century Religious Lyric* (Princeton: Princeton University Press, 1979).

27 Richard Marienstras, "*Jack Juggler*: Aspects de la conscience individuelle dans une farce du 16ᵉ siecle," *Etudes Anglaises* 16 (1963): 329.

28 *Jack Juggler*, in *Four Tudor Comedies*, ed. William Tydeman (Harmondsworth, Middlesex: Penguin, 1984). The number given in parenthesis is the line number.

29 This confusion anticipates that of Richard III, who has a similar lament during his mental agitation the night before Bosworth Field: "What do I fear? Myself? There's none else by. / Richard loves Richard, that is, I am I" (5.3.182–83).

30 B. J. Whiting, *Proverbs in the Earlier English Drama*, Harvard Studies in Comparative Literature 14 (Cambridge, Mass.: Harvard University Press, 1938), p. 201. Why it should surprise anyone with "fascinated horror" I leave the reader to determine.

31 Marie Axton, ed. *Three Tudor Classical Interludes* (Cambridge: D. S. Brewer, 1982), p. 20.

32 See David Bevington, *Tudor Drama and Politics* (Cambridge, Mass.: Harvard University Press, 1968), p. 126.

33 On the debate over transubstantiation in the sixteenth century, see Jaroslav Pelikan, *Reformation of Church and Dogma* (Chicago: University of Chicago Press, 1983); in *Eucharistic Presence and Conversion in Late Thirteenth-Century Franciscan Thought* (Philadelphia: American Philosophical Society, 1984), David Burr provides a useful background of doctrinal conceptions of transubstantiation in the medieval period until 1500.

34 Charles H. George and Katherine George, *The Protestant Mind of the English Reformation, 1570–1640* (Princeton: Princeton University Press, 1961), p. 348.

35 George and George, *The Protestant Mind*, p. 348.

36 James C. Bryant, *Tudor Drama and Religious Controversy* (Macon, Georgia: Mercer University Press, 1984), p. 111. Bryant quotes *The Conflict of Conscience* in the course of his remarks on the Tudor debate over the doctrine of Transubstantiation, pp. 107–11.

37 Quoted in Robert Weimann, "Discourse, Ideology and the Crisis of Authority in post-Reformation England," *REAL: The Yearbook of Research in English and American Literature* 5 (1987): 109–40; p. 121.

38 Karl Marx, *Capital* (New York: International, 1967) vol. 1, p. 105.

39 Gail Kern Paster, *The Idea of the City in the Age of Shakespeare* (Athens: University of Georgia Press, 1985), p. 178.

40 Paster, *Idea of the City*, p. 179.

41 Freedman, "Errors in Comedy," p. 241.

42 Freedman, "Errors in Comedy," p. 242.

43 Richard Henze, "*The Comedy of Errors*: A Freely Binding Chain," *Shakespeare Quarterly* 22 (1971): 40.

44 Relayed in conversation.

45 R. H. Tawney, introduction to Thomas Wilson's *A Discourse Upon Usury* (London: G. Bell and Sons, 1925), ed. R. H. Tawney.

46 David Scott Kastan, "Workshop and/as Playhouse: Comedy and Commerce in *The Shoemaker's Holiday*," *Studies in Philology* 84 (1987): 324–37; p. 325.

47 Kastan, "Workshop," p. 325.

48 Kastan, "Workshop," p. 326.

49 Thomas Dekker, *The Shoemakers' Holiday*, ed. D. J. Palmer (New York: W. W. Norton, 1975). All quotations from the play are taken from this edition.

50 Emile Durkheim, *The Division of Labor in Society* (New York: Free Press, 1984), p. 123.

51 Wedding rings were often inscribed with a motto, of course, but by its size and location (on the inside, away from view) such a motto seems inherently less social than letters on a shoe.

52 Terence Eagleton, "Language and Reality in 'Twelfth Night'," *Critical Quarterly* 9 (1967): 221, n. 1.

53 Susan Stewart and Patricia Fumerton have each discussed the interrelation of token and self in the Elizabethan ornamental miniature, Fumerton drawing connections between the "problems of self and self expression" and the display of these objects throughout the sixteenth century. But if the English court had for some time employed the miniature as a way of understanding political and personal identity, it was not until the late 1590s, I would argue, that these problems became a concern of the popular and private drama. Patricia Fumerton, "'Secret' Arts: Elizabethan Miniatures and Sonnets," in *Representing the English Renaissance*, ed. Stephen Greenblatt (Berkeley: University of California Press, 1988): 95. Susan Stewart, *On Longing: Narratives of the Miniature, the Gigantic, the Souvenir, the Collection* (Baltimore: Johns Hopkins University Press, 1984).

6   THE FARCE OF OBJECTS

1 Thomas Rymer, "A Short View of Tragedy," in *The Critical Works of Thomas Rymer*, ed. Curt A. Zimansky (New Haven: Yale University Press, 1956), pp. 163, 164.

2 Rymer, "Short View," p. 160.

3 Rymer, "Short View," p. 160.

4 Rymer, "Short View," p. 132.

5 Rymer, "Short View," p. 162.

6 See, for example, Lynda Boose, "Othello's Handkerchief: The Recognizance and Pledge of Love," *English Literary Renaissance* 5 (1975): 360–74.

7 Edward Snow, "Sexual Anxiety and the Male Order of Things in *Othello*," *English Literary Renaissance* 10 (1980), p. 392, n. 11.

8 Karen Newman, "'And wash the Ethiop white': Femininity and the Monstrous in *Othello*," in *Shakespeare Reproduced: The Text in History and Ideology*, ed. Jean E. Howard and Marion F. O'Connor (New York: Methuen, 1987), p. 156.

9 See the gloss in *The Riverside Shakespeare*.

10 Newman, "'Ethiop white'," p. 155.

11 John Gay, *The Beggar's Opera*, ed. Bryan Loughrey and T. O. Treadwell (New York: Viking Penguin, 1986), 1.4, p. 50.

12 The *locus classicus* for discussion of property in *Othello* is Kenneth Burke, *A Grammar of Motives* (Berkeley: University of California Press, 1969), p. 414.

13 See James T. Henke, *Courtesans and Cuckolds: A Glossary of Renaissance Dramatic Bawdy* (New York: Garland, 1979), p.304; Eric Partridge, *Shakespeare's Bawdy* (New York: E. P. Dutton, 1948), p. 223.

14 One might witness Cassio's "What do you mean by this haunting of me" immediately before this speech, where it concerns Cassio's mind-set as well as Othello's. For manifestations of the uncanny in Shakespeare's tragedies, see Marjorie Garber, *Shakespeare's Ghost Writers: Literature as Uncanny Causality* (New York: Methuen, 1987).

15 George Steevens, quoted in note to 5.2.269 in The New Variorum *Othello*, ed. H. H. Furness (New York: American Scholar, 1965).

16 Frederick Engels in *The Origin of the Family, Private Property and the State* (New York: International Publishers, 1968); Homer from Richmond Lattimore's translation of the *Odyssey* (New York: Harper & Row, 1967), Book 21, lines 350–53.

17 John Florio, *Second Frutes* (1591) (Gainesville: Scholars' Facsimilies, 1953), p. 143.

18 Partridge, *Shakespeare's Bawdy*, p. 187.

19 Cyril Tourneur [Thomas Middleton], *The Revenger's Tragedy*, ed. R. A. Foakes (Manchester: Manchester University Press, 1986), 2.2.144–45.

20 Henke, *Courtesans and Cuckolds* , p. 250.

21 Here I am indebted to the formulations of "triangular" and "mimetic" desire offered by René Girard in, respectively, *Deceit, Desire and the Novel* (Baltimore: Johns Hopkins University Press, 1965), pp. 5–16, and "The Politics of Desire in *Troilus and Cressida*," pp. 188–209 in *Shakespeare and The Question of Theory*, ed. Patricia Parker and Geoffrey Hartman (New York: Methuen, 1985).

22 Edward Sharpham, *Cupid's Whirligig*, ed. Allardyce Nicoll (Waltham Saint Lawrence: Golden Cockerel Press, 1926), p. 41.

23 See Shell, *Money, Language, and Thought* , pp. 61–63.

24 John Marston, *The Dutch Courtesan*, ed. M. L. Wine (Lincoln: University of Nebraska Press, 1965), p. 3.

25 It is relevant here to compare Mulligrub's anxiety over his bowls – and the way the wags play on his uncertainty – with the score of Tudor proclamations against the exportation of certain commodities (e.g., grain, ordnance, coal, gold and silver, coin) and for preserving the integrity of the coinage. The

"Warning against Foreign Debasement of English Coin" (1587), for example, speaks of gold

> by the sinister and unlawful dealings of wicked persons not only carried out of our realm to foreign countries, and there by divers means diminished of their value and from thence returned hither and paid in lieu of lawful coin for the commodities of our countries, and some other of them embased by clipping, soldering, and other unlawful practices of their due fines, so that both the one sort and the other (by means aforesaid) are brought much inferior to their first true value and goodness; and beside that, many false pieces be counterfeited in foreign parts of the said coins, whereby great and intolerable loss and diminution of the riches of our realm doth daily grow and increase.

From *Tudor Royal Proclamations*, ed. Paul L. Hughes and James F. Larkin, 3 vols. (New Haven: Yale University Press, 1964–69), vol. 2, p. 539.

26 Randle Cotgrave, *A Dictionarie of the French and English Tongues* (1611) (Columbia: University of South Carolina Press, 1950).

27 Thomas Nashe, *Pierce Peniless*, in *The Works of Thomas Nashe*, ed. Ronald B. McKerrow, 5 vols. (London: A. H. Bullen, 1904–1910), vol. 1, pp. 173–74.

28 In relation to the present argument, it seems significant that the title character of Graham Greene's *The Third Man*, a black market adulterator of penicillin (and hence a murderer, for the diluted medicine causes irreversible complications in patients, instead of curing them) is named Harry Lime.

29 MacDonald P. Jackson and Michael Neill, eds., *The Selected Plays of John Marston* (Cambridge: University Press, 1986), note to 2.3.11–12.

30 See the fifteenth tale in *Merry Tales Made by Master Skelton*, in P. M. Zall, ed., *A Hundred Merry Tales, And Other Jestbooks of the Fifteenth and Sixteenth Centuries* (Lincoln: University of Nebraska Press, 1963), pp. 347–48. Skelton concludes: "For through such uses and brewing of wine may men be deceived, and be hurt by drinking of such evil wine" (p. 348).

31 Here I depart strongly from Robert Watson's otherwise persuasive reading of *Bartholomew Fair*: where Watson sees a "generosity in *Bartholomew Fair* toward objects in general, and the specific acceptance of human digestive processes" which shows a "significant deviation from [the] miserly and punitive pattern" of earlier comedies that Edmund Wilson described, in *The Triple Thinkers*, as "anal erotic," I see a Jonson still possessed, in 1614, by the anti-commercial, satiric vision of the *Every Man* plays and *The Alchemist*. Robert Watson, *Ben Jonson's Parodic Strategy: Literary Imperialism in the Comedies* (Cambridge, Mass.: Harvard University Press, 1987), note 1, p. 251. Edmund Wilson's "Morose Ben Jonson" can be found in *The Triple Thinkers and The Wound and the Bow* (Boston: Northeastern University Press, 1984), pp. 213–32.

32 Ben Jonson, *Bartholomew Fair*, ed. G. R. Hibbard (London: Ernest Benn, 1977), 155–59.

33 *Minor Prose Works of King James VI and I*, ed. James Craigie (Edinburgh: Scottish Text Society, 1982), pp. 83–99.

34 Craigie, ed., *Minor Prose*, p. 85.

35 Craigie, ed., *Minor Prose*, pp. 98–99.

36 See Schmidt's *Lexicon*.

37 Peter Stallybrass and Allon White, *The Politics and Poetics of Transgression* (Ithaca: Cornell University Press, 1986), p. 65. A study which has been

influential to my understanding of the Jacobean purity discourse is Mary Douglas's *Purity and Danger: An Analysis of the Concepts of Pollution and Taboo* (1966; New York: Routledge & Kegan Paul, 1988).

38 A rough count of "tobacco" in all its forms in Crawford's concordance to the 1616 Folio of Jonson's works – which does not include, of course, *Bartholomew Fair* – reveals something close to 60 occasions of use. Charles Crawford, *A Complete Concordance to the 1616 Folio of Ben Jonson's Works*, 5 vols. (Microfilm; Ann Arbor: University of Michigan, Library Photoduplication Service). On tobacco in Renaissance England generally, see Jeffrey Knapp, "Elizabethan Tobacco," *Representations* 21 (1988), pp. 26–66.

7 "THE ALTERATION OF MEN"

1 All references to *Troilus and Cressida* are to the New Arden edition, ed. Kenneth Palmer (New York: Methuen, 1982). I should note here that this essay develops some of Raymond Southall's suggestions in "*Troilus and Cressida* and the Spirit of Capitalism," printed in *Shakespeare in a Changing World*, ed. Arnold Kettle (New York: International, 1964), pp. 217–232.

2 Robert Kimbrough, *Shakespeare's "Troilus and Cressida" and its Setting* (Cambridge, Mass.: Harvard University Press, 1964), p. 26. See also John S. P. Tatlock, "The Siege of Troy in Elizabethan Literature, Especially in Shakespeare and Heywood," *Publications of the Modern Language Association* 30 (1915): 673–770. The importance of the turn of the century to the growing anxiety over London and England's future is difficult to overestimate. On eschatology and literature, my argument has benefitted from Frank Kermode's *The Sense of an Ending* (Oxford: Oxford University Press, 1966).

3 Marc Shell, *Money, Language, and Thought* (Berkeley: University of California Press), pp. 47–83, discusses "verbal usury," as well as the effects of commerce generally, in *The Merchant of Venice*. He refers (p. 50, n. 12) to Pompey's statement in *Measure for Measure*: "'Twas never merry world since, of two usuries, the merriest [sexual] was put down, and the worser [monetary] allowed by order of law" (3.2.5–7, Shell's brackets). I would argue that *Troilus and Cressida* protests not their ranking, but rather their conflation.

4 Of course Troy has always conjured up visions of wealth: see, for only one example, Euripides' *Trojan Women* (568ff.) and its picture of Achilles' chariot heaped with the booty of war from the ruined city.

5 George Peele, "The Tale of Troy," *The Life and Works of George Peele*, 3 vols., ed. Charles Prouty (New Haven: Yale University Press, 1952), vol. 1, pp. 229–230.

6 T. J. B. Spencer, "'Greeks' and 'Merrygreeks': A Background to *Timon of Athens* and *Troilus and Cressida*," in *Essays on Shakespeare and Elizabethan Drama in Honor of Hardin Craig*, ed. Richard Hosley (Columbia: University of Missouri Press, 1962), p. 231.

7 So Gary Taylor glosses Pistol's insult to Fluellen in his edition of *Henry V* (Oxford: Clarendon Press, 1982) (5.1.17;28).

8 Quoted from the Johnson-Steevens Variorum edition (London: 1778).

9 Thomas Nashe, *The Unfortunate Traveller* (vol. 2, p. 220), and the "Epistle Dedicatory" to *Have With You to Saffron-Walden*, in *The Works of Thomas*

Nashe, 5 vols., ed. Ronald B. McKerrow (London: A.H. Bullen, 1904–1910), vol. 3, p. 11.
10 Quoted in Chambers, vol. 4, p. 19.
11 Thomas Middleton, *The Old Law*, in A. H. Bullen, ed. *The Works of Thomas Middleton*, 8 vols. (Boston: Houghton Mifflin, 1885), vol. 2, 4.1 (p. 198).
12 Thomas Heywood, *The Dramatic Works*, 2.1 (pp. 113–114).
13 See, for example, René Girard, "The Politics of Desire in *Troilus and Cressida*," in Patricia Parker and Geoffrey Hartman, eds. *Shakespeare and the Question of Theory* (New York: Methuen, 1985), pp. 188–209; Gayle Greene, "Language and Value in Shakespeare's *Troilus and Cressida*," *Studies in English Literature* 21 (1981): 271–85. Among the recent readings I have found valuable are those of Jonathan Dollimore in *Radical Tragedy* (Chicago: University of Chicago Press, 1984), pp. 40–45; Thomas G. West, "The Two Truths of *Troilus and Cressida*," in *Shakespeare as Political Thinker*, John Alvis and Thomas G. West, eds. (Durham: Carolina Academic Press, 1981), pp. 127–43; and Northrop Frye, "The Reversal of Reality" in his *The Myth of Deliverance: Reflections on Shakespeare's Problem Comedies* (Toronto: University of Toronto Press, 1983).
   Many of the studies which have stressed the play's connections with London and Elizabethan society have tended to argue for a more limited range of social concerns. William Poel, famous for his efforts in reviving Elizabethan drama, felt *Troilus and Cressida* to be "Shakespeare's travesty of the Iliad story, as he wrote it in answer to Chapman's absurd claim for the sanctity of Homer's characters," and suggested it is intimately connected to factionalism in Elizabeth's court and government, and to Essex's problems in particular (*Shakespeare in the Theatre* (London: Sidgwick and Jackson, 1913), pp. 106–12). Peter Alexander's argument, still holding a great deal of critical currency, portrays *Troilus and Cressida* as a coterie play designed for Inns of Court performance: "*Troilus and Cressida*, 1609," *Library* 4th series, 9 (1928): 267–86. Tucker Brooke, in "Shakespeare's Study in Culture and Anarchy," *The Yale Review* 17 (1928): 571–77, noted that the First World War had prompted the renewal not only of Shakespeare's bitter comedies generally, but *Troilus and Cressida* in particular. Brooke, in a casual remark very significant to my argument, related: "I cannot help imagining that [Shakespeare] is, however subconsciously, anatomizing the England of the dying Elizabeth: within the wall the febrile Essex type of decadent chivalry; without, the strident go-getters of the newer dispensation: Cecil-Ulysses and Ralegh-Diomed" (p. 576). Brooke, however, goes on to make the leap that so many have made, reading Shakespeare's play as prophecy: "I take it that Shakespeare glimpsed somehow the seriousness of the cleavage between Cavalier and Puritan, sensed in Thersites the lowering shadow of Prynne and the iconclasts" (p. 576). More recent attempts to place *Troilus and Cressida* in one milieu or another can be seen in Abbie Potts, "*Cynthia's Revels, Poetaster*, and *Troilus and Cressida*," *Shakespeare Quarterly* 5 (1954): 297–302, and John Enck, "The Peace of the Poetomachia," *Publications of the Modern Language Association* 77 (1962): 386–96.
14 Eric S. Mallin, *The End of Troy: Elizabethan Dissolution in Shakespeare's Troilus and Cressida* (Ann Arbor: University Microfilms, 1986). See also

Mallin in "Emulous Factions and the Collapse of Chivalry: *Troilus and Cressida*," *Representations* 29 (1990): 145–79.

15 Jeanne Newlin, "The Modernity of *Troilus and Cressida*: The Case for Theatrical Criticism," *Harvard Library Bulletin* 17 (1969): 353–373. Newlin points out that the play received its first major, modern production at the hands of Poel in December of 1912, catching, in her words, "the apprehension of England's intellectuals before World War I" (p. 362); was put on at Cambridge in 1922, reflecting "the weariness of all of Europe" in its war satire; was revived again in Westminster, 1938, "as an anti-war play" (p. 364) – Newlin's second plate of which reveals Michael MacOwan's Cowardesque set and costumes – that, significantly, "there were no productions of *Troilus* in Britain from 1939 through 1945" (p. 365); that, in 1961, "to celebrate the Centennial of the American Civil War, the play was staged and costumed in that period. Priam became 'a whiskery and indecisive Lee.' His opponent, Agamemnon, was made into a cigar-smoking Grant. Cressida, of course, evolved as a Southern belle ... Troilus a young, foolishly idealistic Confederate officer" (p. 369). I quote at such length here only to indicate the sheer malleability of the Troy story, and that versions of what I suggest Shakespeare did with *Troilus and Cressida* have been repeated throughout the twentieth century.

16 T. J. Stafford, "Mercantile Imagery in *Troilus and Cressida*," in Stafford, ed., *Shakespeare in the Southwest: Some New Directions* (El Paso: Texas Western Press, 1969), p. 42.

17 Douglas B. Wilson, "The Commerce of Desire: Freudian Narcissism in Chaucer's *Troilus and Criseyde* and Shakespeare's *Troilus and Cressida*," *English Language Notes* 21 (1983): 15.

18 Sandra K. Fischer, *Econolingua: A Glossary of Coins and Economic Language in Renaissance Drama* (Newark: University of Delaware Press, 1985) p. 29. Her first tier of plays in which economics play a primary role is comprised of *The Comedy of Errors*, *The Merchant of Venice*, and *Timon of Athens*.

19 C. C. Barfoot, "*Troilus and Cressida*: 'Praise us as we are tasted'," *Shakespeare Quarterly* 39 (1988): 46.

20 "Bark" in Troilus' passage does not necessarily mean small ship, as many editors tend to assume. In *King Lear* – "yond tall anchoring bark" (4.6.18) – and *Othello*, where Cassio calls Othello's "bark" (2.1.48) a "tall ship" (2.1.79), the term refers to larger ships. K. R. Andrews, in *English Privateering Voyages to the West Indies, 1588–95* (Hakluyt Society, second series, no. 111, 1956), points out that "The most common type of English privateer in the Spanish war was the ordinary merchantman of some fifty to a hundred tons burden, commonly referred to as a 'bark'," p. 21.

21 Text and translation in *Petrarch's Lyric Poems*, ed. Robert M. Durling (Cambridge, Mass.: Harvard University Press, 1976), number 323.

22 Drayton from J. William Hebel, ed. *The Works of Michael Drayton*, 5 vols. (Oxford: Shakespeare Head Press, 1932), vol 2. Donne from Elegy 19, "To his Mistress Going to Bed," in A. J. Smith, ed. *John Donne: The Complete English Poems* (New York: Penguin, 1971). See also Elegy 18, "Love's Progress," and Shakespeare's *Sonnets*, *passim*. Sidney and Daniel seem to resist the *ricca merce* conceit.

23 Edmund Spenser, *Amoretti* 81, 5–6. See also numbers 15, 76.

24 See *The Taming of the Shrew* 1.2.64–75; *The Merchant of Venice* 1.1.161–176 (Bassanio is compared – by himself and Gratiano, respectively – to Jason at 1.1.172 and 3.2.241); *The Merry Wives of Windsor* 3.4.10, 12–14.

25 Of probable significance here are the idolatry references in play at 2.2.56, 2.3.189 and 5.1.7.

26 See, for example, Chrysalus in *Bacchides*: "*ego sum Ulixes, cuius consilio haec gerunt*" – "I am Ulysses, whose plans direct everything" (940); and Pseudolus: "*Viso quid rerum meus Ulixes egerit*" – "Now I'll see what my Ulysses has pulled off" (1063–64). Menaechmus of Epidamnus also refers to his slave as "*meus Ulysses*" – "my Ulysses." *Comoediae*, Oxford Classical Texts (Oxford: Oxford University Press, 1980), 2 vols. Translations by author.

27 *Epistulae ad Familiares*, 10.13.2: "*Itaque Homerus non Aiacem, nec Achillem, sed Ulixem appellavit ptoliporthon.*"

28 Wolfgang Clemen, *The Development of Shakespeare's Imagery* (Cambridge, Mass.: Harvard University Press, 1951), p. 102. Immediately following this observation Clemen goes on to quote from *Troilus and Cressida* to support his point.

29 William Empson, *Some Versions of Pastoral* (Edinburgh: Edinburgh University Press, 1935), p. 35.

30 Peele, *Life and Works*, vol. 2.

31 Thomas Hughes, *The Misfortunes of Arthur*, ed. Harvey Carson Grumbine (Berlin: 1900).

32 From Lawrence Manley, ed., *London in the Age of Shakespeare: An Anthology* (London: Croom Helm, 1986), p. 53.

33 Manley, *London in the Age*, p. 56.

34 John Speed, *The Historie of Great Britaine* (second edition) (London: 1623). I am grateful to Michael Dobson for bringing this to my attention.

35 Dekker in E. D. Pendry, ed., *Thomas Dekker*, The Stratford-upon-Avon Library 4 (Cambridge, Mass.: Harvard University Press, 1968), pp. 46–47.

36 Pendry, ed., *Thomas Dekker*, p. 42.

37 Pendry, ed., *Thomas Dekker*, p. 41.

38 Pendry, ed., *Thomas Dekker*, p. 41.

39 Thomas Nashe, *Pierce Peniless*, in McKerrow, ed., *Works*, vol. 1, p. 181.

40 See, for example, Hypsipyle – the queen of Lemnos, betrothed to and abandoned by Jason – in Ovid's *Heroides* (6.47–48) and the beginning complaints in Euripides' *Medea* and Seneca's *Medea*.

41 Cicero, *The Republic*, trans. Clinton Walker Keyes in the Loeb Classical Library (Cambridge, Mass.: Harvard University Press, 1951), 2.4.8.

42 Eclogue 4, 31–36. *Virgil*, the Loeb Classical Library, 2 vols., revised; trans. H. Rushton Fairclough (Cambridge, Mass.: Harvard University Press, 1978), vol. 1.

43 William Arrowsmith, ed., *Three Comedies by Aristophanes* (Ann Arbor: Michigan University Press, 1969), p. 3.

44 Henry George Liddell and Robert Scott, *Greek-English Lexicon* (New York: Harper & Brothers, 1869).

45 Appian, *An Auncient History and Exquisite Chronicle of the Romanes Warres, both Civile and Foren*, (London: 1578).

46 Thomas Heywood, *Troia Britanica: or, Great Britaines Troy* (London: 1609;

facsimile, New York: Georg Olms Verlag, 1971). I am in debt to G. Blakemore Evans for the gift of his copy.

47 Samuel Daniel, *The Civil Wars*, ed. Laurence Michel (New Haven: Yale University Press, 1958), 5.4–5. In the 1595 edition, the material of Book 5 is contained in Book 4.

48 George Chapman, *Chapman's Homer*, ed. Allardyce Nicoll, 2 vols. (New York: Pantheon Books, 1956), vol. 1, p. 503, title; p. 504, lines 60–61.

49 James C. Bulman, "*Coriolanus* and the Matter of Troy," in J. C. Gray, ed., *Mirror up to Shakespeare: Essays in Honour of G. R. Hibbard* (Toronto: University of Toronto Press, 1984), p. 243.

50 See, for example, the early remarks of Arthur Acheson in *Shakespeare and the Rival Poet* (New York: John Lane, 1903), pp. 167–206; G. B. Harrison, *Shakespeare at Work, 1592–1603* (London: Routledge & Sons, 1933), pp. 218–228; and Geoffrey Bullough, *Narrative and Dramatic Sources of Shakespeare*, 8 vols. (New York: Columbia University Press, 1957–1975), vol. 6, pp. 87–88.

51 John Channing Briggs, "Chapman's *Seaven Bookes of the Iliades*: Mirror for Essex," *Studies in English Literature* 21 (1981): 61.

52 Briggs, "Chapman's *Seaven Bookes*," p. 73. But Henry M. Weidner, in "Homer and the Fallen World: Focus of Satire in George Chapman's *The Widow's Tears*," *Journal of English and Germanic Philology* 62 (1963): 518–32, argues that Chapman's enthusiasm waned: "In the early 1600's Chapman's embattled Homeric idealism finds outlet in a vicious satire on the wrongheaded dualism of good and evil espoused by misbegotten, often hypocritical absolutists" (p. 522).

53 Quoted in D. M. Palliser, *The Age of Elizabeth: England under the Later Tudors 1547–1603* (New York: Longman, 1983), p. 147.

54 R. B. Wernham, "Elizabethan War Aims and Strategy," in S. T. Bindoff, ed., *Elizabethan Government and Society* (London: Athlone Press, 1961), p. 357.

55 K. R. Andrews, *Elizabethan Privateering* (Cambridge: Cambridge University Press, 1976), p. 223. See p. 73 and n. 1, for further discussion of the *Madre de Dios* incident.

56 Michael Howard, *War in European History* (Oxford: Oxford University Press, 1976), p. 41.

57 Howard, *War in European History*, p. 38.

58 Quoted in Howard, *War in European History*, p. 45.

59 See Felix Schelling, *Elizabethan Drama, 1558–1642*, 2 vols. (Boston: Houghton, Mifflin, 1908), vol. 1, p. 429. This period also saw a theatrical interest in classic plots. G. B. Harrison points out that, in an eighteen-month period around 1601 "the Admiral's men alone had produced *Brute*, *Troy's Revenge*, *Agamemnon*, *Orestes' Furies*, and a version of *Troilus and Cressida* by Dekker and Chettle." Harrison, *Shakespeare at Work*, p. 219.

60 K. R. Andrews, *English Privateering Voyages*, p. 21. See pp. 1–21 for his remarks on the structure and importance of privateering in this period of English history.

61 See C. L'Estrange Ewen, *Lording Barry, Poet and Pirate* (London: Private printing, 1938).

62 Printed in Henry Gee, ed., *The Elizabethan Prayer-Book and Ornaments* (London: Macmillan, 1902), Appendix 3, p. 210.

63 T[homas] M[un], *A Discourse of Trade, From England unto the East Indies* (London: 1621; New York: Facsimile Text Society, 1930).

64 M[un], *Discourse*, p. 29.

65 Robert Wilson, *The Three Ladies of London*, in *A Select Collection of Old English Plays* (Robert Dodsley, 1744, 4th edition; W. Carew Hazlitt; reprinted New York: Benjamin Blom, 1964), pp. 275–276.

66 Girard, "Politics of Desire," pp. 188–209.

67 Girard, "Politics of Desire," p. 200.

68 See Ovid, *Metamorphoses*, 13.200ff.; Aeschylus, fragment 135 (Nauck) [64, Loeb]; Servius, *Commentary*, Book 1, line 474.

69 Vergil, *Aeneid*, trans. W. F. Jackson Knight (New York: Penguin, 1958), 2. 163–168.

70 See Coppélia Kahn's "The Rape in Shakespeare's *Lucrece*," *Shakespeare Survey* 9 (1976): 45–72. In "'Born of Woman': Fantasies of Maternal Power in *Macbeth*," *Cannibals, Witches, and Divorce: Estranging the Renaissance*, ed. Marjorie Garber (Baltimore: Johns Hopkins University Press, 1986), pp. 90–121, Janet Adelman argues for a feminine portrayal of Duncan, pointing out that Macbeth describes himself as Tarquin before he enters Duncan's chamber and thus emphasizes the political and sexual conflation of the approaching *raptus*.

71 Heywood, *The Dramatic Works* , vol. 3., 5.1. (p. 340).

72 W. H. D. Rouse, ed., *Shakespeare's Ovid, Being Arthur Golding's Translation of the Metamorphoses* (Carbondale: Southern Illinois University Press, 1961), Book 11, lines 232–233.

73 Quoted by Appian in his *Punica*, 132. The quotation within the quotation is from the *Iliad*, 6.448–449.

74 Karl Marx, *A Contribution to the Critique of Political Economy* (New York: International Publishers, 1970), p. 216.

75 G. Wilson Knight, "Shakespeare on the Gold Standard," *Shakespearean Dimensions* (Totowa, New Jersey: Barnes & Noble, 1984), p. 68. First published in *Saturday Night* (Toronto), February 17, 1940.

Bibliography

Acheson, Arthur. *Shakespeare and the Rival Poet*. New York: John Lane, 1903.

Adams, Robert. "The Concept of Debt in *The Shipman's Tale*." *Studies in the Age of Chaucer* 6 (1984): 85–102.

Adelman, Janet. "'Born of Woman': Fantasies of Maternal Power in *Macbeth*." In Marjorie Garber, ed. *Cannibals, Witches, and Divorce: Estranging the Renaissance*. Baltimore: Johns Hopkins University Press, 1986: 90–121.

Aers, David. "Rewriting the Middle Ages: Some Suggestions." *The Journal of Medieval and Renaissance Studies* 18 (1988): 221–40.

Chaucer, Langland and the Creative Imagination. London: Routledge & Kegan Paul, 1980.

Community, Gender, and Individual Identity: English Writing 1360–1430. London: Routledge, 1988.

Agnew, Jean-Christophe. *Worlds Apart: The Market and the Theater in Anglo-American Thought, 1550–1750*. New York: Cambridge University Press, 1986.

Alexander, Peter. "*Troilus and Cressida*, 1609." *Library* 4th series, 9 (1928): 267–86.

Andrews, K. R. *English Privateering Voyages to the West Indies, 1588–95*. Hakluyt Society, second series, no. 111, 1956.

Elizabethan Privateering. Cambridge: Cambridge University Press, 1976.

Appian. *An Auncient History and Exquisite Chronicle of the Romanes Warres, both Civile and Foren*. London: 1578.

Arrowsmith, William, ed. *Three Comedies by Aristophanes*. Ann Arbor: Michigan University Press, 1969.

Ashton, Robert. "Popular Entertainment and Social Control in Later Elizabethan and Early Stuart London." *London Journal* 9 (1983): 3–19.

Astington, John H. "The Red Lion Playhouse: Two Notes." *Shakespeare Quarterly* 36 (1985): 456–57.

Auden, W. H. *The Dyer's Hand, and Other Essays*. London: Faber and Faber, 1963.

Auerbach, Eric. *Literary Language and Its Public in Late Latin Antiquity and in the Middle Ages*, trans. Ralph Manheim. London: Routledge & Kegan Paul, 1965.

Mimesis: The Representation of Reality in Western Literature, trans. Willard Trask. Princeton: Princeton University Press, 1974.

Axton, Marie, ed. *Three Tudor Classical Interludes*. Cambridge: D. S. Brewer, 1982.

Bald, R. C. "The Sources of Middleton's City Comedies." *Journal of English and Germanic Philology* 33 (1934): 373–87.

Barber, C. L. *Shakespeare's Festive Comedy: A Study of Dramatic Form and its Relation to Social Custom.* Princeton: Princeton University Press, 1959.

Barfoot, C. C. "*Troilus and Cressida*: 'Praise us as we are tasted'." *Shakespeare Quarterly* 39 (1988): 45–57.

Barish, Jonas. *The Antitheatrical Prejudice.* Berkeley: University of California Press, 1981.

Barker, Francis. *The Tremulous Private Body: Essays on Subjection.* London: Methuen, 1984.

Barnes, Thomas G. "The Prerogative and Environmental Control of London Building in the Early Seventeenth Century: The Lost Opportunity." *Ecology Law Quarterly* 1 (1971): 62–93.

Baudrillard, Jean. *Le Système Des Objets.* Paris: Gallimard, 1968.

Beier, A. L. "Social Problems in Elizabethan London." *Journal of Interdisciplinary History* 9 (1978): 203–21.

"Poverty and Progress in Early Modern England." In Beier et al., eds. *The First Modern Society: Essays in English History in Honour of Lawrence Stone.* New York: Cambridge University Press, 1989: 201–39.

Beier, A. L. and Roger Finlay, eds. *London 1500–1700: The Making of the Metropolis.* London: Longman, 1986.

Belsey, Catherine. *The Subject of Tragedy: Identity and Difference in Renaissance Drama.* New York: Methuen, 1985.

Bentley, Gerald Eades. *The Profession of Dramatist in Shakespeare's Time, 1590–1642.* Princeton: Princeton University Press, 1971.

The Profession of Player in Shakespeare's Time, 1590–1642. Princeton: Princeton University Press, 1984.

Bergson, Henri. "Laughter." In Wylie Sypher, ed. *Comedy.* Garden City, New York: Doubleday, 1956: 61–190.

Bermel, Albert. *Farce: A History from Aristophanes to Woody Allen.* New York: Simon and Schuster, 1982.

Berry, Herbert. "The First Public Playhouses, Especially the Red Lion." *Shakespeare Quarterly* 40 (1989): 133–48.

Bethell, S. L. *Shakespeare and the Popular Dramatic Tradition.* London: Staples Press, 1944.

Bevington, David. *Tudor Drama and Politics: A Critical Approach to Topical Meaning.* Cambridge, Mass.: Harvard University Press, 1968.

Bliss, Lee. *The World's Perspective: John Webster and the Jacobean Drama.* New Brunswick: Rutgers University Press, 1983.

Boose, Lynda. "Othello's Handkerchief: The Recognizance and Pledge of Love." *English Literary Renaissance* 5 (1975): 360–74.

Boulton, Jeremy. *Neighbourhood and Society: A London Suburb in the Seventeenth Century.* Cambridge: Cambridge University Press, 1987.

Bourdieu, Pierre. *Outline of a Theory of Practice*, trans. Richard Nice. Cambridge: Cambridge University Press, 1977.

Braudel, Fernand. *Civilization and Capitalism, 15th–18th Century.* 3 vols. English translation, New York: Harper & Row, 1981–1984.

The Structures of Everyday Life. New York: Harper & Row, 1981.

The Wheels of Commerce. New York: Harper & Row, 1982.

The Perspective of the World. New York: Harper & Row, 1984.

Brecht, Bertolt. "Radio as a Means of Communication: A Talk of the Function of Radio" (1930). In Armand Mattelart and Seth Siegelaub, eds. *Communication and Class Struggle*, vol. 2, "Liberation, Socialism." New York: International General, 1983: 169–71.

Brenner, Robert. "Agrarian Class Structure and Economic Development in Pre-Industrial Europe." *Past and Present* 70 (1976): 30–75.

"The Agrarian Roots of European Capitalism." *Past and Present* 97 (1982): 16–113.

Breton, Nicholas. *Cornu-copiae. Pasquil's Night-cap: or, Antidote for the Headache.* London: 1612.

Pasquil's Mad-cappe. In *The Works in Verse and Prose of Nicholas Breton*, ed. Alexander B. Grosart. 2 vols. Edinburgh: Edinburgh University Press, 1875–79.

Briggs, John Channing. "Chapman's *Seaven Bookes of the Iliades*: Mirror for Essex." *Studies in English Literature* 21 (1981): 59–73.

Bristol, Michael D. *Carnival and Theater: Plebian Culture and the Structure of Authority in Renaissance England.* New York: Methuen, 1985.

Brooke, C. F. Tucker, ed. *The Shakespeare Apocrypha.* Oxford: Clarendon Press, 1918.

"Shakespeare's Study in Culture and Anarchy." *The Yale Review* 17 (1928): 571–77.

Brown, Paul. "'This thing of darkness I acknowledge mine': *The Tempest* and the Discourse of Colonialism." In Dollimore and Sinfield, eds. *Political Shakespeare*: 48–71.

Brown, E. H. Phelps and Sheila V. Hopkins. "Seven Centuries of the Prices of Consumables, Compared with Builders' Wage Rates." In Peter H. Ramsey, ed. *The Price Revolution in Sixteenth-Century England.* London: Methuen, 1971.

Bryant, James C. *Tudor Drama and Religious Controversy.* Macon, Georgia: Mercer University Press, 1984.

Bullough, Geoffrey. *Narrative and Dramatic Sources of Shakespeare.* 8 vols. New York: Columbia University Press, 1957–75.

Bulman, James C. "*Coriolanus* and the Matter of Troy." In J. C. Gray, ed. *Mirror up to Shakespeare: Essays in Honour of G. R. Hibbard.* Toronto: University of Toronto Press, 1984: 242–60.

Burckhardt, Jacob. *The Civilization of the Renaissance in Italy,* 2 vols. (1860) New York: Harper & Row, 1958.

Burckhardt, Sigurd. *Shakespearean Meanings.* Princeton: Princeton University Press, 1968.

Burke, Kenneth. *A Grammar of Motives.* Berkeley: University of California Press, 1969.

Burr, David. *Eucharistic Presence and Conversion in Late Thirteenth-Century Franciscan Thought.* Philadelphia: American Philosophical Society, 1984.

Butler, Martin. *Theatre and Crisis 1632–1642.* Cambridge: Cambridge University Press, 1984.

Campbell, Oscar James. *Comicall Satyre and Shakespeare's "Troilus and Cressida".* Los Angeles: Adcraft Press, 1938.

Carson, Neil. *A Companion to Henslowe's Diary.* Cambridge: Cambridge University Press, 1988.

Cavell, Stanley. *Pursuits of Happiness: The Hollywood Comedy of Remarriage.* Cambridge, Mass.: Harvard University Press, 1981.

   In Quest of the Ordinary: Lines of Skepticism and Romanticism. Chicago: University of Chicago Press, 1988.

Chambers, E. K. *The Elizabethan Stage,* 4 vols. Oxford: Clarendon Press, 1923.

Chapman, George. *Chapman's Homer,* ed. Allardyce Nicoll, 2 vols. New York: Pantheon Books, 1956.

Charnes, Linda. "'So Unsecret to Ourselves': Notorious Identity and the Material Subject in Shakespeare's *Troilus and Cressida.*" *Shakespeare Quarterly* 40 (1989): 413–40.

Chartres, J. A. *Internal Trade in England, 1500–1700.* London: Macmillan Press, 1977.

Cicero, Marcus Tullius. *The Republic,* trans. Clinton Walker Keyes. Loeb Classical Library. Cambridge, Mass.: Harvard University Press, 1951.

Clark, Alice. *Working Life of Women in the Seventeenth Century.* 1919; London: Routledge, 1982.

Clark, Sandra. *The Elizabethan Pamphleteers: Popular Moralistic Pamphlets 1580–1640.* London: Athlone Press, 1983.

Clemen, Wolfgang. *The Development of Shakespeare's Imagery.* Cambridge, Mass.: Harvard University Press, 1951.

Cohen, Walter. *Drama of a Nation: Public Theater in Renaissance England and Spain.* Ithaca: Cornell University Press, 1985.

Cook, Ann Jennalie. *The Privileged Playgoers of Shakespeare's London, 1576–1642.* Princeton: Princeton University Press, 1981.

Cotgrave, Randle. *A Dictionarie of the French and English Tongues* (1611). Columbia: University of South Carolina Press, 1950.

Craigie, James, ed. *Minor Prose Works of King James VI and I.* Edinburgh: Scottish Text Society, 1982.

Crawford, Charles. *A Complete Concordance to the 1616 Folio of Ben Jonson's Works,* 5 vols. Microfilm; Ann Arbor: University of Michigan, Library Photoduplication Service.

Creizenach, Wilhelm. *The English Drama in the Age of Shakespeare.* Trans. 1916; rpt. New York: Russell & Russell, 1967.

Cressy, David. "Describing the Social Order of Elizabethan and Stuart England." *Literature and History* 3 (1976): 29–44.

Daniel, Samuel. *The Civil Wars,* ed. Laurence Michel. New Haven: Yale University Press, 1958.

Davis, Natalie Zemon. *The Return of Martin Guerre.* Cambridge, Mass.: Harvard University Press, 1983.

   "Boundaries and the Sense of Self in Sixteenth-Century France." In *Reconstructing Individualism: Autonomy, Individuality, and the Self in Western Thought,* ed. Thomas C. Heller et al. Stanford: Stanford University Press, 1986: 53–63.

Day, John. *The Works of John Day*, ed. A. H. Bullen; rpt. London: Holland Press, 1963.

Debord, Guy. *Society of the Spectacle*. Detroit: Black & Red, 1983.

Dekker, Thomas. *The Dramatic Works of Thomas Dekker*, ed. Fredson Bowers, 4 vols. Cambridge: Cambridge University Press, 1953–61.

   Thomas Dekker, ed. E. D. Pendry. The Stratford–upon-Avon Library, vol. 4. Cambridge, Mass.: Harvard University Press, 1968.

   The Shoemakers' Holiday, ed. D. J. Palmer. New York: W. W. Norton, 1975.

Demetz, Peter et al., eds. *The Disciplines of Criticism: Essays in Literary Theory, Interpretation, and History* New Haven: Yale University Press, 1968.

Dollimore, Jonathan. *Radical Tragedy: Religion, Ideology, and Power in the Drama of Shakespeare and His Contemporaries*. Chicago: University of Chicago Press, 1984.

Dollimore, Jonathan and Alan Sinfield, eds. *Political Shakespeare: New Essays in Cultural Materialism*. Ithaca: Cornell University Press, 1985.

Doran, Madeleine. *Endeavors of Art: A Study of Form in Elizabethan Drama*. Madison: University of Wisconsin Press, 1954.

Douglas, Mary. *Purity and Danger: An Analysis of the Concepts of Pollution and Taboo*. 1966; New York: Routledge & Kegan Paul, 1988.

Drayton, Michael. *The Works of Michael Drayton*, ed. William J. Hebel, 5 vols. Oxford: Shakespeare Head Press, 1931–41.

Dunkel, Wilbur Dwight. *The Dramatic Technique of Thomas Middleton in His Comedies of London Life*. Chicago: University of Chicago Libraries, 1925.

Durkheim, Emile. *The Division of Labor in Society*. New York: Free Press, 1984.

Durling, Robert M., ed. *Petrarch's Lyric Poems: The Rime Sparse and Other Lyrics*. Cambridge, Mass.: Harvard University Press, 1976.

Dyer, Christopher. *Standards of Living in the Later Middle Ages: Social Change in England c. 1200–1500*. Cambridge: Cambridge University Press, 1989.

Eagleton, Terence. "Language and Reality in 'Twelfth Night'." *Critical Quarterly* 9 (1967): 217–28.

Empson, William. *Some Versions of Pastoral*. Edinburgh: Edinburgh University Press, 1935.

Enck, John. "The Peace of the Poetomachia." *Publications of the Modern Language Association* 77 (1962): 386–96.

Engels, Frederick. *The Origin of the Family, Private Property and the State*. New York: International Publishers, 1968.

Ewen, C. L'Estrange. *Lording Barry, Poet and Pirate*. London: Private printing, 1938.

Fennor, William. *The Counter's Commonwealth* (1617). In Judges, ed. *The Elizabethan Underworld*: 423–87.

Ferry, Anne. *The "Inward" Language: Sonnets of Wyatt, Sidney, Shakespeare, Donne*. Chicago: University of Chicago Press, 1983.

Fineman, Joel. "Fratricide and Cuckoldry: Shakespeare's Doubles." In *Representing Shakespeare*, ed. Murray M. Schwartz and Coppélia Kahn. Baltimore: Johns Hopkins University Press, 1980: 70–109.

   Shakespeare's Perjured Eye: The Invention of Poetic Subjectivity in the Sonnets. Berkeley: University of California Press, 1986.

Finlay, Roger. *Population and Metropolis: The Demography of London, 1580– 1650.* Cambridge: Cambridge University Press, 1981.

Fischer, Sandra K. *Econolingua: A Glossary of Coins and Economic Language in Renaissance Drama.* Newark: University of Delaware Press, 1985.

Fisher, F. J. *London and the English Economy, 1500–1700,* ed. P. J. Cornfield and N. B. Harte. London: Hambledon Press, 1990.

Florio, John. *Second Frutes* (1591). Gainesville: Scholars' Facsimilies, 1953.

Foakes, R. A., and R. T. Rickert, eds. *Henslowe's Diary.* Cambridge: Cambridge University Press, 1961.

Fowler, Alastair. *Kinds of Literature: An Introduction to the Theory of Genres and Modes.* Cambridge, Mass.: Harvard University Press, 1982.

Freedman, Barbara. "Errors in Comedy: A Psychoanalytic Theory of Farce." In Maurice Charney, ed. *Shakespearean Comedy.* New York: New York Literary Forum, 1980: 233–43.

   Staging the Gaze: Postmodernism, Psychoanalysis, and Shakespearean Comedy. Ithaca: Cornell University Press, 1991.

Freud, Sigmund. *Collected Papers,* ed. James Strachey, 5 vols. London: Hogarth Press, 1950.

Freud, Sigmund. *Beyond the Pleasure Principle,* trans. James Strachey. New York: Norton, 1961.

Frye, Northrop. *The Myth of Deliverance: Reflections on Shakespeare's Problem Comedies.* Toronto: University of Toronto Press, 1983.

Fumerton, Patricia. "'Secret' Arts: Elizabethan Miniatures and Sonnets." In Greenblatt, ed. *Representing the English Renaissance*: 93–133.

Furness, H. H. Jr., ed. The New Variorum *Julius Caesar.* Philadelphia: J. B. Lippincott, 1913.

Furness, H. H. Jr., ed. The New Variorum *Othello.* New York: American Scholar Publications, 1965.

Garber, Marjorie. "'Infinite Riches in a Little Room': Closure and Enclosure in Marlowe," in Alvin Kernan, ed. *Two Renaissance Mythmakers: Christopher Marlowe and Ben Jonson.* Baltimore: Johns Hopkins University Press, 1977: 3–21.

   Shakespeare's Ghost Writers: Literature as Uncanny Causality. New York: Methuen, 1987.

Gay, John. *The Beggar's Opera,* ed. Bryan Loughrey and T. O. Treadwell. New York: Viking Penguin, 1986.

Gee, Henry, ed. *The Elizabethan Prayer-Book and Ornaments.* London: Macmillan, 1902.

George, Charles H. and Katherine George. *The Protestant Mind of the English Reformation, 1570–1640.* Princeton: Princeton University Press, 1961.

Giamatti, A. Bartlett. "Proteus Unbound: Some Versions of the Sea God in the Renaissance." In Demetz et al., eds. *Disciplines of Criticism*: 437–76.

Gibbons, Brian. *Jacobean City Comedy.* Cambridge, Mass.: Harvard University Press, 1968.

Gilbert, Alan H. "The Prosperous Wittol in Giovanni Battista Modio and Thomas Middleton." *Studies in Philology* 41 (1944): 235–37.

Girard, René. *Deceit, Desire and the Novel.* Baltimore: Johns Hopkins University Press, 1965.

"The Politics of Desire in *Troilus and Cressida*." In Parker and Hartman, eds. *Shakespeare and The Question of Theory*: 188–209.

Gorges, Arthur. *A True Transcript and Publication of His Majesties Letters Patent. For an Office to be Erected and called the Public Register for General Commerce. Whereunto is Annexed an Overture and Explanation of the Nature and Purport of the Said Office, for their Better Understanding and Direction that Shall Have Occasion to Use It*. London: 1611.

Gosson, Stephen. *Plays Confuted in Five Actions*. In W. C. Hazlitt, ed. *The English Drama and Stage under the Tudor and Stuart Princes, 1543–1664*. London: 1869, 157–218.

Gray, Robert. *A Good Speed to Virginia*. London: 1609.

Greenblatt, Stephen. *Renaissance Self-Fashioning: From More to Shakespeare*. Chicago: University of Chicago Press, 1980.

"Psychoanalysis and Renaissance Culture." In Patricia Parker and David Quint, eds. *Literary Theory/Renaissance Texts*. Baltimore: Johns Hopkins University Press, 1986: 210–24.

Greenblatt, Stephen, ed. *Representing the English Renaissance*. Berkeley: University of California Press, 1988.

Greene, Gayle. "Language and Value in Shakespeare's *Troilus and Cressida*." *Studies in English Literature* 21 (1981): 271–85.

Greene, Thomas. "The Flexibility of the Self in Renaissance Literature." In Demetz et al., eds. *Disciplines of Criticism*: 241–64.

Griswold, Wendy. *Renaissance Revivals: City Comedy and Revenge Tragedy in the London Theatre, 1576–1980*. Chicago: University of Chicago Press, 1986.

Gurr, Andrew. *Playgoing in Shakespeare's London*. Cambridge: Cambridge University Press, 1987.

Hall, John. *The Advancement of Learning*, ed. A. K. Croston. Liverpool: Liverpool University Press, 1953.

Halpern, Richard. *The Poetics of Primitive Accumulation: English Renaissance Culture and the Genealogy of Capital*. Ithaca: Cornell University Press, 1991.

Hannaford, Stephen. "'My Money is my Daughter': Sexual and Financial Possession in English Renaissance Comedy." *Shakespeare Jahrbuch*. West (1984): 93–110.

Harbage, Alfred. "Copper Into Gold." In Standish Henning et al., eds. *English Renaissance Drama: Essays in Honor of Madeleine Doran and Mark Eccles*. Carbondale: Southern Illinois University Press, 1976: 1–14.

Harbage, Alfred, Samuel Schoenbaum, and Sylvia Stoler Wagonheim. *Annals of English Drama, 975–1700*, Third edition. New York: Routledge, 1989.

Harben, Henry A. *A Dictionary of London*. London: Herbert Jenkins, 1918.

Harrison, G. B. *Shakespeare at Work, 1592–1603*. London: Routledge & Sons, 1933.

Heinemann, Margot. *Puritanism and Theatre: Thomas Middleton and Opposition Drama under the Early Stuarts*. Cambridge: Cambridge University Press, 1980.

Heller, Agnes. *Renaissance Man*, trans. Richard E. Allen. New York: Schocken Books, 1981.

Henke, James T. *Courtesans and Cuckolds: A Glossary of Renaissance Dramatic Bawdy*. New York: Garland, 1979.

Henze, Richard. "*The Comedy of Errors*: A Freely Binding Chain." *Shakespeare Quarterly* 22 (1971): 35–41.

Herford, C. H., Percy Simpson, and Evelyn Simpson, eds. *Ben Jonson*, 11 vols. Oxford: Clarendon Press, 1925–52.

Hexter, J. H. *Reappraisals in History: New Views on History and Society in Early Modern Europe*. Chicago: University of Chicago Press, 1979.

Heywood, Thomas. *The Dramatic Works of Thomas Heywood*, 6 vols. London: 1874; rpt. New York: Russell & Russell, 1964.

   Troia Britanica: or, Great Britaines Troy. London: 1609; facsimile, New York: Georg Olms Verlag, 1971.

Hibbard, G. R. "Love, Marriage, and Money in Shakespeare's Theatre and Shakespeare's England." In Hibbard, ed. *The Elizabethan Theatre VI*. Toronto: The Macmillan Company, 1978: 134–55.

Homer. *The Odyssey*, trans. Richmond Lattimore. New York: Harper & Row, 1967.

Horace. *Horace*, ed. E. C. Wickham, 2 vols. Oxford: Clarendon Press, 1903–12.

Horwich, Richard. "Wives, Courtesans, and the Economics of Love in Jacobean City Comedy." In *Drama in the Renaissance: Comparative and Critical Essays*, ed. Clifford Davidson, et al. New York: AMS Press, 1986: 255–73.

Howard, Michael. *War in European History*. Oxford: Oxford University Press, 1976.

Hughes, Paul L. and James F. Larkin, eds. *Tudor Royal Proclamations*, 3 vols. New Haven: Yale University Press, 1964–69.

Hughes, Thomas. *The Misfortunes of Arthur*, ed. Harvey Carson Grumbine. Berlin: 1900.

Jaeger, Werner. *Paideia: The Ideas of Greek Culture*, 3 vols., trans. Gilbert Highet. Oxford: Basil Blackwell, 1939–45.

Jameson, Fredric. *The Political Unconscious: Narrative as a Socially Symbolic Act*. Ithaca: Cornell University Press, 1981.

Jones, Emrys. "London in the Early Seventeenth Century: An Ecological Approach." *The London Journal* 6 (1980): 123–33.

Jonson, Ben. *Bartholomew Fair*, ed. G. R. Hibbard. London: Ernest Benn, 1977.

   Epigrams and The Forest, ed. Richard Dutton. Manchester: Carcanet, 1984.

   Every Man in His Humour: A Parallel-Text Edition of the 1601 Quarto and the 1616 Folio, ed. J. W. Lever. Lincoln: University of Nebraska Press, 1971.

Jonson, Ben, George Chapman, and John Marston. *Eastward Ho!*, ed. C. G. Petter. London: Ernest Benn, 1973.

   The Selected Plays of John Marston, ed. MacDonald P. Jackson and Michael Neill. Cambridge: Cambridge University Press, 1986.

Judges, A. V., ed. *The Elizabethan Underworld*. New York: E. P. Dutton, 1930.

Kahn, Coppélia. *Man's Estate: Masculine Identity in Shakespeare*. Berkeley: University of California Press, 1981.

   "The Rape in Shakespeare's *Lucrece*." *Shakespeare Survey* 9 (1976): 45–72.

Kastan, David Scott. "Workshop and/as Playhouse: Comedy and Commerce in *The Shoemaker's Holiday*." *Studies in Philology* 84 (1987): 324–37.

Kermode, Frank. *The Sense of an Ending*. Oxford: Oxford University Press, 1966.

Kerrigan, William. "The Articulation of the Ego in the English Renaissance." In

The Literary Freud: Mechanisms of Defense and the Poetic Will, ed. Joseph H. Smith. New Haven: Yale University Press, 1980: 261–308.

Keynes, J. M. *A Treatise on Money*, 2 vols. New York: Macmillan, 1930.

Kimbrough, Robert. *Shakespeare's "Troilus and Cressida" and its Setting*. Cambridge, Mass.: Harvard University Press, 1964.

Kinney, Arthur, ed. *Rogues, Vagabonds, and Sturdy Beggars: A New Gallery of Tudor and Early Stuart Rogue Literature Exposing the Lives, Times, and Cozening Tricks of the Elizabethan Underworld*. Amherst: University of Massachusetts Press, 1990.

Knapp, Jeffrey. "Elizabethan Tobacco." *Representations* 21 (1988): 26–66.

Knight, G. Wilson. *Shakespearean Dimensions*. Totowa, New Jersey: Barnes & Noble, 1984.

Knights, L. C. *Drama and Society in the Age of Jonson*. London: Chatto and Windus, 1937.

Leggatt, Alexander. *Citizen Comedy in the Age of Shakespeare*. Toronto: University of Toronto Press, 1973.

Leinwand, Theodore B. *The City Staged: Jacobean Comedy, 1603–1613*. Madison: University of Wisconsin Press, 1986.

Levin, Harry. "English Literature of the Renaissance." In *The Renaissance: A Reconsideration of the Theories and Interpretations of the Age*, ed. Tinsley Helton. Madison: University of Wisconsin Press, 1961.

Playboys and Killjoys: An Essay on the Theory and Practice of Comedy. New York: Oxford University Press, 1987.

Lewalski, Barabara K. *Protestant Poetics and the Seventeenth-Century Religious Lyric*. Princeton: Princeton University Press, 1979.

Liddell, Henry George and Robert Scott. *Greek-English Lexicon* New York: Harper & Brothers, 1869.

Lodge, Thomas. *The Wounds of Civil War*, ed. Joseph W. Houppert. Lincoln: University of Nebraska Press, 1969.

Lodge, Thomas and Robert Greene. *A Looking Glass for London and England*. In Russell A. Fraser and Norman Rabkin, eds. *Drama of the English Renaissance*, 2 vols.; vol. 1: *The Tudor Period*. New York: Macmillan, 1976.

Loengard, Janet. "An Elizabethan Lawsuit: John Brayne, His Carpenter, and the Building of the Red Lion Theatre." *Shakespeare Quarterly* 34 (1983): 298–310.

Loewenstein, Joseph. "The Script in the Marketplace." In Greenblatt, ed. *Representing the English Renaissance*: 265–78.

Machiavelli, Niccolo. *The Prince*, trans. Harvey C. Mansfield, Jr. Chicago: University of Chicago Press, 1985.

Machyn, Henry. *The Diary of Henry Machyn, Citizen and Merchant–Taylor of London*, ed. John G. Nichols. London: Camden Society, 1848; rpt. New York: Johnson Reprint Corporation, 1968.

McLuskie, Kathleen. "The Patriarchal Bard: Feminist Criticism and Shakespeare: *King Lear* and *Measure for Measure*." In Dollimore and Sinfield, eds. *Political Shakespeare*: 88–108.

Macpherson, C. B. "Capitalism and the Changing Concept of Property." In Eugene Kamenka and R. S. Neale, eds. *Feudalism, Capitalism and Beyond*. London: Edward Arnold, 1975: 104–24.

The Political Theory of Possessive Individualism: Hobbes to Locke. Oxford: Oxford University Press, 1962.

Mallin, Eric S. *The End of Troy: Elizabethan Dissolution in Shakespeare's* "Troilus and Cressida". Ann Arbor: University Microfilms, 1986.

"Emulous Factions and the Collapse of Chivalry: *Troilus and Cressida.*" *Representations* 29 (1990): 145–79.

Manley, Lawrence, ed. *London in the Age of Shakespeare: An Anthology.* London: Croom Helm, 1986.

"From Matron to Monster: Tudor-Stuart London and the Languages of Urban Description." In Heather Dubrow and Richard Strier, eds. *The Historical Renaissance: New Essays on Tudor and Stuart Literature and Culture.* Chicago: University of Chicago Press, 1988: 347–74.

Manning, Roger B. *Village Revolts: Social Protest and Popular Disturbances in England, 1509–1640.* Oxford: Clarendon Press, 1988.

Marcus, Leah S. *Puzzling Shakespeare: Local Reading and its Discontents.* Berkeley: University of California Press, 1988.

Marienstras, Richard. *"Jack Juggler*: Aspects de la conscience individuelle dans une farce du 16ᵉ siecle." *Etudes Anglaises* 4 (1963): 321–30.

New Perspectives on the Shakespearean World, trans. Janet Lloyd. Cambridge: Cambridge University Press, 1985.

Marston, John. *The Dutch Courtesan*, ed. M. L. Wine. Lincoln: University of Nebraska Press, 1965.

Martines, Lauro. *Society and History in English Renaissance Verse.* New York: Basil Blackwell, 1985.

Marx, Karl. *Capital*, 3 vols. New York: International, 1967.

A Contribution to the Critique of Political Economy. New York: International Publishers, 1970.

Maus, Katharine Eisaman. "Horns of Dilemma: Jealousy, Gender, and Spectatorship in English Renaissance Drama." *ELH* 54 (1987): 561–83.

"Proof and Consequences: Inwardness and Its Exposure in the English Renaissance." *Representations* 34 (1991): 29–52.

Middleton, Thomas. *The Works of Thomas Middleton*, ed. A. H. Bullen, 8 vols., Boston: Houghton, Mifflin, 1885–86.

The Ghost of Lucrece, ed. Joseph Quincy Adams. New York: Charles Scribner's Sons, 1937.

Michaelmas Term, ed. Richard Levin. Lincoln: University of Nebraska Press, 1966.

A Chaste Maid in Cheapside, ed. R. B. Parker. London: Methuen, 1969.

Middleton, Thomas and Thomas Dekker. *The Roaring Girl*, ed. Andor Gomme. London: Ernest Benn, 1976.

Morse, David. *England's Time of Crisis, from Shakespeare to Milton: A Cultural History.* Basingstoke: Macmillan, 1989.

Mullaney, Steven. *The Place of the Stage: License, Play, and Power in Renaissance England.* Chicago: University of Chicago Press, 1988.

Mun, Thomas. *A Discourse of Trade, From England unto the East Indies.* London: 1621; New York: Facsimile Text Society, 1930.

Nashe, Thomas. *The Works of Thomas Nashe*, ed. Ronald B. McKerrow, 5 vols. London: A. H. Bullen, 1904–10.

Newlin, Jeanne. "The Modernity of *Troilus and Cressida*: The Case for Theatrical Criticism." *Harvard Library Bulletin* 17 (1969): 353–73.

Newman, Karen. "'And wash the Ethiop white': Femininity and the Monstrous in *Othello*." In *Shakespeare Reproduced: The Text in History and Ideology*, ed. Jean E. Howard and Marion F. O'Connor. New York: Methuen, 1987: 143–62.

"City Talk: Women and Commodification in Jonson's *Epicoene*." *ELH* 56 (1989): 503–18.

Nicolson, Marjorie Hope. *The Breaking of the Circle: Studies in the Effect of the "New Science" Upon Seventeenth-Century Poetry*. New York: Columbia University Press, 1960; revised.

Northbrooke, John. *A Treatise Against Dicing, Dancing, Plays, and Interludes*, ed. J. P. Collier. London: Shakespeare Society, 1843.

Nuttall, A. D. *A New Mimesis: Shakespeare and the Representation of Reality*. New York: Methuen, 1983.

Outhwaite, R. B. *Inflation in Tudor and Early Stuart England*, Second edition. London: Macmillan Press, 1982.

Palliser, D. M. *The Age of Elizabeth: England Under the Later Tudors, 1547–1603*. New York: Longman, 1983.

Palmer, Kenneth, ed. *The New Arden Troilus and Cressida*. New York: Methuen, 1982.

Parker, Patricia and Geoffrey Hartman, eds. *Shakespeare and the Question of Theory*. New York: Methuen, 1985.

Partridge, Eric. *Shakespeare's Bawdy*. New York: E. P. Dutton, 1948.

Paster, Gail Kern. *The Idea of the City in the Age of Shakespeare*. Athens: University of Georgia Press, 1985.

Patterson, Lee. "On the Margin: Postmodernism, Ironic History, and Medieval Studies." *Speculum* 65 (1990): 87–108.

Pearl, Valerie. *London and the Outbreak of the Puritan Revolution*. Oxford: Oxford University Press, 1961.

"Social Policy in Early Modern London." In Hugh Lloyd-Jones et al., eds. *History and Imagination: Essays in Honour of H. R. Trevor-Roper*. London: Gerald Duckworth, 1981: 115–31.

Peele, George. *The Life and Works of George Peele*, ed. Charles Tyler Prouty, 3 vols. New Haven: Yale University Press, 1970.

Pelikan, Jaroslav. *Reformation of Church and Dogma*. Chicago: University of Chicago Press, 1983.

Pendry, E. D., ed. *Thomas Dekker*. The Stratford-upon-Avon Library 4. Cambridge, Mass.: Harvard University Press, 1968.

Plautus, T. Maccius. *Comoediae*. 2 vols. Oxford Classical Texts. Oxford: Oxford University Press, 1980.

Pliny. *Natural History*, 10 vols., trans. H. Rackham (Loeb Classical Library) Cambridge, Mass.: Harvard University Press, 1950.

Poel, William. *Shakespeare in the Theatre*. London: Sidgwick and Jackson, 1913.

Potts, Abbie. "*Cynthia's Revels, Poetaster*, and *Troilus and Cressida*." *Shakespeare Quarterly* 5 (1954): 297–302.

Rabelais, Francois. *Gargantua and Pantagruel*, trans. Sir Thomas Urquhart and

Peter Le Motteux (1653–94), 3 vols. Tudor Translations. London: David Nutt, 1900.

Rabkin, Norman. *Shakespeare and the Common Understanding.* New York: Free Press, 1967.

Rappaport, Steve. *Worlds Within Worlds: Structures of Life in Sixteenth-Century London.* Cambridge: Cambridge University Press, 1989.

Rich, E. E. and C. H. Wilson, eds. *The Economy of Expanding Europe in the Sixteenth and Seventeenth Centuries.* The Cambridge Economic History of Europe, vol. 4. Cambridge: Cambridge University Press, 1967.

  eds. *The Economic Organization of Early Modern Europe.* The Cambridge Economic History of Europe, vol. 5. Cambridge: Cambridge University Press, 1977.

Rossiter, A. P. *Angel with Horns and other Shakespearean Lectures.* London: Longmans, 1961.

Rouse, W. H. D., ed. *Shakespeare's Ovid, Being Arthur Golding's Translation of the Metamorphoses.* Carbondale: Southern Illinois University Press, 1961.

Russell, Barry. "Launching the Swan." *Drama* 3 (1986): 11–12.

Russell, Conrad. *The Crisis of Parliaments: English History 1509–1660.* London: Oxford University Press, 1971.

Rymer, Thomas. *The Critical Works of Thomas Rymer,* ed. Curt A. Zimansky. New Haven: Yale University Press, 1956.

Salgado, Gamini, ed. *Four Jacobean City Comedies.* New York: Penguin, 1975.

Saunders, J. W. *A Biographical Dictionary of Renaissance Poets and Dramatists, 1520–1650.* New Jersey: Barnes & Noble, 1983.

Schelling, Felix. *Elizabethan Drama, 1558–1642,* 2 vols. Boston: Houghton Mifflin, 1908.

Schneider, Paul S. "'Taillynge Ynough': The Function of Money in the *Shipman's Tale.*" *Chaucer Review* 11 (1976–77): 201–09.

Sedgwick, Eve Kosofsky. *Between Men: English Literature and Male Homosocial Desire.* New York: Columbia University Press, 1985.

Shakespeare, William. *The Riverside Shakespeare,* ed. G. Blakemore Evans. Boston: Houghton Mifflin, 1974.

Sharpham, Edward. *Cupid's Whirligig,* ed. Allardyce Nicoll, Waltham Saint Lawrence: Golden Cockerel Press, 1926.

Shell, Marc. *The Economy of Literature.* Baltimore: Johns Hopkins University Press, 1978.

  Money, Language, and Thought: Literary and Philosophical Economies from the Medieval to the Modern Era. Berkeley: University of California Press, 1982.

Sidney, Philip. *An Apology for Poetry,* ed. Forrest G. Robinson. Indianapolis: Bobbs-Merrill, 1970.

Silverman, Albert H. "Sex and Money in Chaucer's *Shipman's Tale.*" *Philological Quarterly* 32 (1953): 329–36.

Simmel, Georg. *The Philosophy of Money,* trans. Tom Bottomore and David Frisby. Boston: Routledge & Kegan Paul, 1978.

Slack, Paul. *Poverty and Policy in Tudor and Stuart England.* New York: Longman, 1988.

  The Impact of Plague in Tudor and Stuart England. London: Routledge & Kegan Paul, 1985.

Smith, A. J., ed. *John Donne: The Complete English Poems*. New York: Penguin, 1971.

Smuts, R. Malcolm. "The Court and Its Neighborhood: Royal Policy and Urban Growth in the Early Stuart West End." *Journal of British Studies* 30 (1991): 117–49.

Snow, Edward. "Sexual Anxiety and the Male Order of Things in *Othello*." *English Literary Renaissance* 10 (1980): 384–412.

Southall, Raymond. "*Troilus and Cressida* and the Spirit of Capitalism." In Arnold Kettle, ed. *Shakespeare in a Changing World: Essays on His Times and His Plays*. New York: International Publishers, 1964: 217–32.

Speed, John. *The Historie of Great Britaine* (second edition). London: 1623.

Spencer, T. J. B. "'Greeks' and 'Merrygreeks': A Background to *Timon of Athens* and *Troilus and Cressida*." In Richard Hosley, ed. *Essays on Shakespeare and Elizabethan Drama in Honor of Hardin Craig*. Columbia: University of Missouri Press, 1962: 223–33.

Stafford, T. J. "Mercantile Imagery in *Troilus and Cressida*" in T. J. Stafford, ed. *Shakespeare in the Southwest: Some New Directions*. El Paso: Texas Western Press, 1969: 36–42.

Stallybrass, Peter and Allon White. *The Politics and Poetics of Transgression*. Ithaca: Cornell University Press, 1986.

Stewart, Susan. *On Longing: Narratives of the Miniature, the Gigantic, the Souvenir, the Collection*. Baltimore: Johns Hopkins University Press, 1984.

Stone, Lawrence. "Inigo Jones and the New Exchange." *Archaeological Journal* 114 (1957): 106–21.

The Crisis of the Aristocracy 1558–1641. London: Oxford University Press, 1965.

The Family, Sex and Marriage in England 1500–1800. New York: Harper & Row, 1977.

"The Residential Development of the West End of London in the Seventeenth Century." In Barbara Malament, ed. *After the Reformation: Essays in Honor of J. H. Hexter*. Philadelphia: University of Pennsylvania Press, 1980: 167–214.

Sugden, Edward H. *A Topographical Dictionary to the Works of Shakespeare and His Fellow Dramatists*. Manchester: Manchester University Press, 1925.

Sweeney, John Gordon. *Jonson and the Psychology of Public Theater: To Coin the Spirit, Spend the Soul*. Princeton: Princeton University Press, 1985.

Tatlock, John S. P. "The Siege of Troy in Elizabethan Literature, Especially in Shakespeare and Heywood." *Publications of the Modern Language Association* 30 (1915): 673–770.

Tawney, R. H. *Religion and the Rise of Capitalism*. 1926; rpt. Gloucester, Mass.: Peter Smith, 1962.

Taylor, Gary, ed. *Henry V*. Oxford: Clarendon Press, 1982.

Taylor, John. *All the Works of John Taylor, the Water Poet* (1630). Facsimile; London: Scolar Press, 1977.

Thirsk, Joan. *Economic Policy and Projects: The Development of a Consumer Society in Early Modern England*. Oxford: Clarendon Press, 1978.

Thompson, Roger. *Unfit for Modest Ears: A Study of Pornographic, Obscene and Bawdy Works Written or Published in England in the Second Half of the Seventeenth Century*. London: Macmillan, 1979.

Thomson, Peter. *Shakespeare's Theatre*. London: Routledge & Kegan Paul, 1983.

Tilley, Morris Palmer. *A Dictionary of the Proverbs in England in the Sixteenth and Seventeenth Centuries*. Ann Arbor: University of Michigan Press, 1950.

[Tourneur, Cyril]. *The Revenger's Tragedy*, ed. R. A. Foakes. Manchester: Manchester University Press, 1986.

Tusser, Thomas. *Five Hundred Points of Good Husbandry* (1573). ed. E. V. Lucas. London: James Tregaskis, 1931.

Tydeman, William, ed. *Four Tudor Comedies*. Harmondsworth, Middlesex: Penguin, 1984.

Tyson, Archie Mervin, ed. *Every Woman in Her Humour: A Critical Edition*. New York: Garland, 1980.

Van Lennep, William et al., eds. *The London Stage, 1660–1800*. 5 parts. Carbondale: Southern Illinois University Press, 1965- 68.

Veblen, Thorstein. *The Theory of the Leisure Class*. 1899; New York: Mentor, 1953.

Veltruský, Jiří. "Man and Object in the Theater." In *A Prague School Reader on Esthetics, Literary Structure, and Style*, trans. and ed. Paul L. Garvin. Washington: Georgetown University Press, 1964: 83–91.

Venuti, Lawrence. *Our Halcyon Dayes: English Prerevolutionary Texts and Postmodern Culture*. Madison: University of Wisconsin Press, 1989.

Vergil, *Aeneid*, trans. W. F. Jackson Knight. New York: Penguin, 1958.

Walter, John and Keith Wrightson. "Dearth and the Social Order in Early Modern England." *Past and Present* 71 (1976): 22–42.

Watson, Robert. *Ben Jonson's Parodic Strategy: Literary Imperialism in the Comedies*. Cambridge, Mass.: Harvard University Press, 1987.

Wayne, Don E. "Drama and Society in the Age of Jonson: Shifting Grounds of Authority and Judgment in Three Major Comedies." In Mary Beth Rose, ed. *Renaissance Drama as Cultural History: Essays from "Renaissance Drama", 1977–1987*. Evanston: Northwestern University Press, 1990: 3–29.

Weber, Max. *The Protestant Ethic and the Spirit of Capitalism* 1904–05; rpt., London: Unwin, 1987.

Webster, John. *The Complete Works of John Webster*, ed. F. L. Lucas, 4 vols. Boston: Houghton Mifflin, 1928.

The White Devil, ed. J. R. Mulryne. Lincoln: University of Nebraska Press, 1969.

Weidner, Henry M. "Homer and the Fallen World: Focus of Satire in George Chapman's *The Widow's Tears*." *Journal of English and Germanic Philology* 62 (1963): 518–32.

Weimann, Robert. *Shakespeare and the Popular Tradition in the Theater: Studies in the Social Dimension of Dramatic Form and Function*. (Baltimore: Johns Hopkins University Press, 1978).

"Discourse, Ideology and the Crisis of Authority in post-Reformation England." *REAL: The Yearbook of Research in English and American Literature* 5 (1987): 109–40.

Wells, Susan. *The Dialectics of Representation*. Baltimore: Johns Hopkins University Press, 1989.

Wernham, R. B. "Elizabethan War Aims and Strategy." In S. T. Bindoff, ed. *Elizabethan Government and Society*. London: Athlone Press, 1961: 340–68.

West, Thomas G. "The Two Truths of *Troilus and Cressida*." In John Alvis and Thomas G. West, eds. *Shakespeare as Political Thinker*. Durham: Carolina Academic Press, 1981: 127–43.

Wheeler, John. *A Treatise of Commerce* (1601). Facsimile; New York: Columbia University Press, 1931.

Whiting, B. J. *Proverbs in the Earlier English Drama*. Harvard Studies in Comparative Literature 14. Cambridge, Mass.: Harvard University Press, 1938.

Wiles, David. *Shakespeare's Clown: Actor and Text in the Elizabethan Playhouse*. Cambridge: Cambridge University Press, 1987.

Wilkes, G. A., ed. *The Complete Plays of Ben Jonson*. 4 vols. Oxford: Clarendon Press, 1981–82.

Williams, Raymond. *Culture*. London: Fontana, 1981.

Wilson, Douglas B. "The Commerce of Desire: Freudian Narcissism in Chaucer's *Troilus and Criseyde* and Shakespeare's *Troilus and Cressida*." *English Language Notes* 21 (1983): 11–22.

Wilson, Edmund. *The Triple Thinkers and The Wound and the Bow*. Boston: Northeastern University Press, 1984.

Wilson, Robert. *The Three Ladies of London*. In *A Select Collection of Old English Plays*, Robert Dodsley, 1744, 4th edition; W. Carew Hazlitt; rpt. New York: Benjamin Blom, 1964.

Wilson, Thomas. *A Discourse Upon Usury*, ed. R. H. Tawney. London: G. Bell and Sons, 1925.

Winnicott, D. W. *Playing and Reality*. New York: Basic Books, 1971.

Woodbridge, Linda. *Women and the English Renaissance: Literature and the Nature of Womankind, 1540–1620*. Urbana: University of Illinois Press, 1984.

Woodward, Donald. "Wage Rates and Living Standards in Pre–Industrial England." *Past and Present* 91 (1981): 28–46.

Wrightson, Keith. *English Society 1580–1680*. New Brunswick: Rutgers University Press, 1982.

Wrigley, E. A. and R. S. Schofield. *The Population History of England, 1541–1871: A Reconstruction*. New York: Cambridge University Press, 1989.

Zall, P. M., ed. *A Hundred Merry Tales, And Other Jestbooks of the Fifteenth and Sixteenth Centuries*. Lincoln: University of Nebraska Press, 1963.

Index